C0-CEU-406

Iconoclastic Theology

Plateaus – New Directions in Deleuze Studies

'It's not a matter of bringing all sorts of things together under a single concept but rather of relating each concept to variables that explain its mutations.'
Gilles Deleuze, *Negotiations*

Titles available in the series

Dorothea Olkowski, *The Universal (In the Realm of the Sensible): Beyond Continental Philosophy*
Christian Kerslake, *Immanence and the Vertigo of Philosophy: From Kant to Deleuze*
Jean-Clet Martin, *Variations: The Philosophy of Gilles Deleuze*, translated by Constantin V. Boundas and Susan Dyrkton
Simone Bignall, *Postcolonial Agency: Critique and Constructivism*
Miguel de Beistegui, *Immanence – Deleuze and Philosophy*
Jean-Jacques Lecercle, *Badiou and Deleuze Read Literature*
Ronald Bogue, *Deleuzian Fabulation and the Scars of History*
Sean Bowden, *The Priority of Events: Deleuze's* Logic of Sense
Craig Lundy, *History and Becoming: Deleuze's Philosophy of Creativity*
Aidan Tynan, *Deleuze's Literary Clinic: Criticism and the Politics of Symptoms*
Thomas Nail, *Returning to Revolution: Deleuze, Guattari and Zapatismo*
François Zourabichvili, *Deleuze: A Philosophy of the Event* with *The Vocabulary of Deleuze* edited by Gregg Lambert and Daniel W. Smith, translated by Kieran Aarons
Frida Beckman, *Between Desire and Pleasure: A Deleuzian Theory of Sexuality*
Nadine Boljkovac, *Untimely Affects: Gilles Deleuze and an Ethics of Cinema*
Daniela Voss, *Conditions of Thought: Deleuze and Transcendental Ideas*
Daniel Barber, *Deleuze and the Naming of God: Post-Secularism and the Future of Immanence*
F. LeRon Shults, *Iconoclastic Theology: Gilles Deleuze and the Secretion of Atheism*

Forthcoming volumes:

A. Janae Sholtz, *The Invention of a People: Art and the Political in Heidegger and Deleuze*
Marco Altamirano, *Virtual Ecology: Deleuze and Guattari and the Philosophy of Nature*
Visit the Plateaus website at www.euppublishing.com/series/plat

ICONOCLASTIC THEOLOGY
Gilles Deleuze and the Secretion of Atheism

F. LeRon Shults

EDINBURGH
University Press

Edinburgh University Press Ltd
The Tun – Holyrood Road
12 (2f) Jackson's Entry
Edinburgh EH8 8PJ
www.euppublishing.com

Typeset in Sabon by
Servis Filmsetting Ltd, Stockport, Cheshire,
and printed and bound in the United States of America

A CIP record for this book is available from the British Library

ISBN 978 0 7486 8413 7 (hardback)
ISBN 978 0 7486 8414 4 (webready PDF)

The author of this book has received financial support
from the Norwegian Non-fiction Literature Fund.

Contents

Acknowledgments

I want to thank the many Deleuzian Friends who encouraged me (explicitly or implicitly) in the wake of the fifth International Deleuze Conference in New Orleans in 2012 to contribute a volume to the *Plateaus* book series, and especially its editors Ian Buchanan and Claire Colebrook for supporting the project. Special thanks to Jeff Bell, Joe Hughes, John Protevi, Dan Smith, Nathan Widder, and James Williams. Thanks also to Carol MacDonald and her excellent team at Edinburgh University Press for such a pleasurable publishing experience.

List of Abbreviations

AO	Anti-Oedipus
B	Bergsonism
C1	Cinema 1 – The Movement-Image
C2	Cinema 2 – The Time-Image
CC	Coldness and Cruelty
D1	Dialogues
D2	Dialogues II
DR	Difference and Repetition
ECC	Essays Critical and Clinical
EP	Expressionism in Philosophy: Spinoza
ES	Empiricism and Subjectivity
F	Foucault
FB	Francis Bacon
K	Kafka: Towards a Minor Literature
KCP	Kant's Critical Philosophy
LS	Logic of Sense
N	Negotiations
NP	Nietzsche & Philosophy
PI	Pure Immanence: Essays on a Life
PS	Proust and Signs
SPP	Spinoza: Practical Philosophy
TF	The Fold
TP	A Thousand Plateaus
TR	Two Regimes of Madness
WP	What is Philosophy?

To Gro Anita Homme

my happy atheist

1
Hammering Theology

The impact of Gilles Deleuze's philosophical corpus resounds within and resonates across disciplines as diverse as physics, psychology, political science and the performing arts. Theoreticians and practitioners in these and other fields have been discovering what his literary body can do – and what can be done by extracting the revolutionary force of his massively energetic texts. My project is the extraction of resources for the production of an *iconoclastic* theology. I will argue that Deleuze's whole oeuvre is a *theological* icon-breaking machine that liberates thinking, acting, and feeling from the repressive power of Images of transcendence. His work is not only this, but all of his work is also this. This introductory chapter sets out my plan for tinkering with Deleuzian concepts, connecting them with insights from the bio-cultural sciences of religion, and releasing revolutionary forces that have for too long been domesticated within the discipline of theology.

In his last book with Félix Guattari, *What is Philosophy?*, Deleuze insisted that "Wherever there is transcendence, vertical Being, imperial State in the sky or on earth, there is *religion*; and there is Philosophy only where there is immanence . . . only friends can set out a plane of immanence as a ground from which *idols* have been cleared."[1] Throughout his writings, Deleuze hammered away at all sorts of figures of transcendence, psychological and political as well as priestly. The task of the Deleuzian Friend is clearly a destructive one, especially when it comes to religion. For Deleuze, however, critique and construction always go together. As we will see, many of his most celebrated conceptual creations were engendered by penetrating the thought of philosophers who dealt with religious and theological themes.[2] Obviously, he considered chipping away at the repressive representations of religion to be valuable in and of itself, but Deleuze also found that religion itself produced something of considerable value. "Religions are worth much less than the nobility and the courage of the *atheisms* that they inspire."[3]

Iconoclastic theology, I will argue, has a special role to play in the production of an inspiring atheism. Deleuze claimed that there is "always an atheism to be extracted from religion," suggesting that Christianity *secretes* atheism "more than *any other* religion."[4] Why Christianity? We will explore the reasons for the prodigality of this religion's atheistic secretion as we go along. I hope to show how the creative flows released by Deleuzian critique, such as his rigorous analysis of psychoanalysis and capitalism (*Anti-Oedipus*), can be complemented and intensified by an equally rigorous analysis of religious icons, especially *the* Icon of Christian theology (*Anti-Christ*). I want to illustrate to Friends of Deleuze (from all fields) how productive it can be to poke around the sedentary edifices of traditional theology, as he himself so often did, prying open the cracks in its Iconology, flattening its religious Figures, forging new conceptual tools and weapons with the fragments, and assembling creative atheist machines.

Atheism, religion, theology – these are contentious terms. Their usage becomes even more contested when we try to make transversal connections across disciplines. This sort of endeavor often requires the creation and clarification of new distinctions. Below I will set out a conceptual matrix that will serve as a heuristic device throughout the book. Before starting our extractions from and protractions of the relevant bodies of literature, it is important to begin to unpack the sense in which the Deleuzian corpus may be considered *theological*.

The Science of Non-Existing Entities

Although Deleuze appreciated the contributions of a few select theologians, his attitude toward the discipline as a whole was generally dismissive or even derisive. In his early book on *Nietzsche & Philosophy*, for example, he decried the "theological character" of modern philosophy, the "theological subjection" of thought, and the "theological crime" against the spirit that enslaves it to sadness and *ressentiment*.[5] This is not surprising since, in fact, the term "theology" itself has traditionally been associated with the defense of the religious coalition that Deleuze, like Nietzsche, held most responsible for the establishment of slave morality. Throughout his career, Deleuze often depicted theology as an uncreative mode of thought bound to religious phantasms of transcendence.[6] As we will see, he also consistently worked at overturning the priestly curse on desire, combating the "judgment of God," and leveling images erected and selected as true representations of transcendence.

And so the idea of a *Deleuzian theology* might seem oxymoronic indeed. Nevertheless, Deleuze also made space – indeed space he himself took up – for a "theology" that is both *atheistic* and *productive.* In an appendix to *Logic of Sense* in which he discusses the relation between bodies and language in the work of Pierre Klossowski, Deleuze provocatively suggests that theology can be understood as "the science of non-existing entities, the manner in which these entities – divine or anti-divine, Christ or Antichrist – animate language and make for it this glorious body which is divided into disjunctions" (LS, 322). Now several aspects of this citation are important for our purposes, but let us begin with the definition of theology as the *science of non-existing entities.*

For at least two reasons, this description of the discipline is not as insulting as it might initially appear. First, Deleuze *himself* is a scientist of non-existing entities. Earlier in the main text of *Logic of Sense,* for example, he argues that sense itself is "not of being . . . sense does not exist" (LS, 38). Similarly, he describes the event as "that entity which addresses itself to thought, and which alone may invest it – extra-Being," and sets out an ethics of counter-effectuation, which involves the "liberation of the *non-existent entity* for each state of affairs."[7] As we will see, several of the other key creative concepts in Deleuze's writings – including the problematic, the virtual, ?-being, chaos, the Disparate, the aleatory point, the paradoxical instance, the abstract machine, and the Body without Organs – all designate "entities" (or realities) that do not "exist." These terms refer to the transcendental conditions or sources of genetic determination for the becoming of existing entities. These (very real) "non-existing" entities are immanent causes of the animation of language, the movement of thought, the differentiation of singularities, the differenciation of individuals, the dramatization of concepts, etc. In this sense, Deleuze is the consummate *theological scientist* – albeit of the *Anti-Christ* sort.

A second reason this description of theology is not as offensive as it appears (or at least is not offensive for this most apparent reason) is that it is commonplace even for Christian theologians to acknowledge that there is an important sense in which the object of theological inquiry does not "exist." For example, John of Damascus, in his seventh-century summary exposition of "the orthodox faith," insisted that God does not belong to "the class of existing things" but is "above all existing things, nay even above existence itself" (*De fide Orthodoxa*, I.4). Similar sentiments can be found among most of the leading theologians of the Christian tradition, as well as among scholars from other religious traditions that trace their roots to the axial age.[8] For example, Nirguna Brahman, Sunyata, Wuji, and Dao are not typically conceived as determinate entities that stand-out (ek-sistere) in relation to other finite objects or even finitude as a whole, but as realities that condition all determinate existence.

The absolutely *infinite* cannot be de-fined as standing-out in relation to other finite things, nor even conceived as *a* determinate entity over against finitude as a whole, for then it would be represented as *finite*, i.e., as limited or bounded by another entity or entities that it is *not*, in which case it would not be *absolutely* unlimited. In the case of Christianity, this philosophical insight comes into conflict with religious belief in a God who is represented as an infinite Person in a determinate relation with a finite world that he has created and (at least part of which) he plans to redeem. Jewish and Muslim religious scholars have similar difficulties. Christian theologians, like their counterparts in the other monotheistic traditions that originated in west Asia, have developed a variety of strategies for dealing with this tension within their religious coalitions. I will try to illuminate the motivation for such strategies, and explain the sense in which their failure secretes atheism.

The main point at this stage is that many theologians would not at all be offended at the idea that their discipline deals with that which is "beyond being." The problem they will have with Deleuze is his a-theism; that is, his denial of the reality of a specific kind of non-existent Entity, a personal and transcendent God who establishes moralistic codes for a religious coalition. As we will see in the following chapters, Deleuze is not a big fan of *religion*. From his first (acknowledged) book, on Hume, in which he equates religion with the fanciful and illegitimate use of extensive rules of association (ES, 76), to his last book (with Guattari), in which he argues that monotheism and despotic, imperial States are intrinsically linked (WP, 43), Deleuze rejected modes of argumentation that appeal to dogmatic images of an allegedly transcendent, morally relevant Entity.

So, why would we call what Deleuze is doing – or what I want to do with Deleuze – *theology*? There are good reasons to hesitate.[9] This term is often (indeed usually) identified with debates among rival coalitions over the correct interpretation of the revelation of the God of Jesus Christ, and the correct practice of the rituals through which shared engagement with that God is mediated. We could point out that there is a long precedent for the use of the term "theology" by non-religious philosophers – from Aristotle to Žižek – to describe aspects of their projects.[10] But do we have any good reasons to call *Deleuze* a theologian and, if so, in what sense? Throughout the book I will examine specific elements of his work that illustrate his contribution to the science of non-existing entities that condition real experience. However, it is also important to note that throughout his writings he deals with issues that can be considered "theological" in a wider sense.

Deleuze's speculation on theological themes is evident already in his earliest esoteric (and later repudiated) writings,[11] but our focus will be on his acknowledged works. All of the monographs he wrote on particular philosophers in the 1960s (including Hume, Nietzsche, Kant, Bergson, and Spinoza) dealt with the transcendental conditions for real, finite experience, for which the term "God" (*theos*) has traditionally been used. In fact, Deleuze himself uses this term surprisingly often, although his creation of new concepts radically alters its function. "To anyone who asks: 'do you believe in God?' we should reply in strictly Kantian or Schreberian terms: 'Of course, but only as the master of the disjunctive syllogism . . . the sole thing that is divine is the nature of an energy of disjunctions" (AO, 14). Later in *Anti-Oedipus*, he differentiates between the "schizophrenic God" and the "God of religion," but insists they are related to the same syllogism (AO, 85). In *A Thousand Plateaus* he has Professor Challenger assert that "God is a Lobster" (AO, 45). Such expressions are obviously meant to be humorous – but Deleuze is not joking.

Deleuze is interested in the practical as well as the speculative tasks of theology. For most theologians (of whatever tradition) philosophical reflections on the conditions for the existence of finite reality are connected to pragmatic questions about how to live with (or in) the intensely real experience of being-conditioned as finite. Often such questions are gathered under the heading "spirituality." Deleuze sometimes utilizes such language to describe his own proposals, as when he calls for spiritual repetitions, spiritual becomings, and even a sort of "spiritual philosophy."[12] As with his use of the term "God," however, Deleuze's occasional references to the "spiritual" have nothing to do with disembodied *intentional* forces. What interests him is the intense construction of "a life" in the encounter with infinite intensities of difference. Christian spirituality, of course, answers such questions by appealing to the Spirit of Christ. As we will see in the following chapters, Deleuze's answers include references to demonic geneses, diabolical principles and pacts with the

Devil. Such expressions are obviously meant to be provocative and playful – but, in a sense we will need to unpack as we go along, Deleuze is quite serious.

Anti-Oedipus, Anti-Christ

Throughout his work Deleuze combats forces that restrain thought, regiment behavior and repress desire. This is particularly evident in *Anti-Oedipus*, his first collaborative effort with psychoanalyst Félix Guattari. I will explore this book in more detail in Chapter 5, along with its companion volume *A Thousand Plateaus*. In a sense, however, the whole of Deleuze's philosophy is "Anti-Oedipus," a combat against psychological and social representations that turn life into a tragedy. In several places Deleuze points briefly to parallels between Oedipus and Christ, but he never analyzed the repressive power of the latter in as much detail as that of the former. Let us begin with a brief description of the critical and creative aspects of Deleuze's engagement with "Oedipus" and some of the ways in which my project expands upon his efforts through a more explicit theological engagement with "Christ."

Anti-*Oedipus*? In his collaboration with Guattari, one of Deleuze's most popular targets was a psychoanalytic obsession with the resolution of the Oedipal complex, which he argued reinforces a triangulation of desire within the daddy-mommy-me structure of the "holy family," and serves a colonizing function within the capitalist mode of inscribing the socius. However, the problem is much larger than a particular interpretation of Freudian analysis and the successful resolution of adolescent identity issues during the genital stage of development. "Oedipus" can refer more broadly to representations or "images" that inscribe lack, law, and signification into desire. Deleuze calls this inscription the *priestly* curse on desire. "Every time desire is betrayed, cursed, uprooted from its field of immanence, a priest is behind it. The priest cast the triple curse on desire: the negative law, the extrinsic rule and the transcendental ideal" (TP, 171).

The psychoanalysts Deleuze criticizes so harshly in *Anti-Oedipus* are portrayed as only the latest mediators of this priestly curse. The repressive power of regulative ideals that inscribe deficiency into life saturates the entire field of social-production. Before and after Deleuze, many psychologists and scholars from other disciplines have criticized the Freudian conception of the Oedipal complex for a wide variety of reasons (challenging its phallocentrism, questioning its empirical warrant, etc.). Below I will argue that the Deleuzian project can be rendered even more powerful by linking it to concepts derived from recent theoretical developments based on empirical research in cognitive science and other disciplines. It is important to keep in mind that the critique of psychoanalysis was only a small aspect of Deleuze's lifelong combat with the repressive power of psychological, political, and philosophical "representations."

Anti-Oedipus? Deleuze and Guattari call their project "schizo-analysis" (or pragmatics) and there is no doubt that it has a *negative* task. "Destroy, destroy . . . Destroy Oedipus, the illusion of the ego, the puppet of the superego, guilt, the law, castration" (AO, 342). This comprehensive critique of Oedipus, and all that it "represents," plays a crucial role in their attempt to unveil the reasons why people seem to desire their own repression and even embrace fascism, while disavowing both. However, critique and creation always work together. As we will see, schizoanalysis also has *positive* tasks such as liberating and mobilizing the "schizzes" of desiring-production and assembling revolutionary "machines." Analyzing and producing the break-flows that dissolve Oedipus require aggression, but an aggression that – like Nietzsche's – is always and already an affirmation. Not only *Anti-Oedipus*, but the whole of Deleuze's corpus is an affirmative pragmatic machine that releases the productivity of thinking, acting, and feeling from their bondage to images that are intended to mediate transcendent ideals.

Anti-*Christ*? For the purposes of my project, there are several good reasons for prying into and knocking around within the edifices *Christian* theology. First, Deleuze himself consistently focused on the special role of Christianity in western philosophy and culture throughout his work, and often used the label Anti-Christ to describe aspects of his own proposals. Of course, interest in the psychological and political influence of Christianity on late modernity goes far beyond Deleuze studies. A second reason, then, is that such a focus may contribute to wider conversations among contemporary continental and political philosophers, as well as "new atheists." Third, a set of personal reasons: Christianity is my religious family of origin, the dominant religious force in my social context and one of the areas of study in which I have the most academic expertise. This is not a book about Christian doctrine, but about the secretion of productive atheism that is stimulated by Deleuze's creation of concepts. My interest here is not in the details of intramural doctrinal disputes, but in enhancing that secretion by attending to the repressive function of representations of "Christ" in the mental and social space of *religious* coalitions and the theologies bound to them.

It is important to emphasize that hammering away on *Christ* has very little to do with the historical man Jesus of Nazareth, just as Deleuze's attack on *Oedipus* was only indirectly related to the fictional character in Sophocles' tragic play. Deleuze was interested in the way in which this literary figure was taken up later in the imagination of others, and came to represent a particularly powerful pscyho-social process of repression and oppression. I am interested in how beliefs about the historical figure of Jesus were formed later in the imagination of others, and came to function within the doctrinal formulations and ritual practices of a particular religious coalition, which eventually came to dominate most of the western world. The problem is not Jesus who, as best we can tell, was a relatively compassionate revolutionary with good intentions (who, like Oedipus, apparently had mother issues and struggled with alienation from a Father figure). The problem is the way in which Paul, John and later theologians imaginatively constructed "Christ" as the Son of God, the heavenly High Priest and idealized moral Judge of all humanity. As we will see below, the motivations for such constructions can be illuminated by attending to the human cognitive and coalitional defaults that so easily engender widespread imaginative engagement with supernatural agents (like Christ), which in turn reinforces anxiety about personal and in-group identity.

Anti-Christ? My critique will focus on the way in which "Christ" (as one important example of a religious Image taken as a mediator of transcendence) functions within what I will call *sacerdotal* theology. It is not my intention to destroy the coalitions of Christianity (or any other religion). I am not heralding the coming of the Beast from the thirteenth chapter of the Apocalypse of John, whom the latter envisioned as persecuting believers and dominating the world economy. It is hard to imagine anything less Deleuzian! In his epistles John warns believers that Antichrists have already come into the world, which is a sign that it is "the last hour" (1 Jn. 2:8). Antichrists are those who deny that Jesus Christ has come in the flesh (2 Jn. 1:7). Assuming that this refers to the idea, expressed in the prologue to John's Gospel, that the divine "Logos" became flesh and lived among us, then it is safe to say that, after reading this book, John would consider me and Deleuze to be Antichrists. One of my main concerns in what follows is to show why and how anxiety about properly detecting Christ and anxiety about protecting Christian in-group cohesion are interrelated.

This "Anti-Christ" project is also meant to be constructive as well as destructive. In his book on Nietzsche, Deleuze argues that the opposition of Zarathustra or Dionysius to Christ is a "differential *affirmation* . . . against all nihilism and against this particular form of it."[13] As Deleuze chipped away at Oedipus (as well as the dogmatic image of thought and moral images of transcendence), he also created novel concepts and assembled new, productive schizo-analytic and pragmatic machines. By chipping away at the iconic function of Christ, I hope to help unveil the dynamics that lead people to desire their own *religious* repression. This too will require creating new concepts and making new connections. How does one go about the process of construction? Deleuze recommends that one must begin within the social formation in which one finds oneself. "Lodge yourself on a stratum, experiment with the opportunities it offers, find an advantageous place on it, find potential movements of deterritorialization, possible lines of flight, experience them, produce flow conjunctions here and there, try out continuums of intensities segment by segment, have a small plot of new land at all times" (TP, 178).

The social formation in which I find myself is largely stratified by monotheistic religions, even – or especially – when the role of these coalitional forces is ignored or downplayed. Increasingly one hears the voices of "new atheists" protesting against this stratification. Why is it so easy for most people to ignore these protests? My strategy is to begin from the inside, so to speak, and to work outward, testing Deleuze's suggestive hypothesis that Christianity in particular has a special role to play in the secretion of atheism. What potential movements of deterritorialization, what possible lines of flight can we find already *within* Christian theology itself? As atheists have learned over the centuries, however, poking at problematic doctrinal reasoning or questionable moral practices in religion has surprisingly little effect. If we really want to dissolve the power of *religious* repression, we need more leverage; we need to understand the mental and social mechanisms that surreptitiously produce and automatically reproduce this phenomenon across cultures. Here we are aided by discoveries within the bio-cultural sciences of religion, which have exposed the evolved cognitive and coalitional processes through which the gods (including Christ) are imaginatively born(e).

Anthropomorphic Promiscuity and Sociographic Prudery

I use the phrase "bio-cultural study of religion" to designate the heterogeneous conceptual space within which an expanding number of disciplines are converging in support of the claim that religious phenomena can be explained by the evolution of cognitive processes that over-detect human-like forms and coalitional processes that over-protect socially inscribed norms. The empirical research that supports this sort of hypothesis comes from fields as diverse as cognitive science, archaeology, evolutionary neurobiology, moral psychology, social anthropology, and political theory. I do not have the space here to review all of the various trends in these and other disciplines that bear on these issues.[14] Happily, such a review is not required for our current purpose, namely, providing a conceptual framework derived from this research that we can use as a heuristic device in our analysis of Deleuze and as a wedge for splitting apart two distinctive trajectories in theology.

Figure 1.1 is a coordinate grid that depicts a correlation between cognitive and coalitional tendencies that developed together in mutually reinforcing ways in the evolution of *Homo sapiens*. This

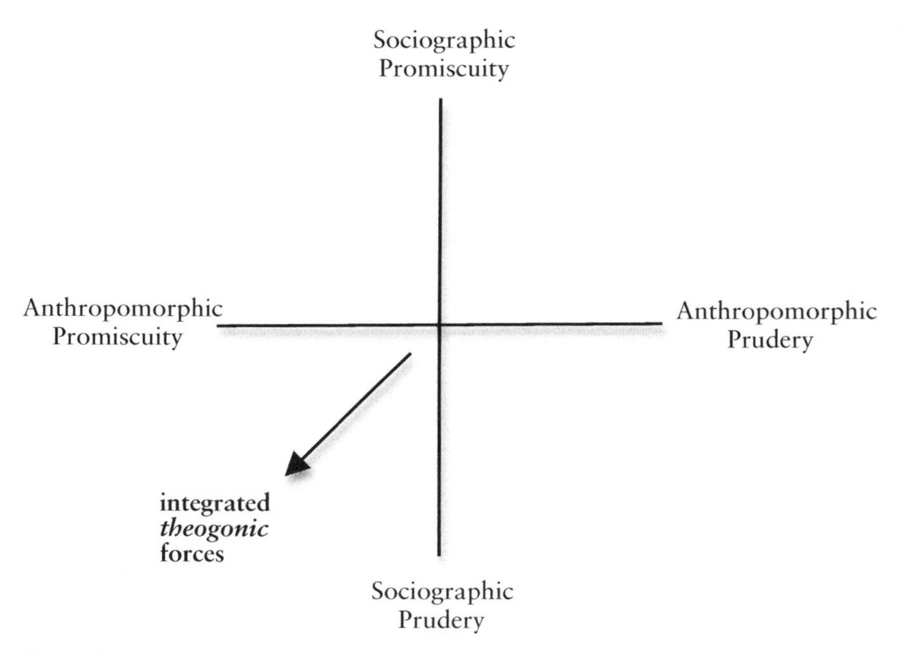

Figure 1.1

framework does not capture all of the important distinctions within and between the various theories in the bio-cultural study of religion, but the distinctions it does make can help us render more explicit the connections between them and more easily link them to Deleuze's project in the chapters that follow. It can also help us unveil the secrets of theogonic reproduction.

The horizontal line indicates a continuum on which we can mark the tendency of persons to guess "human-like intentional force" when confronted with ambiguous phenomena in the natural environment. The anthropomorphically *promiscuous* are always on the lookout, jumping at any opportunity to postulate such agents as causal explanations even – or especially – when these interpretations must appeal to disembodied intentionality, i.e., "supernatural agency" in a sense explained below. The anthropomorphically *prudish*, on the other hand, are suspicious about such appeals. They tend to reflect more carefully before giving in to their intuitive desire to ascribe intentionality to unknown causes.

The continuum indicated by the vertical line registers how a person holds on to conventional modes of inscribing the social field, i.e., to the proscriptions and prescriptions that regulate the evaluative practices of the coalition with which he or she primarily identifies. Sociographic *prudes* are strongly committed to the authorized social norms of their in-group, following and protecting them even at great cost to themselves. They are more likely to be suspicious of out-groups and to accept claims or demands that appeal to authorities within their own coalition. The sociographic *promiscuity* of those at the other end of the spectrum, on the other hand, leads them to be more open to intercourse with out-groups about alternate normativities and to the pursuit of new modes of creative social inscription. Such persons are also less likely to accept moralistic restrictions that are based primarily on appeals to convention.

The evolutionary default is toward the integration of anthropomorphic promiscuity and sociographic prudery. In other words, human beings today are intuitively and naturally drawn into the bio-cultural gravitational field of the integrated tendencies in the lower left quadrant. Why? In the environment of our early ancestors (Late Pleistocene Africa) the selective advantage went to hominids whose cognitive capacities enabled them to quickly detect relevant agents in the *natural* environment, and whose groups were adequately protected from the dissolution that could result from too many defectors and cheaters in the *social* environment. Prior to the pressures exerted by population expansion or by reduced access to ecological resources, hominid groups may well have been less prudish in their sociography. Whatever the unique conditions were that led some groups out of Africa, however, it seems clear that their survival was enhanced by the integration of theogonic forces.

The evolution of cognitive mechanisms like the Hypersensitive Agency Detection Device (HADD) would have helped them survive by increasing their success in avoiding predation and in finding prey, protectors, and partners. However, it also would have made our ancestors prone to perceptual mistakes, such as interpreting a noise in the forest as a tiger when it was only the wind. When it comes to detecting potential agents in the environment it is better to be safe than sorry; better overly sensitive and often wrong than in-sensitive and eaten once. Despite the many false positives, natural selection would have rewarded this perceptual strategy. The interpretation of ambiguous phenomena increasingly defaulted to "intentional force." If no physical tiger could be found, this default would have contributed to the likelihood of guessing "animal-spirit" or some other invisible power like "ancestor-ghost." Such guesses would have been reinforced as other default cognitive processes kicked in, such as the Theory of Mind Mechanism (ToMM) and intuitive dualism, further strengthening the tendency to postulate the existence of disembodied agents with mental and emotional states when confronted with ambiguous phenomena.[15]

Ideas of disembodied intentional forces may have been engendered by overly sensitive cognitive *detection*, but it was overly sensitive coalitional *protection* that determined which ideas were maintained and nurtured by human groups. In other words, imaginative ideas about ghosts, gods or other supernatural agents are easily born in cognition but they must also be borne in cultures. Such ideas multiply rapidly in the mind, but the images that stick around are those that are more easily transmitted across generations and contribute to the cohesion of the group. A variety of theories within the bio-cultural sciences contribute to our understanding of the role of religion in sociographic prudery. For example, belief in ghosts or gods who could always be watching the behavior of the natural agents in the coalition, and who had the power to bring misfortune or blessing, would decrease the likelihood of cheating or defection to other groups. Even if no one else sees me, a god might catch me cheating and I (or the whole group) could be punished.

In addition to enhancing moral behavior, imaginatively intense forms of communal engagement with supernatural agents (e.g., chanting or singing together, dancing or other synchronic movement and other activities that lead to altered states of consciousness) would also have strengthened emotional bonds within human coalitions, enriched social intelligence, and even increased susceptibility to the placebo effects of ritual healing. But religion often involves painful rituals and self-destructive behaviors that do not seem to promote health. At the very least, they take time, energy, and resources that could be used in other ways that would more directly contribute to the survival of the coalition. Such behavior can be illuminated by costly signaling theory. A willingness to undergo painful rituals, perform time-consuming devotional exercises, or express emotional dedication to a god in other ways, powerfully signals a person's commitment to the group. Such persons are more easily trusted and granted status within the group. Archaeological evidence suggests that sometime during the Late Pleistocene, some of these "god-bearing" (theogonic) groups left Africa, eventually out-competing all other hominid species and spreading out across the Levant and into Europe and Asia. All contemporary humans share a phylogenetic heritage that was shaped by adaptations to this ancestral environment, and that still influences social entrainment practices across cultures today. This helps to explain why religion comes so naturally to most people.[16]

The conceptual integration of *bio*-logical and *cultural* aspects of religion within this interdisciplinary field provides an easy point of contact with the Deleuzian project. Deleuze makes similar transversal moves throughout his work, exploring (for example) the relation between bodies and language in *Logic of Sense* and the relation between desiring-production and social-production in *Anti-Oedipus*. At one point in the latter volume, he even suggested that the theory of schizophrenia is "biocultural."[17] Of course, he could not have meant this in the technical sense developed above since the most relevant empirical findings only began to emerge, and the relevant disciplines only began to converge, in the 1990s. In *Difference and Repetition* and *A Thousand Plateaus*, among other places, Deleuze often reached across academic fields and extracted concepts from (for example) mathematics, physics, chemistry, biology, archaeology, and cultural anthropology. There are several creative attempts to demonstrate the importance of Deleuze's philosophy for a wide variety of sciences in the secondary literature, but none have applied it to this constellation of disciplines as they bear on the phenomena of religion.[18]

At one level, my project is meant to contribute to Deleuze studies by reading him at the intersection of fields within what I am calling the bio-cultural study of religion. At another level, it is meant to demonstrate how Deleuzian philosophy can contribute to this interdisciplinary discussion by encouraging more rigorous reflection on the existential conditions and practical implications of some of the findings within these sciences. My primary concern, however, is fabricating an iconoclastic theology out of resources extracted in the process of reading these two bodies of literature together. Given the empirical complexity of the bio-cultural study of religion and the conceptual complexity of Deleuze's philosophy, it will not be possible to provide exhaustive summaries or detailed analysis of even the most important ideas within either. My more modest goal is to demonstrate the way in which integrating concepts derived from both can unveil and weaken the power of the theogonic forces of anthropomorphic promiscuity and sociographic prudery, opening up new creative possibilities for theology.

In the next five chapters, I will follow the increasingly common practice in the bio-cultural study of religion of referring to all disembodied intentional forces postulated across cultures as "supernatural agents" (or "gods").[19] In order to include imagined agents that are temporarily embodied even if they have not always been, no longer embodied even if they once were, or potentially embodied even if they might not ever be, perhaps we should say "contingently-embodied" instead of simply "disembodied." For such a force to play a religious function within a coalition, it must be attributed intentionality or related human-like features, such as consciousness or the capacity for symbolic communication. Moreover, belief in the axiological relevance of the postulated agent must be widely shared and ritually mediated in a way that bears on the normative boundaries and behavior of members of the in-group.

I have argued elsewhere for the appropriateness of using the term *religion* to designate "shared imaginative engagement with axiologically relevant supernatural agents."[20] This is obviously not the only aspect of the complex phenomena wrapped up within and around what is commonly referred to as "religion," but it does pick out a distinctive feature that is particularly relevant for our purposes. I will continue to use this vocabulary here, but for the sake of this experimental exploration of Deleuzian theology I will also refer to the supernatural Agent (or "God") postulated in monotheism as a "transcendent moralistic Entity," for reasons that will soon become clear. Oedipus and Christ; both are born(e) as a result of naturally evolved and socially entrained tendencies that most people are happy to leave secret. Theologians do not have this luxury.

Sacerdotal and Iconoclastic Trajectories

If we think of "religion" as shared imaginative engagement with supernatural agents, Deleuze is quite clearly *not* religious. To understand more clearly why it makes sense to say that he *is* a "theologian," we need to make some more distinctions. We will continue to utilize Deleuze's own (Klossowski-inspired) description of theology introduced above throughout the book, but I would also like to introduce another description that is consistent with his but can more easily be brought into the dialogue fostered by the bio-cultural study of religion. Broadly speaking, we may think of theology as the critique and construction of hypotheses about the conditions for axiological engagement. We find ourselves bound together with others within psychologically complex and shifting social boundaries, enmeshed within ongoing processes of evaluating and being evaluated. What are the sources of determination that account for the existence of all this pragmatic evaluation? What engenders this binding normativity in which we live and move and have our valuing? To use Deleuzian terms, which we will have to unpack in the chapters that follow, what are the transcendental conditions for the real experience of creating new values?

Most hypotheses about the conditions for the real experience of axiological engagement have been of the sort that flow easily from the default tendencies produced by the integration of evolved theogonic forces; they appeal to supernatural agents that care about the survival and flourishing of "our" in-group. These are "hypotheses" in the broadest sense, i.e., abductive inferences or "best guesses" that are shaped by prior experience but whose plausibility depends on their ongoing explanatory and pragmatic functions. In small-scale societies, the tendency to guess "animal-spirit" or "ancestor-ghost" when confronted with ambiguous phenomena comes naturally and is reinforced by emotionally arousing rituals, participation in which provides an ongoing opportunity to signal commitment to the group. Ideas about this sort of "god" are minimally counter-intuitive, which makes them easy to remember and transmit across generations.[21] In such contexts, beliefs about supernatural agents are not held onto as "hypothetical" in a narrower sense (postulates that might or might not be true) because everyone in the group *knows* about the *powers* of these disembodied intentional forces.

When all humans lived in such coalitions, there was no need for theology. As societies grew in size and complexity, however, new strategies were needed for dealing with an increasing plurality of competing abductive inferences (whose gods?, which spirituality?). Appealing to the relatively small supernatural agents of local coalitions no longer sufficed. Bigger gods were needed for bigger cultures to manage difference and doubt. This required "high gods" who were smarter and stronger, who could judge commitment to the shared moral codes of the larger culture more accurately, and whose power to punish or reward behavior reached across the in-groups that were being subsumed into such civilizations. Within the complex literate states that came into dominance during the axial age, we find the emergence of the idea of an all-encompassing Force, which in some way transcends finite, human existence and originates, orders and orients any and all axiological engagement whatsoever. This is an example of a retroductive hypothesis.

As inferences that "lead away from" (ab-ducere) old and toward new inductions and deductions, *abductive* hypotheses often work automatically – as long as they work. *Retroductive* hypotheses intend to "lead back" (retro-ducere) from more or less stable abductive hypotheses about a phenomenon to the conditions without which the phenomenon could not be as (or become what) it is. In other words, they are claims about that which renders a phenomenon possible (or actual). Theology makes retroductive inferences about the conditions for the existence of finite axiological engagement itself. Because it makes abductions explicit, however, retroductive argumentation also automatically alters the conditions that affect their plausibility and stability. This means that theology is "about" the pragmatic conditions of axiological engagement as well. That is to say, insofar as its theoretical hypothesizing is wrapped up within and around the abductive inferences operative in the practices of human coalitions, theology *makes a difference* in the conditions for thinking, acting, and feeling. In this sense, theology can engender *new* conditions for axiological engagement.[22]

In east and south Asia, retroductive theological hypotheses included concepts like Dao and Dharma. In the major religious traditions that arose in west Asia, however, the dominant hypotheses that emerged involved appeals to a much more person-like and coalition-favoring supernatural Agent. As we will see, the obsession with identifying

One source of determination was influenced in part by the Platonic and Aristotelian categories that influenced the intellectual leaders of these religions. However, belief in one Personal God, whose law-giving and care-giving are mediated within and by a particular group, was also shaped by the way in which the identity of Jewish, Christian, and Muslim coalitions was tied to narratives about the creation of Adam and the call of Abraham (paradise lost, and found, in west Asia). The main debates among these coalitions revolve around the extent to which Moses, Jesus or Muhammad mediate the revelation of and ritual access to the one true God. Monotheism is anthropomorphic promiscuity and sociographic prudery gone wild – taken (and applied) to infinity. When theologians from these traditions operate under the influence of the bio-cultural gravitational pull of the integrated theogonic forces, they are following what I call the *sacerdotal* trajectory of theology (cf. Figure 1.2).

This trajectory is "sacerdotal" in the sense that it is nurtured by and reinforces shared imaginative engagement with a transcendent moralistic Entity, whose "making-sacred" of a coalition is mediated by "priests"; that is, by religious leaders who interpret divine revelation and codify or police the rituals of the group. My project here focuses on the sacerdotal trajectory within Christian theology and

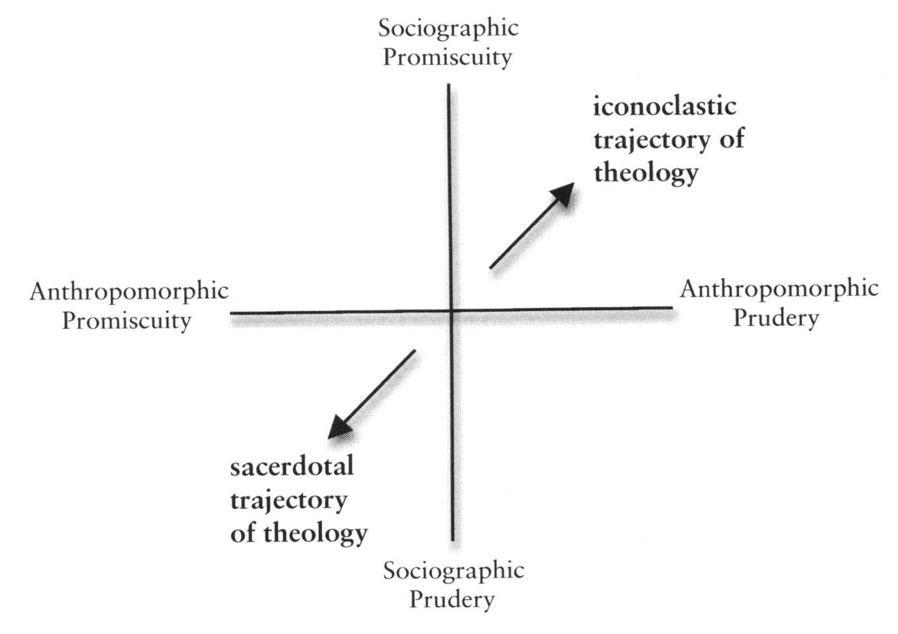

Figure 1.2

the function of the image of *Christ* in the priestly mediation of divine intentionality.

However, this is not the only sort of trajectory in theology. Appealing to a supernatural Agent detected by a particular religious coalition is not the only way to construct retroductive hypotheses about the conditions for axiological engagement. In fact, even among Christian theologians one finds hypotheses that do not rely upon, and sometimes even challenge, the idea of an infinitely wise and powerful Person whose final eschatological redemption is limited to a select Group. At the end of Chapter 2, I will explore some of the ways in which the anthropomorphic promiscuity and sociographic prudery that support or protect privileged religious representations are sometimes resisted by members of Christian coalitions, especially logicians, egalitarians, and contemplatives. Such resistance follows (at least partially) what I will call the *iconoclastic* trajectory of theology. The problem, however, is that these voices are almost always ignored, repressed, destroyed or domesticated by the overwhelming forces of the sacerdotal trajectory.

As we will see, Deleuze follows the iconoclastic trajectory radically or, I should say, rhizomically. His retroductive hypotheses about the conditions for real experience are exceptionally anthropomorphically prudish and sociographically promiscuous. In the following chapters, we will see that he sometimes refers to transcendent*al* conditions, by which he most definitely does *not* mean transcend*ent* conditions. His vocabulary shifts throughout his writings, but Deleuze will consistently argue against portrayals of the "non-existent entities" that animate language (and all that comes and goes with it) that represent them as transcendent to or as models of that which they condition. Values are not distributed and hierarchically organized by a moral Being; rather, the pure becoming of univocal being *is* the creation of new values. I hope to show how this sort of theological hypothesis, which breaks *icons* of transcendence and creates new *clastic* assemblages made up of productive fragments, can be rendered more plausible and productive in dialogue with the bio-cultural study of religion.

As the critique and construction of retroductive hypotheses about the conditions for axiological engagement, in the sense explained above, "theology" only became necessary (and perhaps only became possible) as societies became more complex and densely populated, creating new psychological and political challenges in the axial age. The sort of hypothesis that eventually came to dominate most of west

Asia and Europe (and much of the rest of the globe) relied on appeals to a transcendent moralistic Entity, imaginative engagement with whom reinforced the hopes of souls and empires for immortality. This strategy was motivated, in part, by anxiety about the doubt that began to secrete within pluralistic encounters. Why do other groups have such different gods? Why does our god not seem to be helping us? Sacerdotal hypothesizing works hard at defending the truth of "our" interpretation of supernatural Agency, and the necessity of "our" ritualized engagements with that Agency.

A quite different sort of strategy emerges when one begins to resist the default forces of theogonic reproduction. Perhaps we can explain ambiguous phenomena and create shared values without appealing to the authority of a supernatural Agent. Perhaps axiological engagement has nothing to do with gods. Naturalism, secularism, and atheism were also born in the axial age, but they were very nearly starved to death. In our late modern globalizing context, which is characterized by ever more complexity and plurality, it will be increasingly important to explore the sort of theoretical and pragmatic hypotheses that are produced by the iconoclastic trajectory of theology. Theology may have evolved within particular religious traditions, but like all of the other sciences, it too can escape the domination of religious coalitional authorities, and have its own productive life. It may well be, however, that some of the most productive hypotheses that flow from this iconoclastic trajectory will be those that begin by poking around the cracks in the conceptual edifices erected within a particular monotheistic Coalition.

The Secrets of Theism

In *Nietzsche & Philosophy*, Deleuze wrote that the atheism secreted by Christianity is that of a bad conscience and *ressentiment* (NP, 154). In his later works, however, he came to see this secretion as potentially more positive. In his book on the painter *Francis Bacon*, for example, he suggested that "Christianity contains a germ of *tranquil atheism* that will *nurture* painting."[23] We will explore this relation between atheism and artistic expression in more detail at the end of Chapter 5, but Deleuze's comments on painting and philosophy can help us introduce his broader point. In his 1980 lectures on Spinoza, he insisted that "atheism has never been external to religion: atheism is the artistic power at work on religion." Deleuze argued that when Renaissance painters began to take seriously the claim that God could not be represented, they felt freed to portray figures, even and especially the Figure of Christ, in a plurality of strange and creative ways. He suggests that, in a similar way, the struggle with the idea of "God" in philosophy provided it with an irreplaceable opportunity to free concepts from the constraints of "representation."[24] This suggests that it is precisely here, in the process of revealing the failure of theistic attempts to represent the infinite that the aesthetic power and philosophical productivity of atheism can begin to flow.

First, what is the relation between theist secrets and atheist secretion? Deleuze describes secrets in a way that resists a simple binary distinction between the secret and its disclosure. A secret is not a static content that is *either* hidden in a box *or* out in the open. It is the nature of secrets that something oozes out of the box and that something is perceived through or in a partially opened box. Secrets are always in motion, always being secretly perceived. "The secret as secretion" (TP, 317). Deleuze was partial to the literary form of the novella, whose very form is Secrecy (What Happened?), and he saw the "becomings" of secrets as playing an important role in his own authorship.[25] For our purposes at this stage, the important point is a distinction Deleuze makes in the ways in which societies treat their secrets. The secret has its origin in the nomadic war machine, where it is treated with celerity – always in motion, molecularized, becoming imperceptible in a pure moving line. Within the State apparatus or a monotheistic religion, however, secrets are treated with gravity – acquiring an infinite form, a molar organization protected by a paranoiac insistence on absolute imperceptibility. However, "the more the secret is made into a structuring, organizing form, the thinner and more ubiquitous it becomes, the more its content becomes molecular, at the same time as its form dissolves" (TP, 319).

We will unpack some of this language in more detail in Chapter 5, but we can already pose the key questions: How does theism treat its secrets? What does theism secrete? In this context, my interest is in two types of secret, or two modes of secretion, both of which have to do with the issue of *representing* the infinite God of orthodox Christian doctrine. This supernatural Agent is not as easy to bear as the finite gods that have populated most human coalitions throughout history and, indeed, that continue to populate the imaginative worlds of most Christians; e.g., heavenly saints, angelic messengers, demonic tempters and, in a distinctive sense we will unfold throughout the book, Christ himself.

The first type of secret in theism is connected to the problem of *revelation*, and is primarily related to anthropomorphic promiscuity. Sacerdotal coalitions are held together, in part, by shared engagement with an ambiguously perceived supernatural Agent. Classical theism asserts that God is impassible, immutable and transcendent to creation. But how can one comprehend an infinite Person? How can such a God be detected? On the one hand, most theologians want to maintain divine infinity (to avoid limiting God), and so insist that a God comprehended is no God (the apophatic move). That may well be, but a wholly incomprehensible God is axiologically irrelevant. Religious people need to know, at least, *that* God somehow knows something about them in some sense. However, it seems that a supernatural Agent with infinite knowledge (omniscience) would know everything all at once about everyone in any and all coalitions, past, present, and future; such knowledge has little practical import in the quotidian life of a religious coalition. So, on the other hand, sacerdotal religious leaders make all sorts of positive assertions (multiple kataphatic moves), claims about specific things we can know about God and about specific things that God knows about us, both of which are required in order to render divine knowledge relevant for daily practice.

Without some appeal to revelation, members of the group would be ignorant about God, and it would dissolve as a *religious* coalition. It is no secret that sacerdotal theology depends heavily upon divine revelation. Enormous energy is spent trying to discern what God *meant* to reveal in Scripture, what the revelation of Christ *means* for everyday life. However, precisely by treating this problem with such gravity, a suspicion secretes within this monotheistic Religion: is anyone really able to detect the intentions of a transcendent moralistic Entity? Christianity cannot hide this secret, nor does it try. The various coalitions within Christianity cohere precisely because of these ongoing lively debates about the meaning of divine revelation. However, not much can be said about a wholly transcendent, infinite Person, and so hyper-active cognitive default mechanisms latch onto more anthropomorphic and socially relevant supernatural agents. Christ in particular plays a key role in revealing secret divine knowledge because he is imaginatively engaged as the ideal *representative* of the infinite God. The problem of ignorance about the latter is dealt with by appealing to special revelations of the former, which are only properly detected and interpreted by members of the in-group. However, such appeals also allow the secret to ooze more freely: the infinite deity allegedly revealed in Christ is so maximally counter-intuitive that its detection plays no relevant role in the lives of most Christians.[26]

A second sort of secret has to do with the problem of *ritual* in sacerdotal coalitions, and is more closely related to sociographic prudery. The orthodox God of Christian theism is portrayed as omnipotent as well as omniscient. However, an infinite God whose all-powerful will pre-ordains everything from all eternity is also not of much use when it comes to holding together a religious coalition on a daily basis. How can such infinite power be mediated? On the one hand, an absolutely powerful God can eternally protect the in-group and eternally punish defectors and out-groups. Sociographic prudery writ large. On the other hand, why would it even be necessary (and how would it be possible) to ritually engage a transcendent Entity whose moralistic determinations are irresistible? It is hard to make sense, for example, of the effect that prayer could have on such an Agent. Oddly enough, divine omnipotence is equivalent to divine impotence, when it comes to the everyday management of axiological engagement within a religious coalition – except insofar as the intellectually costly profession of belief in such apparently absurd ideas signals a strong commitment to spiritual kith and kin and thereby reinforces in-group cohesion.

Without some ritual mediation of the power of God, the smaller coalitions within a monotheistic Religion would dissolve as *religious* groups. It is no secret that the rituals of Christianity do not always work. Baptisms do not always produce holy people. The Eucharist does not create a unified Church. Prayers seem to go unanswered. One of the purposes of sacerdotal theology is to explain these ritual failures. The implausibility of such explanations is less interesting than the fact that the explanations themselves secrete the flow of atheism, precisely by displaying the apparent irrelevance of an infinite supernatural Agent. The sorts of small-scale societies in which our ancestors evolved were held together, in part, by shared participation in rituals with just the right balance of sensual pageantry, emotional arousal, frequency and perceived involvement of human-like, coalition-favoring supernatural agents.[27] A transcendent moralistic Entity gets no traction with these evolved cognitive and coalitional mechanisms. As we will see, this is why Christian sacramental rituals and other related practices (such as joint worship and prayer, Bible studies, etc.) so quickly default to shared imaginative engagement with more human-like and coalition-favoring "gods" who could appear out of nowhere at any time to give concrete guidance or to punish cheaters. The risen Christ surprises Saul on the road to Damascus and blinds him because he is persecuting in-group members (Acts 9). Ananias and Sapphira fall down dead because they lied to the Holy Spirit about their donation to the church (Acts 5:1–6). This is the sort of supernatural agent that encourages group cohesion.

In Christianity, the image of Christ is at the center of revelation and ritual. He is imaginatively engaged as the *representation* of the infinite God, manifesting and mediating divine intentionality, which always remains secretive even as it is ambiguously perceived. Those who follow the sacerdotal trajectory treat these secrets with gravity, working hard to keep them from dissolving the molar organizations of the Religion. To follow the iconoclastic trajectory is to treat these secrets with celerity, sending them flying into contact with other hypotheses that challenge their anthropomorphic promiscuity and sociographic prudery or, in Deleuzian terms, clearing the ground of idols of transcendence in order to create new concepts on a plane of immanence.

Scholars familiar with the complexities of the historical development of Christian doctrine, and the nuances of Christology in particular, might already be wincing at some of my generalizations and are sure to wince further as the argument unfolds. For the purposes of this project, however, the utilization of such generalizations is both necessary and sufficient. It is necessary because of the limitations of space and the nature of the intended audience. It is sufficient because the argument I am trying to make about the function of Christ in Christian theology and religious imagination is not dependent on the details of any particular formulation of doctrine. In fact, one of the main take-away points of the project is that the attempt on the part of theologians to pull the conversation back into debates over the "right" interpretation of Christian revelation or the "best" way to organize Christian rituals and polity is itself an excellent illustration of the operation of the theogonic forces within the sacerdotal trajectory. The iconoclastic theologian refuses to be pulled in, and stays focused on the extent to which an enterprise that appeals to supernatural agents, which are detected only by members of the in-group it helps to protect, remains a plausible and productive way of explaining the natural world and inscribing the social world in an increasingly complex and pluralistic global environment.

An allegedly transcendent moralistic Entity who is unknowable and immutable might as well not exist. Nietzsche wondered whether the gods died laughing. The God of Christian theism dies of boredom. Iconoclastic theology has little or no interest in his death. It is much more interesting to explore how this God is – or fails to be – born(e) in human minds and culture, and to develop new non-religious hypotheses about the conditions for axiological engagement. Deleuze's hypotheses are varied and complex. I will not argue that he is "right" or "best" but that he is "productive." Deleuzian secretions get us moving. Connecting them to insights derived from the bio-cultural study of religion can move us even further: "one can never go far enough in the direction of deterritorialization: you haven't seen anything yet – an irreversible process" (AO, 353).

For Deleuze, the philosopher's critique is not a re-action, but an active mode of existence, a way of being-philosopher that "intends to wield the differential element as *critic and creator* and therefore *as a hammer*."[28] Likewise, iconoclastic theologians wield hammers in ways that are constructive as well as destructive. In fact, there are many ways of using a hammer. Nietzsche himself hammered gently as well as forcefully, creatively "sounding out" the world as well as smashing idols. At one place Deleuze cautions against using a "sledgehammer" in the dismantling of repressive organizations as one makes for oneself a Body without Organs (TP, 177). However, it would be quite un-Deleuzian to make this a universal rule, especially since in so many other places he celebrates the creative power of Nietzsche's more violent atheist hammering[29] and consistently works to flatten icons of transcendence. Hammers can also be used to play musical instruments, and the human ear has one that enables it to listen. When used skillfully with an anvil, with the right mixture of heat and pressure, a hammer can help forge other tools or weapons.

Sometimes one needs to tinker and make new connections, or to tap and create new resonances. Sometimes one needs to knock down walls, or to crack apart the oppressive structures that bind thought, action, and desire. We do not yet know what theological hammers can do.

2

Breaking Theological Icons

This chapter introduces the first and perhaps most obvious sense in which Deleuze's theology is *iconoclastic*: it hammers away at the Platonic notion of *icons* as good copies of ideal models. In fact, his whole philosophical project contributed to the inversion or "reversal of Platonism," a phrase Deleuze borrows from Nietzsche but develops in his own way. Here, as elsewhere, his hammering is both critical and constructive. Deleuze aims to destroy both copies *and* models "in order to institute the chaos which *creates*, making the simulacra function and raising a phantasm – the *most innocent of all destructions*, the destruction of Platonism."[1]

Exploring Deleuze's passion for overturning Platonism is also a good place to start because it further clarifies the sense in which his iconoclasm is *theological*. He rejects Plato's hypotheses about the conditions for the experience of axiological engagement, challenging the way in which they appeal to iconic representations of idealized and morally determinative transcendent entities. Deleuze is even more combative toward the appropriations of Plato among later Christian theologians and philosophers who attempt to represent the infinite as a personal creator and legislator. As we will see, Deleuze's own theological proposals will attempt to invert the entire domain of representation.

This chapter also explores a first sense in which a Deleuzian inspired iconoclastic theology can be considered "Anti-Christ." Deleuze would expose and flatten every putative *image* of transcendence, and he is well aware of the way in which "Christ" has functioned as such an image in Christianity. I will extend Deleuze's creative critique by exploring in more detail how the portrayal of Christ as *the Image* (Icon) of God in sacerdotal theology illustrates what he calls the hidden dualism that motivates Platonic representation. I will also return to the cognitive and coalitional tendencies unveiled by the bio-cultural study of religion, this time attending to the integrated theolytic (god-dissolving) forces of sociographic promiscuity and anthropomorphic prudery, both of which are unleashed in Deleuzian philosophy.

Deleuze finds resources for inverting Platonism in many writers (including Plato himself), but in this chapter I focus on his critical appropriation of three philosophers – Kant, Spinoza, and Nietzsche – in part because of the way in which they deal with difference and desire in relation to "God."[2] Finally, I point to modes of iconoclastic intensification present *within* sacerdotal theology, whose resistance to theogonic forces already initiates the overturning of religious Figures, precisely by exposing the secrets of theism. The rest of the book links Deleuzian concepts to insights from the bio-cultural sciences of religion, intensifying the productive flow of atheism. The first step, however, is introducing the general icono-clasmic force of Deleuze's philosophical (and theological) corpus.

The Inversion of Platonism

Plato's attempts to distinguish the intelligible from the sensible, essence from appearance, and Ideas from images have been the subject of extensive critique from Aristotle onward. However, Deleuze argues that this misses the real drive behind Plato's philosophy, which he discovers in a different sort of distinction. The context in which Plato tried to think, the Greek city, had invented "the agon" as the "rule of the community of free men as rivals" (WP, 9). Any citizen could lay claim to something, and new modes of adjudicating between these claims also had to be invented. Deleuze argues that Plato applied this new challenge to thought itself; how can one choose between rival concepts? There must be some way to judge between a true and a false friend, a just and an unjust state, Socrates and the sophist. To solve this problem, Plato creates the philosophical concept of the Ideas (or the Forms). Deleuze argues that for Plato the primary value of the realm of *Ideas* was not its opposition to the whole realm of *images*, but its provision of models by which to validate the claims of rival mental images. For example, what is justice? The Idea of justice itself, which must be "recognized" through the use of dialectic, is the ground for choosing between competing representations (or images) of justice. For Plato, then, the more important dualism is between two types of image: *icons*, which are true copies of the Idea and always well founded, and *phantasms*, which are false simulacra always engulfed in dissimilarity.

In Plato's dialogues, Socrates (or another friend of truth, such as the Eleatic Stranger) is often portrayed as testing the rival concepts proposed by his interlocutors, exposing the simulacra and trying to track down the icon, the true image that shares in the reality of the Idea. Adjudicating between rival images requires identifying the icon (or copy), which possesses in a secondary way, or "participates" in, the abstract determination that is possessed in a primary way by the Idea (or model) itself. The phantasms, on the other hand, do not truly resemble or participate in the being of the model; their power lies in their capacity to deceive. In other words, according to Deleuze, the basic motivation of Plato's creation of the concept of the Ideas was to provide models, to establish grounds for *selecting between* the good images (icons, which have an internal resemblance as true pretenders) and the bad images (simulacra, disguised and displaced false pretenders). Deleuze calls this Plato's "Eidetic" framework, or the "domain of representation," and argues that most of western philosophy has remained trapped within it ever since.

As we will see in Chapter 3, in a more detailed discussion of *Difference and Repetition*, Deleuze does not simply reject Platonism tout court. He inverts its basic motivation, creating a new concept of Ideas as immanent and differential, rather than transcendent and identical. In fact, Deleuze finds intimations of the reversal of this hidden Platonic dualism already in Plato himself, especially toward the end of the *Sophist* when "the different" almost unhinges the entire discussion of the universal genera and escapes the Eidetic framework, but then falls back and becomes merely the difference *of* things. Overturning Platonism involves a denial of the primacy of original over copy, of model over image; it heralds the "twilight of the *icons*" (DR, 128). However, it also involves an *affirmation* of the *being* of simulacra, and a glorifying of their reign as they flip over the copies *and* the models. Everything becomes simulacrum, but this becoming is not a participation *in* or resemblance *of* anything, but "the act by which the very idea of a model or privileged position is challenged and overturned" (DR, 69).

In *Logic of Sense* Deleuze argues that "to reverse Platonism is first and foremost to remove essences and to substitute events in their place, as jets of singularities" (LS, 64). There he describes the rising of the simulacra in relation to the eternal return, which "reverses representation and destroys the icons" (LS, 302). We will return to these themes in a closer reading of this book in Chapter 4. In that context, Deleuze finds resources in the Stoics (and Epicureans) for challenging Platonists (and Aristotelians, and just about everybody else). The pre-Socratics, with their attempts to find the foundational essence of reality, were philosophers of "the depths." Those who follow Plato out of the cave and seek idealized essences are philosophers of "the heights." The Stoics, on the other hand, are philosophers of "the surface," extending singularities and releasing events, stretching out to make new connections with(in) endlessly cavernous multiplicities.

In Chapter 5, we will find that Deleuze's interest in overturning Platonism is still at work in his collaboration with Félix Guattari in the *Capitalism and Schizophrenia* project. Deleuze is particularly critical of the "image" of Oedipus, the ideal held up by psychoanalysis for resolving sexual and other drives. This image itself is produced by social-machines that "fall back" upon desiring-machines and repress their production by "representing" desire in various ways. The territorial, despotic and capitalist machines code, overcode and decode the flows of desire, leading to quite different representations of desire, as we will see. For Deleuze, "Oedipus" illustrates what he calls the "priestly" curse on desire, a curse that inscribes lack, law, and idealization into desire (castration, incest, fantasy). I will unpack this terminology as we go along, but my focus in each chapter will be on demonstrating how the repressive function of Christ as the Image (or Logos, Incarnation, Judgment) of God functions even more effectively than Oedipus, or other non-religious representations, in part because of the surreptitious forces of theogonic reproduction.

Throughout his writings Deleuze challenges the Platonic dogma that escaping mere opinion (*doxa*) and achieving real knowledge (*episteme*) requires making judgments between rival images that participate more or less truly in transcendent ideal models. Whether or not they called themselves Platonists, Deleuze argues that philosophers have too quickly accepted their task as selecting the right *eidolon*, rejecting the false simulacra and identifying the true copy. Aristotle, for example, may have focused in more detail on genera and specific differences than Plato but he continued to operate within the Eidetic framework. He continues to select among pretenders in a way that excludes the divergent and privileges an allegedly superior finality that grounds or orients the entire domain (the Unmoved Mover). Deleuze complains that philosophy has, for the most part, remained bound by this framework; his favorite exceptions include some of the Stoics and Epicureans, Duns Scotus, Spinoza, and Nietzsche. The problem, for Deleuze, is not images per se, which are real and productive, as he makes clear (for example) in his books on *Cinema*.[3] The problem is treating them only as "representative," which represses their creative power of fabulation. In other words, the problem is judging images as *either* true copies *or* false simulacra *of* something else that transcends them.

It is important to emphasize the sense in which Deleuze's beef with Plato is *theological*. As we saw above, Deleuze depicts theology as the science of non-existent entities and the way in which they animate language (or engender thought, effectuate propositions, condition social-production, etc.) and make for it a body divided into disjunctions. This fits with the broader description of theology I proposed in the first chapter: the critique and construction of retroductive hypotheses about the conditions for axiological engagement. In this sense, Plato is a theologian too. What is it that conditions all experiences of valuation whatsoever? One of Plato's most influential hypotheses was that this imaginative process is ultimately conditioned by the Form or Idea of the Good, which grounds all other Forms or Ideas, in relation to which (the rational part of) the soul is able to adjudicate between true and false images, distinguishing copies from simulacra. On this hypothesis, the value of the images depends on their resemblance to and participation in an Idea.

Plato hinted in Book V of the *Republic* that the Good is "beyond being" (509[b]), a notion later taken up and developed by Plotinus and carried over into Christian Neo-Platonism. This postulated "non-existing" Entity was conceived as the condition for being itself – a transcendent reality that makes knowledge possible (and so animates language, etc.). Deleuze's theological hypotheses, as we shall see, are quite different. Indeed, they are inversions of Plato's Eidetic framework. At this stage, I want to emphasize that *every* Platonic icon is by definition a true imitation (copy) of a transcendent, eternal Idea. In this sense, *all* icons are theological. However, this does not mean that all theology must be iconic. Indeed, Deleuzian theology is intensely iconoclastic. And his iconoclasm is intensely theological.

Deleuze is particularly critical of the way in which Plato, and all those who followed him, treated the concepts of difference and desire. First, Plato privileged sameness over *difference*. "Everything depends," Deleuze argues, on a decision between two formulas: "only that which resembles differs" or "only differences can resemble each other." These are two distinct readings of the world. "The first formula posits resemblances as the condition of differences . . . according to the other formula, by contrast, resemblance, identity, analogy and opposition can no longer be considered anything but effects, the product of a primary difference or a primary system of differences" (DR, 116). Plato promoted the first formula, inviting us to think of difference from the standpoint of a prior similitude or identity: sameness is the condition for imagining differences. Deleuze champions the second formula, inviting us to think of sameness as the product of a deep disparity. He will argue that the condition for our real experience of evaluating things as similar (for example) is conditioned by the complex repetition of pure difference.

Deleuze also blames Plato for taking the wrong step at the beginning of philosophy's long labor over the concept of *desire*. In *Anti-Oedipus*, for example, he insists that "the traditional logic of desire is all wrong from the very outset: from the very first step that the Platonic logic of desire forces us to take, making us choose between *production* and *acquisition*" (AO, 26). Given his broader conception of the domain of representation, in which images lack the reality of the ideal objects they imitate, it makes sense that Plato would think of desire in terms of acquisition. Knowledge is acquired when the soul attains the ideal object it desires. Deleuze is critical of the way in which this inscribes lack (as well as law and idealization) into desire. As we will see in the following chapters, he develops a positive concept of desiring-*production*, unchaining thought and liberating the actor from transcendent regulative Ideals.

What heuristic function can theogonic reproduction theory play here? Like all other members of the species *Homo sapiens*, philosophers inherit the tendency to be anthropomorphically promiscuous and sociographically prudish. One characteristic distinctive of philosophers, however, is that they often intentionally resist these cognitive and coalitional biases, reflecting critically on their hypotheses about the natural and social worlds. Nevertheless, the operation of theogonic forces is usually not difficult to find. For example, in the *Timaeus* Plato portrays the creative demiurge, and even the "Father" of all, in somewhat obviously anthropomorphic terms. The *Republic* attempts to identify the one, ideal way to inscribe normativity in the social field. One can also see traces of theogonic forces in Aristotle's concept of the Unmoved Mover (thought thinking itself) and his ambivalent attraction toward regimes of the despotic type, such as that of his most (in)famous student Alexander the Great.

However, neither Plato nor Aristotle attempted to represent *the infinite*. For them, it would make no sense to try since by definition the limitless (*apeiron*) could not have a form that was *representable*. Deleuze argues that Christianity extends the philosophical intoxication with representation to infinity. As we will see below, he especially has in mind the attempts among Christian philosophers to represent the infinitely small (Leibniz) and the infinitely large (Hegel). Deleuze has little use for Hegel, but borrows and reworks several ideas from Leibniz's philosophy. However, he is critical of both for remaining in the domain of representation. They illustrate the problematic fact that philosophy "always pursues the same task, *Iconology*, and adapts it to the speculative needs of Christianity" (LS, 297). But Deleuze does not go into much detail regarding the question of *how* Christianity was able to impose its speculative needs so easily onto philosophy. This can be explained in part by the power of the sacerdotal trajectory within that Religion, which felt itself compelled by the evolutionary tide of theogonic forces to represent the infinite as a transcendent moralistic Entity whose intentions were revealed by an Icon with whom its coalitional members could imaginatively engage in shared rituals.

Christ as the Image of God

As I emphasized in the introductory chapter, chipping away at the iconic *Christ* is not meant as an attack on the man Jesus of Nazareth or on those who are inspired by revolutionary aspects of his teaching and way of life. No doubt one can extract valuable forces from the sayings of or texts about Jesus (or Moses, Muhammad, Buddha, Confucius, Lao-Tse, and so many others). However, my intention is indeed to challenge the way in which selecting one such Figure as a true image of an infinite supernatural Agency functions within the mental and social worlds of religious in-groups and the theologies bound to them. "Christ" is a dominant example of theogonic forces run wild in the Eidetic framework. In *Difference and Repetition* Deleuze briefly alludes to the patristic doctrine of the image (and likeness) of God, but he does not deal with it in any depth. His broader concern is with flipping over the copies and raising the simulacra as "demonic images, stripped of resemblance" (DR, 127). We will return to his general project below, but let us first begin the process of analyzing how a particular religious Icon can bind the imagination of a Coalition.

The books of the New Testament were written during the period now called "middle Platonism," characterized by a mixture of (mostly) Platonic, Aristotelian, and Stoic philosophy. It is not difficult to discern the influence of the Platonic interest in selecting the right images of transcendent models. Paul, for example, describes Christ as the "image" (*eikon*) of the invisible God (Colossians 1:15).

The one true God, he declares, predestined and foreknew those who would be "conformed to the *image* of his Son" (Romans 8:29). Human persons are judged by the extent to which they copy, imitate, or participate in that image. Unbelievers are blinded by the "god of this age," and cannot see "the glory of Christ, who is the *image* of God" (2 Corinthians 4:4). Like all children of Adam, believers "have borne the image of the earthly man," but they "shall bear the image of the heavenly man" (1 Corinthians 15:49), i.e., the image of Christ who is the "last Adam." Paul was not alone here. The epistle to the Hebrews asserts: "The Son is the *reflection* of God's glory and the *exact imprint* God's being, sustaining all things by his powerful word" (1:3). The Apocalypse of John warns that those who worship the rival image of the Beast, and follow the false prophet, will be thrown into the lake of fire and tormented forever "in the presence of the Lamb" (14:9–11). The basic thrust of the entire New Testament is that Christ is the one true image (icon) of the one true transcendent moralistic Entity, the only mediator between humanity and the supernatural Agent he called "Father."

During the rise and eventual dominance of what is now called "Neo-Platonism" during the third and fourth centuries after Jesus' death, the notion of Christ as the image of God became even more important. We will revisit this prevailing philosophical framework in the next chapter, but the important point here is the way in which it set the terms of the debate: what is the relation between the One (which is beyond differentiation) and the many (whose differentiation still somehow depends upon and is oriented toward participation in the One)? For Christian theologians, the problem of mediation was complicated by a desire to conceive of the One as the Father of the particular (differentiated) man Jesus. The solution seemed to be identifying the latter with the eternal divine Image of the former; in other words, with the eternal Son who resembles and is of the same nature as the Father. The difficulties with such a position were already obvious to patristic theologians and, as we will see, fueled the debates and anathemas surrounding the ecumenical councils.

It is important to recognize the impact that the concept of *image* had on interpretations of the broken relationship between human beings and God. The idea that humanity is created in the "image and likeness" of God was derived from the first creation myth in the book of Genesis (1: 26–7). In the early fifth century, Augustine folded this claim into his interpretation of the second creation myth, which he read as an historical "fall" that corrupted human nature. On this hypothesis, Adam and Eve, who had been created in the image and likeness of God, lost this similitude after disobeying the divine command not to eat of the fruit of the tree of the knowledge of good and evil. The first parents' transgression corrupted human nature itself, which no longer reflected the divine. This deformed sinful nature was passed on to all of their offspring, transmitted through the sexual act. Every soul was born deficient and guilty, incapable of achieving a properly regulated relation to a transcendent ideal. For Augustine, the only way for human souls to be restored is by being conformed to the image of the eternal Son, which is possible only by entering into the ritual mediations administered by the Mother Church, thereby satisfying the demands of the Eternal Father. Oedipus in Neo-Platonic heaven.

Christian theology came to have a more distinctly Aristotelian character during the Middle Ages, as a new awareness and appreciation of his philosophy arose out of dialogue with Muslim and Jewish scholars. Nevertheless, Thomas Aquinas's thirteenth-century formulations of Christ as the image of God remained within the Platonic Eidetic framework, presupposing a transcendent model as the ground for selecting among rival images. Thomas made a stronger distinction between image and likeness than Augustine had, suggesting that the image was lost but some likeness remained. Still, the basic point was that Christ is the true likeness (and image) of God, beating out all rivals as *the* Icon to which all humans ought to conform. Participation in that Image, which requires the ritual mediation of the Church, is the (only) road to transcendence. Differences between Luther and Calvin on this doctrine reflected the differences between Augustine and Thomas but, as we will see in the following chapters, Reformation theologians continued to operate within the domain of representation, appealing explicitly to the supernatural Agent detected within their religious coalitions.

One still finds some contemporary conservative Christian theologians who equate orthodoxy with doctrinal formulations forged in Platonic categories, but today fewer theologians than ever would embrace the label "Platonist." In the Deleuzian sense, however, *all* sacerdotal theologians are Platonic dualists, insofar as they continue to try to distinguish between true and false images of transcendence. The classical doctrine of the image of God as created similarity to God (usually tied to righteousness or rationality) lost its textual warrant when critical biblical scholarship discovered that the term "image" in the context of the original redactors of Genesis would have most likely referred to the representation of a regional despot who claimed dominion over a particular area. Adam and Eve were God's "images" (political representatives) on earth. In the twentieth century, it became popular to interpret the phrase "image of God" in eschatological rather than protological terms. In other words, it is not a quality in human nature that was lost in the past but the destiny of human nature that will fully appear in the future. However, this shift in temporal focus does not escape either the Eidetic framework or reliance on a transcendent model of a moralistic Entity who is concerned about a coalition.

It is also important to stress the fact that my use of the term "iconoclastic" to describe a trajectory within theology has nothing to do with the debates among sacerdotal theologians about the appropriateness or value of the use of "icons" (paintings, statues, etc.) common in many forms of eastern Christianity. Well, almost nothing to do with it. The term has sometimes been used to refer to historical examples of Christians who literally broke such manufactured figures. There were certainly political issues tied up in such demolitions, but among the motivations and justifications for such behavior was the claim that any attempt to represent or mediate divine transcendence via a finite, created object was an offense against the Creator, whose infinite glory cannot be represented. Such figures were nothing more than "idols" and must be destroyed. Transcendence is mediated through Christ alone, through the rituals he sanctioned (Baptism and Eucharist), the proclamation of the Word and the inner witness of his Spirit. Such reactions are directly opposed to what I am calling the *iconoclastic* trajectory; by rejecting particular eastern modes of representing the infinite, and insisting on their own modes of imaginatively engaging a supernatural Agent, they remain firmly within the *sacerdotal* trajectory.

It is easy to get distracted by the debates among factions within this latter trajectory, such as the disputes between primarily Latin speaking western theologians and primarily Greek speaking eastern theologians as they attempted to solve the problem of relating to a transcendent moralistic Entity by relying on various mixtures of Platonic and Aristotelian categories, disputes which eventually led to the mutual excommunications of the eleventh century. I will return in the following chapters to some of these issues, but the far more interesting point for our purposes is the *similarity* between these (and all other) Christian factions.

As *religious* coalitions, they are held together by imaginative engagement with axiologically relevant supernatural agents. As coalitions tied to a monotheist *Religion* that traces its roots to the west Asian axial age, however, they are also shaped by a long tradition of attempts to detect the Highest God possible – an *infinite* supernatural Agent. The conceptual problems with such an idea are tricky enough, but the practical problems are a nightmare. It is hard to relate to a moralistic Entity whose intellect contains absolutely everything (simultaneously) and whose will determines absolutely everything (eternally). Christ as the image or representative of this God provides believers with a mediating supernatural agent in relation to whom the cognitive and coalitional defaults that hold together religious groups can more easily be activated.

Christ has an even more significant role in the Iconology of western *philosophy* than Deleuze acknowledges. He clearly recognizes that the attempts to represent the infinite by Leibniz and Hegel, for example, are influenced in part by their relationship to Christianity. Deleuze interprets the grand Leibnizian analysis as an introduction of the finite Self into the development of the infinite, and the grand Hegelian synthesis as the introduction of the infinite into the operation of the finite Self. They amount to the same thing. Both finite synthetic Self and divine analytic Substance trap the infinite within some kind of God-Man (or Man-God) permutation (DR, 58). However, Deleuze does not point out how deeply Leibniz and Hegel are tied to the specific idea of Christ as *the* image (or representation) of God.

He suggests that there were "theological exigencies" that hindered Leibniz from taking the concept of incompossibility in the direction Deleuze himself wants to take it,[4] but does not spell out what these exigencies were. In the section on "Conformity of Faith with Reason" in his *Theodicy*, Leibniz explicitly accepts the assumption that humanity has "received the divine grace through Jesus Christ," asserting that it suffices to affirm the Mysteries such as the Trinity and the Incarnation as words not "altogether devoid of meaning" even if one cannot comprehend them completely.[5] What *theological* function did the concept of compossible worlds play? It provided an (Eidetic) framework in which God could choose the "best possible world," the one in which Christ is sent to remedy the sin of Adam. In his *Monadology* Leibniz refers to human minds as "*images* of the divinity itself," and it is not accidental that Adam is his primary example, there and throughout his letters, of the status of an individual in a compossible world.[6] The role of Christ in Hegel's Trinitarian-shaped philosophy is evident throughout, but shines through perhaps most clearly when he explicitly links the second element of the Absolute or Consummate Religion, "*Representation*" (the "appearance" of the eternal Idea, or differentiation within the divine life), to the *incarnation* of the Son of God.[7]

One can certainly also find lines of flight within the work of these two Christian philosophers that lead in the direction of the iconoclastic trajectory. This is true of most Christian theologians as well. The problem is that when imagination fails, when it threatens to break on the infinite, it is all too tempting to give in to the default psychological and political pressures of the sacerdotal trajectory. Even Leibniz and Hegel eventually appealed to a particular image of an axiologically relevant Entity (Creator of a pre-established Harmony, and Absolute Spirit, respectively). The need to represent the infinite as a supernatural Agent is driven by the cognitive and coalitional tendencies we have been discussing. Even if the likeness of the divine to human persons is greatly reduced and the favor of the deity is extended to all human persons, we are still dealing with *an Agency* that is axiologically relevant for *a Group*. As we will see, however, this is not the only way to go about making "theological" hypotheses.

Anthropomorphic Prudery and Sociographic Promiscuity

Like most scholars whose academic work is not bound to a particular religious in-group, Deleuze resists appeals to contingently-embodied human-like forces in theoretical explanations of the natural world, and resists appeals to coalition-favoring authorities in normative prescriptions for the social world. In other words, he is anthropomorphically prudish and sociographically promiscuous (see Figure 2.1).

When these cognitive and coalitional tendencies are integrated, as indicated in the upper right quadrant, they have an intensified "theolytic" or god-dissolving effect, which can destabilize the function of religious images in human minds and cultures. It takes a great deal of energy to challenge the evolutionary defaults, but it can be and has been done.

Even though these tendencies are not always (or even usually) explicitly acknowledged in the academy, they play a role within every discipline. If a scientist working on a chemistry experiment, for example, is confronted with an ambiguous result, she will probably

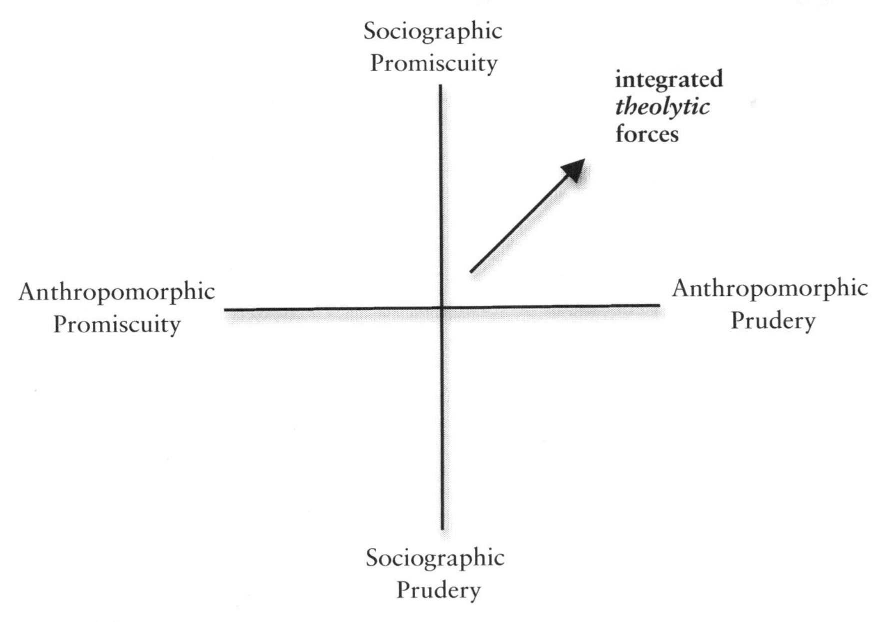

Figure 2.1

not immediately jump to the hypothesis that a discarnate intentional entity such as a ghost caused the anomaly. If she is pressured to carry out her experiments in conformity with the cultic purity codes of some members of her research team, she will probably not immediately comply. Those are rather silly examples, but the serious point is that scientists typically resist the evolved defaults – at least when they are doing science. This is just as true in the social sciences, where human agents and in-group dynamics are actually the subject matter of academic research. When it comes to verifying the results of inquiry, the fewer appeals to hidden intentional powers, and the more triangulation of findings from different research coalitions, the better. In this sense, anthropomorphic prudery and sociographic promiscuity are promoted throughout the scholarly community.

As we will see in the next three chapters, the Deleuzian project takes these theolytic tendencies to the extreme. All attempts to determine the transcendental as *consciousness*, argues Deleuze, think of it "in the *image* of, and in *resemblance* to, that which it is supposed to ground . . . but this requirement does not seem to be at all legitimate."[8] He is also critical of what he calls "theological" phantasms, or aggregates of simulacra that produce the mirage of a false infinite because they are perceived in a minimum of sensible time (image), which cannot capture their movement below this minimum, in what Epicurus called the *clinamen*. "Our belief in gods rests upon simulacra which seem to dance, to change their gestures, and to shout at us promising eternal punishment – in short, to *represent the infinite*."[9] His prudence in relation to anthropomorphism goes so far that even when confronted with the ambiguous natural phenomena of actual *human* agency he resists guessing "human-like agents," at least in the traditional sense of substantial or self-identical subjects. What we experience as our own subjective identity, Deleuze will argue, is a phantasm that is represented in consciousness as the cause of intentionality, whereas in fact it is the effect of a series of passive syntheses of flows of intensity, or emissions of impersonal and pre-individual singularities.

How far does his sociographic promiscuity go? As we saw in the introductory chapter, Deleuze suggests in *Anti-Oedipus* that "one can never go far enough in the direction of deterritorialization" (AO, 353). Much of his critique in that volume is aimed at three basic social-machines that produce "representations" that fall back on and repress desiring-machines. Schizoanalysis (or pragmatics) aims to liberate desire from the reterritorializations of the primitive, despotic, and capitalist modes of social inscription. In *A Thousand Plateaus*, Deleuze promotes the rhizomic, the molecular, and the nomadic in contrast to the arboreal, the molar, and the sedentary. He calls for resisting the State apparatus of capture and the priestly curse on desire by constructing a plane of consistency (in combat with a plane of organization) and for making and populating a smooth space (out of a striated space). We will explore this vocabulary in more detail in Chapter 5. In Chapters 3 and 4 as well, we will find a consistent resistance to pre-judicial and prudish regulations of thought and behavior that appeal to socially mediated ideals.

Insights from the bio-cultural study of religion can enhance and extend Deleuze's critique of the Platonic domain of representation in which images so easily take on a repressive function within social groups. In fact, essentialism and colonialism are reinforced by the cognitive and coalitional tendencies that are integrated in what I have called theogonic reproduction. The mental capacity to quickly subsume new phenomena into basic categories (or genera) improved the chances of survival and so provided a selective advantage. Identifying a moving object as an animal automatically generates a series of other inferences, such as "needs to eat" or "is edible."

Placing something, even an ambiguously perceived animal-spirit or ancestor-ghost, in the category of person automatically leads to the attribution of other qualities, such as "remembers things" and "may get angry."

This same default cognitive process is applied to groups of people; members of in-groups and out-groups are *essentially* different. Such perceptions make it easier to justify stereotypes and even violence against or domination over "others." The human mind evolved to classify things automatically and quickly, and it was rather efficient for survival. Platonic essentialism follows this classifying logic as far as it will go, hypothesizing that even classes themselves *are*. Aristotle's *Politics* (Book I) illustrates the way in which this mode of essentialist classification so easily slides into a "colonizing" of others; he argued that it is appropriate for slaves and women, for example, to be subjugated within a household because, compared with free, male members of the community, they are *by nature* deficient. These tendencies are activated all the more strongly when woven together in shared imaginative engagement with supernatural agents.[10]

In *What is Philosophy?* Deleuze distinguished science (as well as art and philosophy) from religion by the way in which the latter invokes "dynasties of gods, or the epiphany of a single god . . . figures of an *Urdoxa* from which opinions stem" (WP, 202). Religion always thinks through "figures" that are essentially paradigmatic, projective, and hierarchical. Art and science also set up figures, but treat them in a different way. The aesthetic figures of art are "percepts" or forces of sensation on planes of composition, while the figural "functives" of science operate on planes of coordination. What sets the artistic and scientific engagement with figures apart from religion is that the former resist the temptation to transcendence. Philosophy, on the other hand, has nothing to do with figures. It is the creation of "concepts." In each case, Deleuze means philosophy, art or science when they do what they – and only they – can do.

For our purposes, the important point is that, for Deleuze, religion *always* has to do with figures, which are represented as transcendent and projected onto a plane of immanence. "Religions do not arrive at the concept without denying themselves, just as philosophies do not arrive at the figure without betraying themselves" (WP, 92). Deleuzian philosophy leaves no religious Figures standing. At the end of this chapter, I will point to some of the forces *within* Christianity that have (partially) followed the iconoclastic trajectory, more or less intentionally challenging the way in which the figure of Christ functions in sacerdotal theology and practice. Examining the fractures produced by such movements within a Religion is a good place to start experimenting in iconoclastic theology.

The integration of the tendencies represented in the upper right quadrant of the grid above somewhat obviously has a dissolutive effect on religious coalitions. However, these theolytic forces can also have a powerfully *creative* effect. This is easier to see when one notices the way in which they can be correlated to naturalism and secularism. We will explore this possibility in the concluding chapter, in the context of clarifying the sense in which iconoclastic theology promotes the secretion of a *productive* atheism. Of course, atheists are people too, and are also susceptible to cognitive and coalitional biases. This is true whether or not they are also scientists, artists or philosophers. The question is how one relates to these biases. As the forces of theogonic reproduction are increasingly exposed, it is easier to resist their power. Repression works best when its causes are, well, repressed. Disclosing them is a first step toward liberation. Unveiling these mechanisms helps us make a clearer distinction between the sacerdotal and iconoclastic trajectories of theology, and moves the discussion of the plausibility (and pragmatic feasibility) of their distinctive hypotheses to a new level of critical self-awareness.

What I hope to show in the following chapters is that bringing concepts derived from the bio-cultural study of religion and concepts derived from Deleuzian philosophy into more explicit dialogue can elucidate the distinctions between these two trajectories. Along the way, it will become increasingly clear how the findings of these sciences can help atheist Friends of Deleuze understand why people are so resistant to challenging their own religious repression. The value of making explicit retroductive hypotheses about axiological engagement when engaging these scientific findings will also become ever more apparent. First, however, I want to introduce three of the philosophers in (or behind) whom Deleuze found inspiration for inverting Platonism, and whose influence we will observe throughout the development of his theologically iconoclastic project.

Kant and the Genitality of Experience

In his search for resources to help overturn the domain of transcendence within which Platonic retroductive hypothesizing operates, Deleuze turned early to Kant. Already in 1956, he indicated that he wanted to follow through on what he saw as a fundamental tendency of Kant's approach – the attempt to "ground" (*fonder*) the "infinite tasks" of reason in *this* present world.[11] Deleuze argues that Kant simply did not follow through on what he started. His Copernican revolution destabilized the mythological foundations that had come to dominate western philosophy, but Kant replaced them with anthropological foundations. As we will see in the following chapters, Deleuze complains that appealing to the identity of the human Self (as that which grounds knowledge, recognition, etc.) is no better than appealing to the identity of a divine Subject. Moreover, he will argue that insofar as Kant (and others) search for the conditions of all *possible* experience, they are presupposing that those conditions *transcend* what *actually* happens. Deleuze's hypotheses are about the transcendent*al* conditions for *real* experience, conditions that are entirely *immanent*.[12] Deleuze would later refer to his early monograph on *Kant's Critical Philosophy* (French, 1963) as a book about an "enemy" (N, 6). In philosophy too, perhaps, the enemy of one's enemy can be a friend. And Deleuze saw Kant as an enemy of Platonism. Kant's hypotheses about the conditions for axiological engagement are a significant resource for Deleuze as he develops new concepts of difference, desire and "God."

First, Deleuze credits Kant with a crucially important role in the development of the philosophy of *difference*. In his critique of Descartes, Kant inserted difference immediately into thought. The Cartesian *cogito* involved two logical values: a determination (I think) and an undetermined existence (I am). The former determines the latter. Thinking determines the ego as an existing thinking subject. Challenging the Cartesian assumption that determination can bear directly on the determined, Kant asked how the undetermined could be *determinable*. Deleuze argues that this third logical value, the form of the determinability of the undetermined by the determination, "amounts to the discovery of Difference." Instead of an (empirical) difference between two determinations, with Kant we now have "the form of a transcendental Difference between the determination as such and what it determines; no longer in the form of an external difference which separates, but in the form of an internal difference which establishes an a priori relation between thought and being" (DR, 86). Deleuze acknowledges the sense in which Plato had already tried to include difference within thought, but notes that he had immediately subjected it again to "the mythical form" of *resemblance* and *identity*.

Kant, on the other hand, inserted difference immediately into thought without appealing to a transcendent Determination – at least in the first Critique (*of Pure Reason*). In the context of discussing the latter, Deleuze argues that for Kant the three logical values are interiorized within Ideas. However, just as a fracture retains that which it fractures, or as "difference immediately reunites and articulates that which it distinguishes," Ideas contain their "dismembered moments" (the undetermined, the determinable, and determination) as an "internal problematic objective unity" in which they are neither identified nor confused. Deleuze suggests that Kant "incarnated" these moments within three distinct Ideas: "the Self is above all undetermined, the World is determinable, and God is the ideal of determination" (DR, 170). In the second Critique (*of Practical Reason*) these Ideas regained a certain transcendence, especially "God" as eternal judge and "the I" as immortal soul. Understandably, Deleuze rejects this return to a traditionally "theological" way of approaching the problem, which in Kant "amounts to a supreme effort to *save the world of representation*."[13]

Even in the first Critique, however, Deleuze does not think Kant went far enough. He did not develop a *concept* of difference in itself. This is related to Deleuze's complaint that Kant's treatment of the conditions for thought in the first Critique does not attain the point of view of *genesis*. For Deleuze, it is the *genitality* of thought that must be accounted for; how is thinking created or engendered? "To think is to create – there is no other creation – but to create is first of all to engender 'thinking' in thought" (DR, 147). What forces us to think? As we will see in Chapter 3, for Deleuze thinking is engendered within thought only by means of a complex repetition of *pure difference*, which is the form of the determinable or the pure and empty form of time.

Deleuze is also appreciative of Kant's contributions toward a revolution of the concept of *desire*. Whereas Plato had conceptualized desire as acquisition, inscribing it with lack, Kant argued for the productivity of desire. In *Anti-Oedipus*, for example, Deleuze applauds Kant's description of desire in the third Critique (*of Judgment*) as the "faculty of *being*," as in some sense "the *cause* of the reality of the objects" of its representations.[14] In general Deleuze is more appreciative of Kant's third Critique, which he views as a praiseworthy example of an older philosopher's willingness to take up previous themes in a new way. In his earlier book on *Kant's Critical Philosophy*, Deleuze had examined the relation between the three Critiques in some detail. What forces one to think? In the third

Critique, it is the *aesthetic Idea*, which goes beyond all concepts. While the first two Critiques focused on the faculties of reason and desire, the third Critique uncovers a "deeper free and indeterminate accord of the faculties as the condition of the possibility of every determinate relationship" (KCP, 68). The discordant "accord" of imagination and reason is not assumed; "it is genuinely *engendered*, engendered in dissension" among the faculties (KCP, 51).

One can think of Deleuze's own attempt in *Difference and Repetition* to create a concept of difference in-itself (and of repetition for-itself) as a re-working of Kant's first Critique, and his theory of desiring-production as a re-working of the second Critique. It is likely that both of these Deleuzian texts were at least partially inspired by the new direction he perceived in Kant's third Critique.[15] Despite these advances, Deleuze argues that Kant does not go far enough in his conception of desire as a productive power in itself. Although he no longer relies on a "theological principle" or a divine foundation in the third Critique, what Kant calls "physical theology" is still given "a 'final' *human* foundation" (KCP, 69). It is no longer God, but the Self that serves as the principle of "finality," the condition for judgment. In other words, difference and desire are finally still grounded in a Self that is attributed a certain transcendence. The third Critique resists invoking a God with infinite faculties to guarantee a harmony between subject and object, but Kant still places the "special genesis" in the Self, which is able to know and fulfill "the law."

Deleuze treats this latter theme in more detail in his book on Masochism and Sadism, *Coldness and Cruelty*. There he observes that Kant provided for the first time a radical new conception that challenged the classical conception of "law" that was founded by Plato. The latter (and those who followed him) dealt with "*the laws* according to the various spheres of the Good or the various circumstances attending the Best," but Kant postulates "the Law," that is, "the form of the law," which cannot be grounded in a higher principle, so now the Good (and Best) revolve around the Law. Deleuze suggests this is perhaps a more important Copernican revolution than Kant's placing of the subject, rather than the object, at the center of the epistemological universe. For Deleuze, however, such an approach to morality remains within the domain of representation. He finds in Sade and Masoch a more serious revolutionary treatment of desire, a subversion of the law that "turns Platonism upside down" (CC, 87). In his later collaboration with Guattari, Deleuze will carry out his own revolutionary overturning of what he will come to call the "priestly" curse on desire: lack, law, and signification.

Deleuze's interest in Kant's (somewhat) revolutionary treatments of these themes is clearly *theological*. For our purposes, the most important aspect of Kant's "theology" extracted and reworked by Deleuze is the link between the idea of *God* and the *disjunctive syllogism*. In the context of the same essay in *Logic of Sense* where he describes theology as the "science of non-existing entities," he takes Kant to task for missing the full import of this link. Deleuze alludes briefly to the way in which the Self, the World, and God are correlated in Kant's first Critique. Kant makes the idea of "the World," as that which conditions the attribution of the category of causality to all phenomena, correspond to the principle of the hypothetical syllogism. "The Self" is the idea that corresponds to the category of substance, and therefore to the principle of the "categorical syllogism, insofar as this relates a phenomenon determined as a predicate to a subject determined as a substance." What is left, asks Deleuze, for God as the third idea? It must be assigned the task of ensuring "the attribute of the category of community, that is, the *mastery of the disjunctive syllogism*. God is here, at least provisionally, deprived of his traditional claims . . . and now has what is but an apparently humble task, namely, to enact *distinctions*, or at least to found them" (LS, 335).

Deleuze follows out a line of thought initiated by Klossowski and argues that "It is not God but the *Antichrist* who is the master of the disjunctive syllogism." Escaping the demand that conceptual conditions be based on the identity of a God, a Self or even a World, this syllogism "accedes to a *diabolical* principle and use, and simultaneously the disjunction is affirmed for itself without ceasing to be a disjunction; divergence and difference become objects of pure affirmation."[16] In the chapters that follow, we will return often to the implications of these two very different uses of the disjunctive syllogism (or synthesis), and to the variety of ways Deleuze employs terms like God, Antichrist, demonic, and diabolical, etc. At this stage, we simply point to the fact that the three syllogisms Deleuze derives from Kant are re-worked in each of the main texts we will be exploring in the chapters that follow. In *Difference and Repetition*, they lie behind his treatment of the passive syntheses of imagination, memory, and thought. In *Logic of Sense* and the *Capitalism and Schizophrenia* project they are linked to what he calls the connective, conjunctive, and disjunctive syntheses, albeit in quite different ways. There is a lively debate among Deleuze scholars about the consistency of his use of these designations across texts, but the key point that is most important for our project is quite clear: in each of these texts (and several others), Deleuze consistently emphasizes the distinctly different ways in which the disjunctive synthesis operates under the order of "God" (negatively, exclusively) and the order of "the Antichrist" (affirmatively, inclusively). As we will see, he does not imagine either of these to be a *transcendent* or an *intentional* force.

Despite Kant's limitations, it is important to acknowledge that his philosophy does indeed have a productive theolytic force. In the first Critique, he went to great pains to articulate a hypothesis about the transcendent*al* conditions for thought without appealing to a transcend*ent* moralistic Entity. In the *Prolegomena to Any Future Metaphysics*, he explained his resistance to "dogmatic anthropomorphism" in more detail. Even in the second Critique, Kant displays some sociographic promiscuity insofar as he tries to establish the conditions for practical reason without appealing to the authority of any particular religious coalition. Nevertheless, at every point he is tempted back by theogonic forces. The second Critique does finally postulate an Author and Governor of the world, and Kant eventually claims that the doctrine of Christianity "even when not regarded as a religious doctrine, gives a concept of the highest good (the Kingdom of God), which is *alone* sufficient to the strictest demand of practical reason."[17] The *Prolegomena* famously concludes by allowing for a "symbolic" anthropomorphism that relies on analogy. And even in the preface to the second edition of the first Critique, Kant points out that the purpose of his limitation of knowledge (pure theoretical reason) was "to make room for *faith*."[18]

As in his treatment of Leibniz and Hegel, Deleuze does not focus on the way in which *Christ* functions in Kant's philosophy. Christ may not have played a dominant role in the second Critique, but the notion of an ideal representative who can in fact fulfill the universal categorical imperative of the supreme lawgiver seems to be lurking in the background. It leaps into the foreground in *Religion within the Limits of Reason Alone*. In that context, after referring to several biblical passages, Kant suggests that the complete moral perfection of "Man, so conceived" that is "alone pleasing to God" is found in no created thing but only in "His only-begotten Son." Kant is clearly operating in the Eidetic framework when he insists that "it is our universal duty as men to *elevate* ourselves to this ideal of moral perfection, that is, to this *archetype* of the moral disposition in all its purity."[19] Christ is the archetype, the true icon of a transcendent model engendered by an omnipotent moral Being. Perhaps we should not be surprised that Kant remained an enemy. But Deleuze found other Friends.

Spinoza and the Vertigo of Immanence

Deleuze describes Kant as a "public" philosopher, but places Spinoza in that line of "private thinkers" who "overturn values and construct their philosophy with *hammer blows*."[20] Kant's Copernican revolution challenged the Platonic reliance on iconic participation in transcendent models as the foundation for knowledge, but the infinite is still represented as a transcendent moral Entity, even if only as a postulate of practical reason. Deleuze calls Spinoza the "prince of philosophers" because he never compromised with transcendence, flattening everything onto a plane of immanence traversed by infinite intensive movements, a plane not immanent *to* anything but itself.[21] In his early monograph on *Expressionism in Philosophy: Spinoza*, Deleuze refers to immanence as "the very vertigo of philosophy" (EP, 180). This vertigo results not from a dizzying encounter with the heights, or from a suffocating plunge into the depths, but from an unlimited movement across the absolute surface of the plane of immanence. In *What is Philosophy?* Deleuze would describe Spinoza himself as "the vertigo of immanence from which so many philosophers try in vain to escape" (WP, 48). Deleuze's last (completed) published essay, "Immanence: A Life," once again calls for a reintroduction of Spinozism into philosophy.[22]

Deleuze's fascination with Spinoza is clearly connected to the latter's *theology*; that is, to his hypotheses about the conditions for the real experience of axiological engagement. What animates language (thought, affect, etc.) and makes for it a body divided with disjunctions? To put the question in more classical terms, how are we to conceive of that which causes beings? Medieval philosophers had distinguished between immanent, emanative, and transitive (or creative) causes, and Christian theology utilized these distinctions in its depiction of the causal relation between God and the World. An immanent cause remains within itself as it produces and so do its produced effects. An emanative cause also remains within itself as it produces, but its effects are external to it. A transitive cause goes outside itself to produce, and its product remains outside of the cause itself. In contrast to the first type of causality, the latter two types both depict the cause as transcendent to its effects.[23] Each of these types posed its own problems for Christian theologians who wanted to maintain *both* the real distinction between God and the World *and* the real presence of God to (or in) the World.

In *Expressionism*, Deleuze analyzes the history of these philosophical and theological debates in some detail. Spinozism, he argues, cannot be understood "apart from the contest it carries on against negative theology, and against any method proceeding through equivocation, eminence and analogy."[24] As we will see in the following chapters, the sacerdotal trajectory of Christian theology commonly appeals to "analogy" as a middle way between equivocity (which seems to make God too transcendent) and univocity (which seems not to leave God transcendent enough). Deleuze argues that any such appeal "is unable to conceal the equivocation from with it sets out, or the eminence to which it leads" (EP, 104). Creationist (transitive) causality was at the core of most Christian hypotheses; all existing entities are distinct from the *transcendent* God who created them. However, this leaves open the question of the relation between divine causality and creaturely effects. Some answers utilized the concept of emanative causality, reworking the Neo-Platonic idea of the many emanating from the One (mediated by the Nous) into the idea of the plurality of creatures emanating from the One Father of All (mediated by the Son). Others hypothesized that the idea of the World eternally existed as a model in the divine Mind, and that it was created and is continually upheld by an act of the divine Will. Each of these last two formulations smacks of immanent causality, especially the latter, which all too easily leads to pantheism. This is why they were usually immediately qualified in ways that emphasized the distinction between the transcendent mystery of the divine Creator and the effects of his creative act.

More than any other philosopher (or theologian) before him, suggests Deleuze, Spinoza's hypothesizing consistently shuns appeals to transcendence, thereby challenging the Platonic domain of representation within which philosophy had so far labored. "The significance of Spinozism seems to me this: it asserts immanence as a principle and frees expression from any subordination to emanative or exemplary causality. *Expression itself no longer emanates, no longer resembles anything*" (EP, 180). Spinoza's concept of a "real distinction" is key here. Instead of explaining the plurality of attributes as emanating from an eminent Unity or created from a transcendent Exemplar,

Spinoza unites the (really distinct) infinity of attributes and absolute Substance, which together constitute expression. Substance and attributes are expressed "modally," which is always and only a *quantitative* differentiation. The attributes are really distinct but this real distinction is immediately (without eminence or imitation) the *qualitative* composition of an ontologically single Substance. "Detached from all numerical distinction, real distinction is carried into the absolute, and becomes capable of expressing difference within Being" (EP, 39).

Deus sive Natura. Deleuze does not seem to mind that Spinoza uses the term "God." In his lectures on Spinoza, Deleuze suggests that he called the one substance described in the *Ethics* "God" precisely because it is "absolutely infinite."[25] As we saw above, Kant sometimes used the term "God" to indicate an immanent causality that has nothing to do with supernatural Agency. Deleuze himself will continue to use the term God in a variety of ways in his own constructive work, with and without Guattari. However, he is (usually) careful to distinguish between this sort of philosophical usage and "what most people call 'God' from a religious viewpoint," a moral lawgiver and judge. In this sense, Deleuze notes, "Spinoza is clearly an atheist" (EP, 253). And so is Deleuze. What makes Spinoza's "theological" hypothesis (or Deleuze's reading of it) so important is the attempt to develop a theory of immanent causality that consistently avoids appeals to something that transcends the multiplicity of beings. Multiplicities *are* what exists. What animates them? The modal expression of the absolute Substance that *is* infinitely multiple. Deleuze argues that this Spinozist move can only be achieved from the perspective of univocity, which rejects the emanation inseparable from negative theology and the analogy inseparable from kataphatic theology.[26]

Spinoza's contribution to the philosophy of *difference* is connected to his role in the history of the elaboration of the univocity of being. In *Difference and Repetition*, Deleuze points to Duns Scotus as the first principal moment in this history. He "neutralized" being itself as an abstract concept, rendering it indifferent to the distinction between created and uncreated, finite and infinite. Scotus' motivation, in part, was to overcome the limitations of negative theology and analogical theology, neither of which could make univocal affirmations about the divine being or attributes. As a Christian theologian, however, Scotus had to maintain the transcendence of the Creator and so, in order to avoid pantheism, his conception of univocal being remained neutral and indifferent. With Spinoza, on the other hand, univocal being becomes "truly expressive" and an object of "pure affirmation," predicated in one and the same sense of substance and modes.[27] Scotus tried to escape the demands of emanative causality, but remained submissive to the demands of creative causality. Spinoza frees himself from both with a consistent theory of immanent causality, in which no causes (or beings) are transcendent to any others.

As the title of his smaller book *Spinoza: Practical Philosophy* suggests, Deleuze insists that Spinoza's hypotheses are practical as well as speculative. Here we can begin to see why he also found Spinoza to be a valuable resource for developing a productive concept of *desire*. The key question is: what can a body *do*? (*Ethics*, III.2s). For Spinoza, Deleuze argues, the affections are always active, or expressive. What are the affections? They are "the modes themselves," or to put it the other way, the modes "are the affections of substance and its attributes" (SPP, 48). Modal essences are degrees of power, or degrees of intensity. A modal essence is not a "possibility," but a physical reality that "lacks nothing" (SPP, 98). The essence of an existing mode is determined as a degree of power, or *conatus*. In other words, *conatus* is the power of modes, under certain determinations, to persevere in existence. Desire is "the *conatus* having become conscious, the *cause* of this consciousness being the affection" (SPP, 60).

The important thing to notice here is that desire is consistently treated within the context of an *immanent* causality. Desire is not caused by ideal objects external to it, in relation to which it is deficient or lacking in being. Desire is an expression of reality (substance and modes). The problem is that consciousness so easily succumbs to the "theological illusion of finality," taking the ideas of affections as truly primary, that is as "true final causes," teleologically ordered by a provident God. Desire can then appear "secondary in relation to the idea of the thing judged good" (SPP, 60). Deleuze reads the *Ethics* as the presentation of a "typology of immanent modes of existence," arguing that Spinoza intended for ethics to replace *morality*, "which always refers existence to transcendent values" (SPP, 23), to a final judgment between good and evil. Morality is linked to Law, which "is always the transcendent instance that determines the opposition of values (Good-Evil)," but Ethics, for Spinoza, is linked to knowledge, which is "always the *immanent* power that determines the qualitative difference of modes of existence (good-bad)."[28]

Theolytic forces are powerfully at work in Spinoza's thought. At least in the *Ethics*, Spinoza clearly rejects any "law" for inscribing the social field that would appeal to the final judgment of a supernatural Agent (of any coalition). Spinoza is also critical of the way in which (sacerdotal) theologians had interpreted God as a personal Creator with an infinite intellect and will. He argues that this is based on a failure to distinguish between attributes and *propria*, which are adjectival properties derived from biblical revelation (e.g., wise, loving, jealous, vindictive) and applied to the divine nature. The *propria* are supposed to express the nature of God yet, as a transcendent Creator, God must also be considered eminent in relation to them. As Deleuze points out, once *propria* are ascribed "an expressive value they do not have, one ascribes to divine substance an inexpressible nature which it does not have either" (EP, 57). When moralistic *propria* are applied to God, it results in absurdities that have compromised theology – and philosophy – as a whole. Deleuze calls this theology's most basic and serious error: confusing obeying and knowing (SPP, 106). Imperative signs interpreted as effects of revelation (grounds for obedience) are confused with the modally expressed attributes of "God" (grounds for knowledge).

No wonder Spinoza got into so much trouble. I began my comments on Spinoza's anthropomorphic prudery and sociographic promiscuity in the last paragraph with the qualification: at least in the *Ethics*. In fact, there are places where theogonic forces seem to take over in Spinoza's writings. In *A Theologico-Political Treatise*, for example, he explicitly accepts the revelation of God to and in Christ and insists that this revelation was necessary because of the limits of reason, thereby at least partially immunizing Scripture from rational critique.[29] This is the dark side of the distinction between attributes and *propria*; the latter can be taken over within the sacerdotal trajectory of theology in order to protect the coalition's detection of its supernatural Agent. In *Expressionism in Philosophy*, Deleuze somewhat curiously limits his comments on *A Theologico-Political Treatise* to the endnotes. He examines the role of the "Word of God" in Spinoza's philosophy in great detail, and observes that his references to Christ in the *Ethics* are "barely Christian."[30] Elsewhere, however, they are almost boldly Christian.

For the purposes of my project, this is important to notice; even the "prince" of the philosophers felt the bio-cultural gravitational pull of the evolved theogonic forces. Of course, he was not alone. Christianity in general, and the concept of Christ in particular, played a dominant role in seventeenth-century political philosophy (e.g., Locke and Hobbes in England, or Hugo Grotius in Spinoza's Holland). From Deleuze's perspective, Spinoza did more to overturn Plato than Kant. Still, he did not go far enough. In *What is Philosophy*?, Deleuze refers to Spinoza as the "Christ of the philosophers" (WP, 60). Quite clearly, he has no intention of setting up Spinoza as a philosophical "savior." Philosophy does not need salvation – it needs to get moving. In his own attempts to put new concepts of desire, difference, and even "God" into motion, when push comes to shove, Deleuze will leave the Christ of the philosophers and follow the Anti-Christ of the philosophers.

Nietzsche and the Rising of the Simulacra

It is in Nietzsche that Deleuze seems to find the most inspiration for the inversion of Platonism. He acknowledged in "A Letter to a Harsh Critic" that buggery did not quite work with Nietzsche as it did with the other philosophers whom he engaged in his early books. "You just can't deal with him in the same sort of way. He gets up to all sorts of things behind *your* back. He gives you a perverse taste . . . for saying simple things in your own way, in affects, intensities, experiences, experiments" (N, 6). In his early book on *Nietzsche & Philosophy* (French, 1962), Deleuze emphasized that for Nietzsche philosophical critique is not a re-action (born of *ressentiment*), but an active attack, an expression of the "natural aggression of a way of being." This way of being is that of the philosopher insofar as she wields "the differential element as critic and creator and therefore *as a hammer*" (NP, 3). In this sense, philosophizing (or theologizing) with a hammer is simultaneously destructive and constructive. In that context, Deleuze suggested that the only properly philosophical way of thinking involves a "principle of violent atheism" (NP, 4). Deleuze's own atheism became more tranquil over the decades but no less combative and even more productive.

We have already noted that Deleuze accepts Nietzsche's challenge "to reverse Platonism," but takes this to mean tracking down Plato's real motivation, which he argues is the search for a way to select between rival images, to screen intellectual claims (pretensions) and distinguish the false from the true pretender, the simulacrum from the icon. As we will see in more detail in Chapters 3 and 4, Deleuze's creative reading of the Nietzschean concept of *eternal return* takes on a central role when he first moves beyond philosophical portraiture and writes more explicitly in his own voice (in *Difference and Repetition* and *Logic of Sense*). His interpretation of this concept, which borrows heavily from Klossowski,[31] is controversial. Deleuze argues that those few statements about the eternal return of "the same" in *Thus Spake Zarathustra* are eventually refuted by Zarathustra; he insists Nietzsche's own position was not opposing a circular order to chaos but rather affirming the power of chaos in its tortuous circularity in which only the new, only "difference" returns. "Nietzsche was right when he treated the eternal return as his own vertiginous idea, an idea nourished only by esoteric Dionysian sources, ignored or repressed by Platonism" (LS, 301).

For the purposes of the current project, it is less important to decide whether or not Deleuze got Nietzsche right than it is to determine what he did with the concepts he extracted from the Nietzschean corpus. At this stage, our main concern is to highlight the way in which Deleuze reads Nietzsche as moving beyond both Kant and Spinoza in his contributions to the philosophy of *difference* and the concept of *desire*, both of which have powerful ramifications for "theological" hypothesizing. We saw above that Deleuze identified Spinoza as the second principal moment (after Duns Scotus) in the elaboration of the univocity of being. Although his affirmation of univocity was more radical, there remained a difference *between* substance and modes in Spinoza's philosophy, which makes the modes appear dependent on substance and substance appear independent of the modes.

A third moment was needed, in which substance (or being) was univocally said of – and only of – the modes. This would require a more radical reversal in which being revolves around Becoming, and identity around the Different. Only this sort of Copernican revolution could make it possible for difference to have its own concept instead of merely being inscribed within and between concepts that are already considered identical. Identity and sameness must be conceived as dependent on *difference*, as products of the "repetition" of becoming itself. The same and the similar would then be said *of* the different, which is all that "returns." Deleuze suggests that "Nietzsche meant nothing more than this by eternal return" (DR, 41). Here univocal being is not merely thought (Scotus) or affirmed (Spinoza) but "effectively realized." The third moment in the development of univocity of being: "Being is said in a single and same sense, but this sense is that of eternal return as the return or repetition of that of which it is said. The wheel in the eternal return is at once both production of repetition on the basis of difference and selection of difference on the basis of repetition" (DR, 42).

In an appendix to *Logic of Sense*, "Plato and the Simulacrum," Deleuze argues that to reverse Platonism means "to *make the simulacra rise* and to affirm their rights among icons and copies."[32] The task of philosophy within Plato's Eidetic framework is to bring about the triumph of the icons over the simulacra. The concept of Ideas was invented to impose a limit on becoming, forcing it into an orderly relation to the Same and the Similar. The model is the "Same" and the copy is the "Similar." Simulacra, on the other hand, are false pretenders. Raising the simulacra, affirming their being and power of fabulation, inverts the Platonic domain of representation. The rising of the simulacra does not provide a new foundation, but engulfs all foundations and assures "a universal breakdown (*effondrement*), but as a joyful and positive event, as an un-founding (*effondement*)."

As the simulacra "rise to the surface," they make the model *and* copy (the Same and the Similar) fall under the fabulating power of the phantasm. This renders the whole order of "participation" and the "hierarchy" of being impossible. Everything becomes simulacra. But simulacra are not illusions (or appearances in *opposition* to icons), but the "power of producing an *effect*" (LS, 300). As we will see in more detail in the next chapters, this fabulating power is not simply negative. The eternal return is the infinite power to *affirm* divergence and decentering and "makes this power the object of a superior affirmation" (LS, 302). Understood in this way, simulation is "inseparable from the *eternal return*, for it is in the eternal return that the reversal of the *icons* or the subversion of the world of *representation* is decided."[33] In later writings, Deleuze will create new vocabularies and place less emphasis on the concepts of simulacra and the eternal return, but he will never stop working to overturn Plato's subordination of difference.

Although the impact of Nietzsche's philosophy on Deleuze's concept of *desire* is evident in the *Capitalism and Schizophrenia* project and beyond, it is perhaps easiest to demonstrate in the early monograph on *Nietzsche & Philosophy*. There Deleuze emphasizes two principles of Nietzsche's philosophy of the will: creation and joy. He refers to them as "the two ends of a *hammer head* that must drive in and pull out."[34] Willing is essentially creative and productive of joy. "Will to power does not mean that the will wants power." The idea of willing as seeking something represented by established values is a conception that is determined by slave morality. Deleuze argues that for Nietzsche, "power is the genetic and differential element in the will" (NP, 85). The active forces of willing are liberative and joyful. Zarathustra's "true teaching of will and liberty" is that willing liberates joy. Thus spoke Zarathustra: "my will always comes to me as my *liberator* and bringer of *joy*."[35] Zarathustra's concern is not "man," but the "overman," which Deleuze suggests is defined by "*a new way of feeling*" (as well as thinking and evaluating). Here it is not a question of shifting one's desire from one set of values to another, but of a "transvaluation" that creates new values (NP, 163).

Nietzsche's own hypotheses about the conditions for axiological engagement are propelled by a powerful integration of the theolytic forces. First, his anthropomorphic prudery in relation to "God" is legendary. Zarathustra and other "madmen" in his writings are aware that God is dead. His corpus is full of colorful, imaginative characters (spirits, demons, and devils as well as gods), but quite clearly Nietzsche's use of such imagery has nothing to do with the actual detection of contingently-embodied morally-relevant intentional forces. Taking seriously the threats and promises of "spirits" reinforces slave morality. For Nietzsche, the conditions for the real experience of valuation are not supernatural agents, but the creative force of the will to power, which produces new values. Like Kant and Spinoza, Nietzsche occasionally (albeit rarely) uses the term "God" in a positive but non-religious sense,[36] a philosophical habit that Deleuze himself will adopt later. The key point, however, is that Nietzsche never tries to represent the infinite as a moralistic intentional Entity; in fact, he does not try to "represent" it at all.

Deleuze suggests that Nietzsche was "the first to see that the death of God becomes effective only with the dissolution of the Self" (DR, 58). In the first Critique, Kant had displaced God (in the traditional sense) as the condition for thought, but replaced him straightaway, placing the Self in the center. For Nietzsche, however, the "identity" of both the infinite and the finite Self are undone by the vicious circularity of the eternal return of difference that produces the new. Hence, Nietzsche's interest in what comes after "Man," as well as what comes after God. What about the World? In Kant, God, the Self and the World were held together. As we will see, Deleuze lets all three go, performing a sort of (anti)metaphysical trifecta in his "diabolical" use of the disjunctive synthesis, which casts off these identities: "the Grand Canyon of the world, the 'crack' of the self and the dismembering of God" (LS, 201). As with Nietzsche, however, these dissolutions release life from forces that separate it from what it can do, and are therefore affirmative and creative, inventing and producing new forms of life.

Nietzsche's sociographic promiscuity is equally legendary. In his *Genealogy of Morals* and elsewhere, he tirelessly fights against the herd-morality represented in Christianity and for a transvaluation of values "beyond good and evil." Deleuze's book on *Nietzsche & Philosophy* begins with the somewhat surprising claim that Nietzsche's most general project is "the introduction of the concepts of sense and value into philosophy." Of course, for centuries values (as well as sense) had been discussed in great detail in moral philosophy. However, Nietzsche's concept of value introduces a *critical* reversal. An evaluation seems to presuppose some values as the basis for appraisal. Yet, values also seem to presuppose evaluations, perspectives of appraisal from which value is derived. For Nietzsche, argues Deleuze, "the problem of critique is that of the value of values, of the evaluation from which their value arises, thus the problem of their *creation.* Evaluation is defined as the differential element of corresponding values, an element which is both critical and creative" (NP, 1). A transvaluation of values is critical of the evaluations from which values arise, and creative of new values that engender productive evaluations. For Nietzsche, the "value of values" derives not from the morality of the herd, with its *ressentiment* and denial of life, but from an affirmation of life that produces new values.

Far more than in his treatment of Kant or Spinoza (or Leibniz or Hegel), Deleuze is more attentive to the way in which Nietzsche treats *Christ.* In part, this is due to the fact that Nietzsche himself was much more explicit about the role of Christ in his own philosophy: Dionysius vs. the Crucified. Nietzsche's target is Christian "nihilism," the denial of life, the internalization and justification of pain and sadness. Deleuze seems to follow Nietzsche in placing the blame on Paul of Tarsus, rather than Jesus of Nazareth, for the Christian form of slave morality, in which *existence* itself is evaluated from the standpoint of "bad conscience." The problem is the *image* of the Crucified articulated in Christian theology and moral philosophy. "Dionysian laceration is the immediate symbol of *multiple affirmation*; Christ's cross, the sign of the cross, is the *image of contradiction and its solution*, life submits to the labor of the *negative.*"[37] Christ is the representation of a transcendent moralistic Entity who judges creaturely existence to be lacking, requiring pity and protection; Anti-Christ is the joyful affirmation of the creative power of existence itself.

In the chapters that follow, we will continue to observe the influence of Kant, Spinoza and Nietzsche on Deleuze's iconoclastic theology. We will return in more detail to the ways in which he connects "God" to the disjunctive synthesis, develops his own complex theory of immanent causality, and raises simulacra that invert Platonism. All of this clearly has a dissolutive effect on the Eidetic framework within which Christian theology has erected its Icon of transcendence. On the other hand, the resilience of the Platonic domain of representation, to which Deleuze so affirmatively applies his hammer, is due in part to the significant role played by "Christ" in western theology and philosophy. Paying closer attention to this Image, in light of insights derived from the bio-cultural sciences, can complement the Deleuzian project and inject a new critical creativity into the evaluation of theological hypotheses.

Overturning Religious Figures

As we have seen, Deleuze argues that religion has a special relation to *figures*. Thinking in religion projects transcendence onto the plane of immanence, and "populates it with Figures." The result is "a wisdom or a religion – it does not much matter which. It is only from this point of view that Chinese hexagrams, Hindu mandalas, Jewish sephiroth, Islamic 'imaginals' and Christian icons can be considered together: thinking through figures" (WP, 89). From the point of view of the bio-cultural sciences of religion, it is important to note that the *use* of the figures in what Deleuze calls "wisdom" traditions is normally wrapped up in shared imaginative engagement with supernatural agents, and so "religious" in the sense I am using the term here. In this context, however, my main focus will continue to be on overturning "Christ," a particularly resilient Figure who is interpreted within the sacerdotal trajectory of Christian theology as *the* image of God, in relation to which all human beings are evaluated.

This may seem overly aggressive. As Deleuze notes, however, when the simulacra overturn copies and models, "*every thought* becomes an aggression."[38] On the other hand, aggression is not necessarily violent. Gentle tinkering, slow leveraging, sudden flipping – we cannot know ahead of time what our iconoclastic bodies can do. Fragmentation and fabulation, critique and creation, destruction and construction come (and go) together. In its affirmation of difference, desire, and existence itself, the iconoclastic trajectory of theology can root out vestiges of Plato's hidden dualism in sacerdotal coalitions, hidden in plain sight where no one sees them, simultaneously produced and obscured by the surreptitious forces of theogonic reproduction. If Deleuze is right that Christianity secretes more atheism than any other religion, it makes sense to start here. "Only friends can set out a plane of immanence as a ground from which idols have been cleared" (WP, 43).

I have suggested that bringing Deleuzian concepts into dialogue with the bio-cultural study of religion can help us understand why people so easily accept, even embrace and defend, their own religious repression. In the following three chapters, I extract conceptual resources for overturning religious Figures by focusing primarily on *Difference and Repetition* (Chapter 3), *Logic of Sense* (Chapter 4) and the *Capitalism and Schizophrenia* project (Chapter 5), with occasional reference to Deleuze's other writings, with and without Guattari, as we go along. As the final sub-section of each of those chapters indicates, this mode of presentation provides a framework for exploring the way in which Deleuze's work liberates thinking, acting, and feeling. This should not be interpreted as an attempt to force these texts into the classical loci of epistemology, morality, and metaphysics, terminologies and boundaries he worked so hard to transgress. Thinking, acting, and feeling are bound *together* – and liberated *together*. My use of the term "axiological" is intended to designate all of our reciprocally related and mutually engaged intellectual, ethical, and aesthetic valuations.

Despite its limitations, selecting these Deleuzian texts and focusing primarily (though not exclusively) on these aspects of their revolutionary force, has other heuristic values. For example, it can help us draw attention to lines of flight *within* Christianity that follow the iconoclastic trajectory. These movements are almost always pulled back by the integrated sacerdotal forces, but their very existence produces cracks in religious Iconology, challenging the way it functions within the imagination of the coalition.

One type of iconoclastic line of flight within Christianity (and other monotheistic religions) pushes primarily for the liberation of *thinking*. Here we find an intensification of conceptual analysis about the coherence of the coalition's ideas about the Figure. As we observed in the introductory chapter, most of the leading theologians within such traditions recognized the logical problems with the notion of an infinite supernatural Agent who favors a particular coalition. If "the infinite" cannot be thought as an Entity distinct from "the finite," else it would be limited by the finite and so itself be finite in that very limitation, then *a fortiori* the infinite cannot be thought of as one supernatural Person distinct from other persons, who favors one Polity distinct from other polities. Nevertheless, even the most rigorous of logicians would only follow this line of flight so far before appealing to another source of knowledge, immunized from logic: revelations and rituals to which only members of the religious in-group had access.

Another line of flight that (partially) escapes sacerdotal forces and begins to follow the iconoclastic trajectory presses toward the liberation of *acting*. Often this movement is motivated by concerns about the way in which authoritative interpretations of the religious Figure are utilized to justify hierarchical social inscriptions that reinforce the oppression of sub-groups within the coalition or the colonization of out-groups. Here we find an intensification of compassionate action that resists the dominating policies of the coalitional elite that oppress others on the basis of (for example), race, class or gender. This can involve calls for distributive justice, or challenges to the idealization of "white, affluent male," which is so easily reinforced by the detection and protection of priestly images of Christ. Nevertheless, even the most strident of egalitarians usually only follow this line of flight so far, urging more sociographic promiscuity but replacing one image of a human-like supernatural agent with another.

One also finds pathways toward the liberation of *feeling*, a third sort of movement within monotheistic coalitions that can open up iconoclastic lines of flight. This is often characterized by an intensification of contemplative awareness, which can lead to experiences that alleviate anxiety about being-limited by an infinite person-like supernatural Agent. The mystics of many traditions have described a sense of feeling connected to, or even becoming united with, "everything" – or "nothing," it does not much matter which. In such experiences, the absolute or the infinite is no longer an "object" at all, much less a Person who prefers a particular Polity. In Christian theology, mysticism is often linked to the apophatic (or negative) way, which doxologically denies the power of human language to comprehend the essence of a transcendent Entity. Nevertheless, even the most apophatic of contemplatives will usually follow this line of flight only so far before also expressing her confidence in kataphatic (or positive) statements about the eminent way in which that moralistic Entity possesses anthropomorphic attributes.

In other words, in every case the risky adventures of the iconoclastic trajectory were pressured to submit to the integrated forces of the sacerdotal trajectory. Logicians, egalitarians, and contemplatives who refused to be domesticated were censored, excommunicated, exiled or worse. It makes sense that these intensifications of thinking, acting, and feeling would be so threatening to a religious coalition. They challenge the way in which its members imaginatively engage the supernatural Agent who is detected as protecting them. The theogonic forces are naturally activated when the psychological or political structures that aid survival are threatened. Moreover, they reinforce one another. Anxiety about the safety of one's group activates anthropomorphic promiscuity, stimulating hyper-active detection of supernatural agents. Anxiety about one's relationship to supernatural agents activates sociographic prudery, stimulating a hyper-active protection of one's in-group and decreasing empathy toward out-group members.

In his own way, Deleuze was a logician, an egalitarian, and a contemplative. Yes, in his own, idiosyncratic way. However, he never gave into the integrated forces of theogonic reproduction in the development of his retroductive hypotheses about the conditions for real experience. All theological hypotheses have to deal with infinity, intensity, and intentionality. Hypotheses that follow the sacerdotal trajectory postulate an infinite intentionality as the *transcendent* condition for the intense experience of axiological engagement. Deleuze will develop hypotheses in which the infinite movements of intensities of difference (or of emissions of singularities, or of break-flows of desiring-machines) are postulated as the transcenden*tal* conditions of intentionality, that is, as *immanent* causes that engender (or animate, or produce) axiological engagements. This sort of iconoclastic theology is intense; it is the intentional intensification of theolytic forces as one encounters the infinite becoming of differences of intensity.

Deleuze quite often uses *devious* language to designate the genetic element of intentionality. This brings me to another reason for presenting his theological hypotheses in the context of his attempts to liberate thinking, acting, and feeling. In Chapter 3, we will see that he rejects the dogmatic image of thought and argues for the "demonic" genesis of thinking. In Chapter 4, we will see that he rejects morality for its appeals to transcendence and argues for a "diabolical" principle that conditions ethics. In Chapter 5, we will see that he rejects the judgment of God and the priestly curse on desire, and praises the flights of the sorcerer who makes pacts with "the Devil." Examinations of this sort of language in Deleuze's work are few and far between in the secondary literature, and usually do not focus on the function of the demonic in religious coalitions.[39] We may not be sure about Deleuze's purpose in using this diabolical vocabulary, but for my purposes it can serve as another point of contact with the biocultural study of religion.

Up to this point, my discussion has for the most part referred to those types of supernatural agents who are detected as loving protectors or partners. However, in most cultures religious imagination is also populated with contingently-embodied entities that are perceived as dangerous, more like predators who must be avoided or turned into prey. In fact, intentional forces that must be manipulated and controlled to protect the coalition are one of the most prevalent types of supernatural agent. This is due, in part, to the way in which the fear evoked as they are represented within a religious Imaginary helps to protect the cohesion of an in-group.[40] In Christianity, for example, the Devil and his minions are often held responsible for the torments, tribulations, and temptations experienced by believers. These mischievous supernatural agents are represented as masters of disguise, which makes it difficult to see through their deceit. All the more need for hyper-sensitive detection. Thought, behavior, and pleasure must be carefully restrained, regulated, and repressed in order to avoid being led astray. All the more need for hyper-sensitive protection of coalitional norms.

This is why the liberation of thinking, acting, and feeling seems so dangerous. The fear of evil spirits is natural, perhaps even more natural than longing for a savior – but neither is necessary. If the goal is the secretion of a productive atheism, picking away at the one true Icon of Christ will not suffice. We must also attend to the way in which the monotheistic religions to which sacerdotal theological trajectories are bound also rely on the detection of spiritual simulacra, of a multitude of malevolent monsters that must be kept at bay. The church is particularly vibrant in contexts where such detection is rampant. Of course, many Christian theologians reject the existence of such beings as do an increasing number of laypeople in more secular contexts. And that is exactly the point. Reflecting on the implausibility of guessing "demon" when confronted with ambiguous phenomena and the dissolution of the binding power of a religious coalition go hand in hand.

Speak of the Devil. This is another way to unveil the forces of theogonic reproduction that make it so easy for us to accept our own religious repression. Does Christianity really secrete atheism more than any other religion? That would be a difficult claim to prove. But it secretes it quite a lot, as I hope to show. Deleuze's "Anti-Christ" theology provides conceptual resources for overturning religious Figures and intensifying this secretion. Understanding how they are erected in the first place and what keeps them in place can further enhance our iconoclastic efforts. Let us find out what else theological hammers can do.

3

Loosening Theological Chains

Breaking icons (re)commences the inversion of Platonism by exposing the obsession with adjudicating between bad and good images based on their putative relation to idealized models. But this is not the only use for a theological hammer. Like the "instructor" in Plato's allegory of the cave, the Deleuzian Friend is interested in loosening the chains that bind thinkers in the dark. Like Glaucon, she will agree with Socrates that these prisoners will naturally be distressed when they become aware of the extent to which their shackles have limited their perspective. For her, however, the problem is not that thinkers are fettered in such a way that they can only see simulacra, and the solution is not leading them out of the cave and up into the light so that they can contemplate the source of true knowledge. The Friend works instead to disclose and dissolve a much more powerful and far less easily perceived Chain that ties thinkers, along with their aspiring Platonist saviors, to an image of thought that is always and already itself bound up within the domain of representation, and bound to judgments based on transcendent ideals.

In *Difference and Repetition*, Deleuze loosens the fetters that constitute this theological Chain, encouraging us to become thinkers of the eternal return who refuse "to be drawn out of the cave, finding instead another cave beyond, always another in which to hide" (DR, 67). In this volume, published in French in 1968, he moves beyond the philosophical portraiture style of his early books, some of which we reviewed in Chapter 2. As Deleuze put it in the Introduction to the English edition (1994), this was his first attempt to "do philosophy." In this chapter we will have the opportunity to observe several continuities between his earlier writings and *Difference and Repetition*. As we will see in Chapters 4 and 5, some of these continuities persist in his later work, both with and without Guattari, despite radical shifts in vocabulary. Our main task, however, is not sketching the genealogy or development of Deleuze's conceptual creations but extracting their revolutionary force and coupling them with insights from the bio-cultural study of religion in the ongoing production of iconoclastic theology.

Like much of Deleuze's work, *Difference and Repetition* is resistant to quick summarization, and even an outline of all of the key aspects of his argument is not possible in a single chapter.[1] My goal here is much more modest. I focus on Deleuze's dissolution of what he calls a quadripartite yoke that binds thinkers within the dogmatic (or moral) image of thought. Although this yoke is treated throughout the book, he spells out its postulates in most detail in Chapter III. Deleuze himself went out of his way to draw readers' attention to this chapter, which he suggested was "the most necessary and the most concrete, and which serves to introduce subsequent books up to and including the research undertaken with Guattari."[2] In that chapter he hammers away at the four shackles of the Platonic world of representation that imprison thinking: "identity with regard to concepts, opposition with regard to the determination of concepts, analogy with regard to judgment, resemblance with regard to objects" (DR, 137).

In what sense are these fetters *theological*? In what ways are they chaining *theology*? If theology is the science of "non-existent entities," and the way in which they animate language and engender thought, then *Difference and Repetition* is clearly a theological volume. Deleuze introduces a variety of concepts that indicate real yet "non-existing" entities that bear on the conditions for and genesis of thinking (e.g., "virtual" and "problematic" fields). He describes the "expressible" as an "ideal event," about which "we *cannot say that it exists in itself*: it insists or subsists, possessing a *quasi-being* or an *extra-being*, that minimum of being common to real, possible and even impossible objects."[3] In such statements, we can hear echoes of his engagement with Spinoza and anticipations of his constructive work in *Logic of Sense*, to which we will turn in Chapter 4. Here I focus on how the four fetters of the dogmatic image of thought are dissolved by four interrelated "theological" concepts in *Difference and Repetition*: difference in-itself, repetition for-itself, univocity of being and the positivity of (non)-being.

This is one way of unpacking Deleuze's hypothesis about the conditions for the real experience of thinking, which he explicitly links to the *eternal return* – a theological concept if ever there was one – as that which loosens the four fetters of the "moral" image of thought forged by Plato, segmented by Aristotle, and soldered together in Christian theology. Deleuze suggests that "difference is crucified" on these quadripartite branches (DR, 137). As we will see, he also refers to a "demonic" genesis of thinking and urges us to discover the Anti-Christ in every believer. I defer an exploration of the shock value of such statements (which are, indeed, both shocking and valuable) to the end of the chapter. Despite these suggestive comments, Deleuze rarely engages Christian theology in any detail. In what follows, I attempt to complement his efforts to loosen these shackles by demonstrating the extent to which they have been welded together and reinforced in western thought by the image of Christ as the *Logos* of God. Drawing on insights from the bio-cultural study of religion will help us understand even more clearly why the fragmentation of the Eidetic framework is so alarming to those whose sense of psychological or political security depends upon the selection of one particular religious Figure over all its rivals. The first step, however, is unveiling the Chain itself.

The Dogmatic Image of Thought

Deleuze begins Chapter III ("The Image of Thought") by observing the importance that philosophers have attached to beginning by identifying and attempting to eliminate all presuppositions. However, it seems that most philosophers, even (or especially) when they consciously try to avoid *objective* presuppositions, bring along their own *subjective* presuppositions to this allegedly new beginning. However, later philosophers who criticize these presuppositions (of either kind) in order to begin again inevitably bring along their own presuppositions, hidden to them but revealed by the next generation of philosophers. It appears that philosophy will always be caught in this Circle. How, then, can it truly begin? Deleuze also wants to challenge presuppositions, but he does so without attempting to secure a new grounding that will stop the Circle, or pretending to start without presuppositions, which only continues the same Circle. Instead, he suggests that the problem lies in presuppositions *about* the circularity itself, which ignore its truly tortuous and productive nature. Deleuze writes that we must indeed conclude that "there is no true beginning in philosophy, or rather that the true philosophical beginning, Difference, is in-itself already Repetition" (DR, 129). We will return to these concepts below.

At this stage, it is important to draw attention to Deleuze's claim that philosophy has, for the most part, presupposed a *pre*-philosophical image of thought, according to which thought has a "natural" affinity with the true. Thought, according to this image, "formally possesses the true and materially wants the true. It is *in terms* of this image that everybody knows and is presumed to know what it means to think" (DR, 131). Deleuze calls this the *dogmatic* image of thought, which he argues presupposes a *moral* grounding of the relation between thought and truth. In this context, his project is the liberation of thinking from moralistic epistemologies that pretend to ground dogmatic knowledge. For Deleuze, the true beginning of philosophy is the commencement and recommencement of a struggle *against* the dogmatic image of thought, an authentic repetition in a "thought without Image" that liberates thinking *within* thought.[4] In the Conclusion, he calls for a revolution in thought like that which took art from representation to abstraction (DR, 276). Only through such a revolution, only when thought is liberated from the dogmatic *image*, Deleuze argues, can thought begin, and continually begin again, to think.

As his title suggests, Deleuze's assessment of the problem and his constructive proposal center around the concepts of difference and repetition. In the "pre-philosophical" approach of the moral image of thought, it seems natural to begin with the identical, the similar, the analogous or the opposed, as the basis for any consideration of differences. In the domain of representation, "*difference becomes an object of representation always in relation to a conceived identity, a judged analogy, an imagined opposition or a perceived similitude*" (DR, 137). Throughout the book, Deleuze criticizes this image of thought for the way in which its four shackles force difference into "mediation," in which it is always "subordinated to identity, reduced to the negative, incarcerated within similitude and analogy," always subjected to "the four iron collars of representation: identity in the concept, opposition in the predicate, analogy in judgment and resemblance in perception."[5] These fetters also make it difficult to conceive of repetition for-itself. Under these conditions, repetition is always represented as something that happens outside of and to things that are conceptually identical, perceived in terms of equality or perfect resemblance, and explained negatively as a real opposition or a relative limitation *of* the same and the similar, whose variants are interpreted analogically.[6]

Deleuze's project extends Klossowski's creative reading of Nietzsche's "eternal return," and develops the concepts of *pure difference* and *complex repetition* in a such a way that they mutually resolve one another, thereby escaping the constraints of the Platonic domain of representation. Demonstrating this bondage and initiating this escape were central aspects of Chapter I ("Difference in Itself") and Chapter II ("Repetition for Itself"). In the latter, he also spelled out the idea of a *dynamic genesis*, building on Bergson's description of the three syntheses of time (present, past, future) and critically applying them to Freud's passive syntheses (Habitus, Eros, Thanatos). Although not in the foreground, one of the most important things going on here is Deleuze's re-working of Kant's attempt to identify the *a priori* grounds of the possibility of experience (and knowledge). In the first Critique, Kant had outlined the three syntheses of apprehension, reproduction, and recognition as part of his deduction of the pure concepts of understanding. Deleuze rejects Kant's appeal to the apperception of an active "I" and argues that the third synthesis inevitably fails because the Ego cannot control the Crack inscribed within it. In this sense, Kant is too "Oedipal" (DR, 87). We will return to these syntheses at various points in the next two chapters, including our discussion of *Anti-Oedipus* in the context of "assembling theological machines."

At the end of Chapter III, Deleuze insists that the act of thinking, the thought that is *born* in thought, is a thought "without image" that is "neither given by innateness nor presupposed by reminiscence but *engendered* in its *genitality*."[7] This is why he goes beyond Kant and proposes what he calls a *static genesis*. Deleuze's hypothesis about the conditions for – and *genesis* of – thinking is outlined in Chapter IV ("Ideas and the Synthesis of Difference"). In this context, he argues that the static genesis takes place between "the virtual and its actualization" and not between two actualized terms. Here Ideas are described as "differentials of thought," as "multiplicities" or "reciprocal syntheses of differential relations," which are "*real without being actual, differentiated without being differenciated, and complete without being entire*" (DR, 214). Some of these distinctions are spelled out in more detail in Chapter V ("Asymmetrical Synthesis of the Sensible"), where he describes an "ideal-virtual" field made up of differential relations. It is important to note that Deleuze also introduces several other concepts to which he will give more attention in *Logic of Sense*, such as paradox, intensity, and the relation of the eternal return as a transcendental or volcanic *spatium* to the "surface" of the world. I delay treatment of these to the next chapter on "releasing theological events."

The arguments of *Difference and Repetition* are exceedingly complex. There is no space here to review all the elements of Deleuze's argument or even to present some his most fascinating concepts, such as "indi-drama-differen*t*/*c*itation." In what follows, I limit myself to brief synopses of those concepts that most clearly illustrate the main point of my reading of Deleuze: many of his most interesting proposals are responses to *theological* questions. What animates language and makes for it a body of disjunctions? What dramatizes individuations? What determines the actualization of ideal-virtual differential relations? His answers have to do with a (tortuously) complex repetition of the syntheses of pure difference. Several of Deleuze's most profound "theological" concepts are introduced and defended in the first two and the last two chapters, such as the univocity of being, the extra-being of the virtual and problematic fields, and the positivity of (non)-being. We will return to these below in the context of outlining some of the ways in which Deleuze works to dissolve the theological Chain of the dogmatic (or moral) image of thought.

In the central chapter (III) of *Difference and Repetition*, Deleuze argues that this distorted and distorting image of thought is reinforced by eight postulates. The whole book works to invert them, thereby liberating thinking from its bondage within the domain of representation. In their philosophical form, Deleuze describes them as the postulates of *Cogitatio natura universalis*, of common sense as the *Concordia facultatum*, of recognition, of representation, of error, of the proposition, of solutions, and of knowledge.[8] Deleuze's reworking of the dynamic genesis seems to be focused on overturning the first four postulates, while his theory of the static genesis more directly addresses the last four.

Our focus, however, is on the way in which all of these postulates are wound together to form the *four shackles* of the dogmatic image of thought. The order in which Deleuze lists the components of this quadripartite yoke varies throughout the book, shifting as he emphasizes one or more of them for some particular purpose in his argumentation. My presentation will trace them from the top to the bottom of "Porphyry's tree" (Figure 3.1).

Porphyry was among the most well-known students of Plotinus, the third-century CE philosopher whose integration of (mostly) Platonic and Aristotelian themes initiated the movement that later came to be called Neo-Platonism. Porphyry's *Isagoge*, from which the tree is derived, was an attempt to integrate the Platonic idea of emanation and Aristotle's theory of categories. It significantly shaped the notion of a "great chain of being," which came to dominate and set the parameters for debate in medieval philosophy and theology.

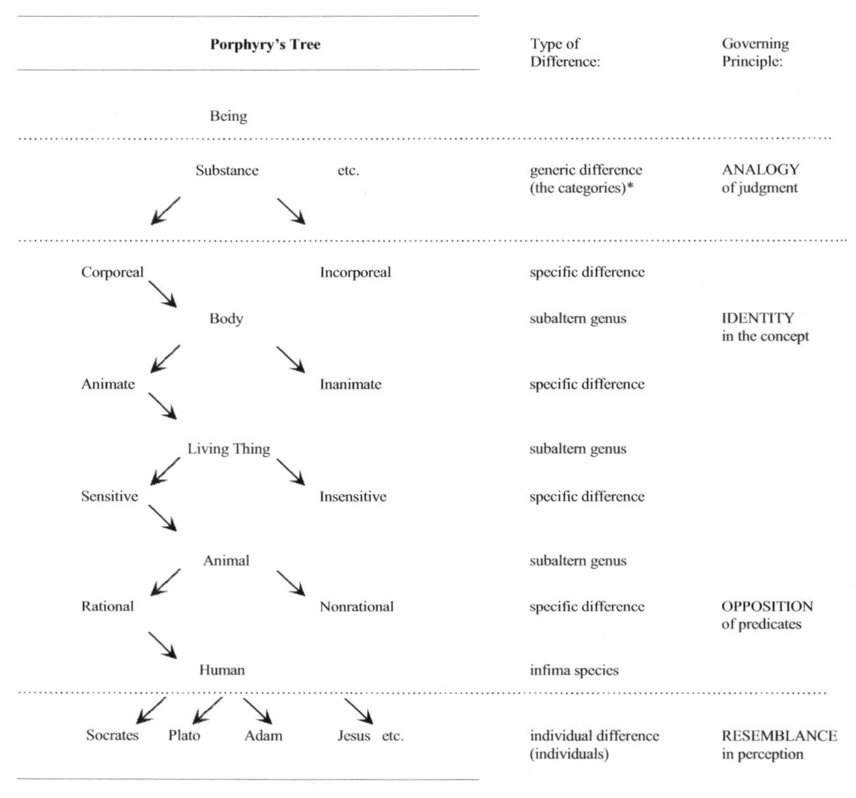

Figure 3.1 This diagram of Porphyry's tree is adapted from Daniel Smith, *Essays on Deleuze* (Edinburgh: Edinburgh University Press, 2012, p. 39), based on the analysis of E.M. Curley, *Spinoza's Metaphysics* (Cambridge, MA: Harvard University Press, 1969).

Presenting the shackles of the dogmatic image of thought in relation to this Chain (or Tree) serves several purposes in this context. It makes it easier to illustrate Deleuze's criticism of the upright and hierarchical (or Arboreal) nature and structure of this Image. It also helps us visualize the interrelation and reciprocal reinforcement among the four fetters, as well as the points at which his own constructive hypotheses about the genitality of thinking dissolve the Chain. Finally, and perhaps most relevant for the current project, Figure 3.1 provides a framework that can guide our discussion of the ways in which one particular religious Figure has been imaginatively used to hold together (and obscure) the "moral" image of thought for nearly two millennia.

Christ as the Logos of God

The most obvious attempt to link the individual man Jesus and the divine Logos in the New Testament is found in the prologue of the Gospel of John: "In the beginning was the Word (*logos*) and the Word was with God, and the Word was God . . . and the Word became flesh and dwelt among us" (1:1, 18). However, the idea of Christ as the ordering principle of creation is clearly expressed elsewhere as well. For example, in his letter to the Colossians, Paul writes that Christ is "the *image* of God, the *firstborn of all creation*." All things were created in him, through him and for him. "He himself is before all things, and in him *all things hold together* . . . through him God was pleased to reconcile to himself all things" (1:15–20). Holding together and reconciling *all things* – this is a job for the creative, regulative and eternal Word of God. These biblical authors were already identifying this Word with the created, obedient, and temporal man Jesus of Nazareth.

This emphasis on the "Word" of God is shared by the other monotheistic religions that emerged in west Asia. The relation of Moses, Jesus, and Muhammad to the Word of God is understood quite differently, which is reflected in the distinctive attitudes toward the Torah, the New Testament, and the Qur'an within these traditions. However, what they all have in common is the notion of the *revelation* of a transcendent moralistic Entity whose intentions and influence are mediated through shared *rituals* in a religious community. The history of the various attempts within Christian theology to identify Jesus with the divine Logos is exceedingly complex, but at least one aspect of this history is clear and relatively simple to understand: all such attempts involve the detection of a supernatural agent who protects a human coalition. The forces of theogonic reproduction work so smoothly and silently, however, that they usually go unnoticed. Sacerdotal theologians are able to focus their energy on how to manage their coalition's rituals and articulate their interpretation of the revelation of the Word of God in (more or less polemical) engagement with their philosophical contemporaries.

During the centuries in which Christological doctrine was forged, those contemporaries were mostly Neo-Platonists and so it is no surprise to find that many theologians were tempted to insert Christ into the metaphysical and epistemological role played by Plotinus' Nous (or Logos), the first emanation of the One. Some even appealed to Paul's description of Christ as the "firstborn of creation" to support this move. On this model, Christ is taken to be the mediator between the immutable One (Being beyond difference) and the plurality of animated individuals (differentiated beings). The problem, however, is that to accomplish this feat as the Logos of God, Christ must be both at the top and at the bottom of Porphyry's tree (Figure 3.1). He must simultaneously be Being beyond generic differentiation *and* an individual man. Moreover, as the one who "holds all things together," Christ must also be construed as the regulative principle that distributes the Aristotelian categories among beings, differentiates species, and orders the hierarchies of subaltern genera.

We will see how difficult it was for sacerdotal theologians to stretch Christ across this tree, as they tried to imagine how a divine Being that transcends generic differences could be united in the person of Jesus to a particular instance of the *infima species* "Human." It is important to see how the concept of a divine Logos as the ultimate creative and ordering principle of the cosmos is clearly *theological*, even in Deleuze's sense of the term. It is a claim about that which animates language (and thought) and makes for it "a glorious body divided into disjunctions." The Logos is not merely one existing entity in relation to others but that Entity that distributes being to existing entities and orders the hierarchy of categories by which thought is (morally) bound to think them. This sort of sacerdotal hypothesis about the conditions for axiological engagement appeals to Christ as the *representation* of God and Man. He is *the* representative of the Creator to human creatures *and* of human creatures to the Creator, the mediator between the eternal Father and his temporal children. Deleuze will offer a quite different sort of hypothesis that inverts the whole domain of representation.

It is not hard to understand why Christian theologians resisted many aspects of Stoicism and Epicureanism and hooked up instead with a philosophical machine composed primarily of parts extracted from Plato and Aristotle, whose anthropomorphic promiscuity and sociographic prudery we noted above. The Idea of the Good beyond Being and the Unmoved Mover as "thought thinking itself" lend themselves to the assemblage of idealized religious Figures much more easily than Stoic physics or Epicurean naturalism. Both of these latter philosophical schools also produced ethical and political theories that were harder to domesticate within a normative inscription of the social field that was based on appeals to shared imaginative engagement with the supernatural Agent of Christianity. Once this particular religious coalition was incorporated into the political power structures of the Roman Empire, the Stoics and Epicureans hardly had a chance.

My main interest here, however, is not with the rather obvious role that Neo-Platonic categories played in shaping Christology, but with the role of *Christ* – as a religious Figure with whom an increasingly dominant in-group imaginatively engaged in ways that regulated and oriented its axiological engagement – in shaping the reification of the Neo-Platonic Chain of being and knowing that came to dominate western philosophy. While contemplation of the One, and even in some sense participation in the Logos (or Nous), would have been encouraged by Neo-Platonic philosophers and may even have cemented their camaraderie, *qua* philosophers they would not have considered this to be ritual engagement with a person-like agent who favors their coalition. Monotheistic coalitions, on the other hand, are held together by imaginatively engaging the "Word" of a transcendent moralistic Entity.

Insofar as this Entity is considered immutable and attributed *infinite* knowledge and power, it cannot function the way a *finite* supernatural agent does – ambiguously appearing now and then in the spatiotemporal social field of the coalition, watching and waiting for opportunities to curse cheaters or bless the obedient. This is why such coalitions must also postulate some mediating Logos, a "Word" revealed by that Entity that can be ritually transmitted, as well as a host of other less powerful, less intelligent and less good supernatural agents, such as angels, demons, jinn, etc., which are more conducive to theogonic reproduction. The sort of hammering away at the conceptual constraints of (Neo)-Platonism we find in *Difference and Repetition* can be rendered even more effective by paying closer attention to these evolved default tendencies. On the one hand, grafting Christ onto the Porphyrian tree made it more resilient and harder to challenge, especially once Christianity took over the Empire. On the other hand, once the Logos is conceived as *Personal* and concerned about a *Group* the conceptual difficulties exponentially increase.

And so, naturally, do the heresies. Quite often the heretics were simply trying to make logical sense of the coalition's core doctrines. In other words, they were tempted to follow lines of intellectual flight that would unleash thinking from the sacerdotal trajectory. Many were also religious leaders concerned about the impact of apparently incoherent and irrelevant doctrines on the real axiological engagement of their local communities. During this period, heretics were often logicians and sometimes contemplatives, but only rarely egalitarians. The important point here is that those judged "heretical" were usually those who pressed the logic of the authorized interpretations of the revelation and ritual mediation of Christ too far. Such pressure brings too much of the wrong kind of attention to the secrets of theism, unveiling the ignorance of the community and the impotence of its supernatural Agent to hold it together. It threatens to unleash the flow of atheism. To ensure the survival of the coalition, the sacerdotal machines get to work reinforcing the dams of orthodoxy. In the history of Christology, by far the most important of these dams was (and is) the Definition of Chalcedon.

The Council of Chalcedon was convened in 451 CE to block the flow of two heretical streams, which had been secreting from the two dominant approaches to Christology during the preceding centuries. Oversimplifying greatly, I will refer to these as the Antiochene and the Alexandrian streams or "schools" of Christology. These streams overlapped considerably since they both relied heavily on Neo-Platonic philosophy. Nevertheless, one can discern a tension in the patristic debates between those who emphasized either some of its Platonic or some of its Aristotelian elements. For the sake of conceptual analysis, we can designate these streams by associating them with Antioch and Alexandria, respectively. It is important to recognize that both groups had their orthodox champions, who had succeeded in enforcing their views during earlier councils, and both had their embarrassing black sheep who had been branded heretics. For example, the Alexandrian school prevailed at Nicea in 325 but the Antiochene emphasis dominated at Constantinople in 381. We will return below to some of the ways in which this tension shaped the material debates about the nature of Christ as the Logos of God.

None of the ecumenical councils had succeeded in unifying these schools, a desideratum with obvious political benefits for the Empire. Despite their efforts, new heresies kept secreting. As we will see, by the middle of the fifth century the Nestorians and the Eutychians had come to represent the logical excesses of the Antiochene and Alexandrian streams respectively. The Chalcedonian Definition did not solve the conceptual problem of uniting the Logos with Jesus of Nazareth either, but it did make the limits of orthodoxy more clear. The most important sentence of the Creed, sometimes called the Symbol of Chalcedon, whose material claims we will examine below, is parenthetically enclosed by appeals to unity on the basis of authority. It begins: "We, then, following the holy Fathers, all with one consent, teach people to confess . . ." and concludes: ". . . as the prophets from the beginning have declared concerning Him, and the Lord Jesus Christ Himself has taught us, and the Creed of the holy Fathers has handed down to us." As is evident in the extracts and condemnations surrounding the council, the machinations of the sacerdotal trajectory were hard at work, trying to plug the heretical holes by praising those who support the newly authorized formulation of belief in the one Lord Jesus Christ as the Logos of God, and threatening those who do not with damnation.[9]

It was not just philosophical clarity that was at stake, but the political coherence of a particular religious coalition and its ability to maintain psychological control over its members within the Empire. The installation of Christ as Logos into the Neo-Platonic metaphysical machine did not really work conceptually, as the continued debates and appeals to mystery over the centuries amply illustrate. Moreover, abstract creedal arguments about the divine and human natures of Christ would hardly have been relevant for everyday believers in the fifth century (anymore than they are today). However, Chalcedon could "work" psychologically and politically because *Christ* could simultaneously function within ecumenical debates as the maximally counter-intuitive Logos of Neo-Platonic theologians, and within small-scale congregations as a minimally counter-intuitive supernatural agent of the sort who could be more easily engaged in imaginative rituals. The apparent irrelevance of the immutable Entity one was called upon to confess could be (and easily was) overcome by regular participation in sacramental practices that activated theogonic reproduction.

Christology continued to operate within the categories of Neo-Platonism (broadly understood) in the late Middle Ages and the Renaissance. This is evident, for example in Nicholas of Cusa's depiction of Christ the Word in *On Learned Ignorance* as the paradigmatic "implication" of God in the world, the symbolic and mysterious meeting point between the enfolding (or "complication") of all things in God and the unfolding (or "explication") of God in all things. Cusa was suspected of denying divine transcendence, but avoided condemnation, at least in part because of his consistent appeal to the mystery of Christ as the coincidence of opposites (the finite and the infinite). Others, like Pico della Mirandola, got into more trouble when they began to spell out this "implication" in ways that encouraged the practice of magic (engaging divine powers in *this* world). Deleuze himself sometimes appropriates aspects of this "hermetic" tradition, and even reworks the terminology of complication, implication, and explication for other uses in *Difference and Repetition* and elsewhere.[10] For him, of course, there is no appeal to transcendence and these terms are used to articulate an ontology of purely immanent causality. Here he was anticipated by Giordano Bruno, who had also followed out the logic of some of Cusa's insights, and concluded he must reject the idea of Christ as the Logos of a transcendent God. Bruno was burned at the stake in 1600.

At this point some sacerdotal theologians might cry out: but we are not Neo-Platonists, and we would never burn anyone! Indeed, many of the Christological proposals that have emerged in the last couple of centuries explicitly reject the language of substance metaphysics and the notion of the great Chain of being upon which so much prior doctrine had been hung. Some of these proposals creatively utilize some of the more relational, dynamic, and holistic categories that have come to play such a significant role in late modern philosophy. However, such defenses of sacerdotal theology miss the deeper point of Deleuze's critique. For him, the problem is not Porphyry's formulation in particular but *any* attempt to choose between rival images as true or better representations of a transcendent reality. In this sense, *all* Christian theology operates in the Platonic domain of representation.

A defensive portrayal of those aspects of one's tradition that affirm non-violence misses the point of the critique derived from the bio-cultural study of religion as well. Shifting from Neo-Platonic to other categories to explain the relation of Christ to a personal God who protects a coalition is still an expression of the hyperactivity of the evolved forces of theogonic reproduction, which automatically reinforce the tendency to detect supernatural agents and activate anxiety about defectors and out-groups, which does in fact often lead to the intensification of emotional or physical violence and the sanctification of war despite the intellectual objections of (some) theologians within the tradition.

In the following four sub-sections of this chapter, I treat each of the shackles of the dogmatic image of thought in turn, showing how these segments of Porphyry's tree were simultaneously reinforced and weakened when theologians used Christ as the Logos of God to prop it up. I also demonstrate how Deleuze's proposals in *Difference*

Quadripartite Fetters	Christ as Logos	Deleuzian Dissolutions
Analogy of Judgment	The Mediator (of divine and human being)	Univocity of being
Identity in the Concept	The Same (substantially God and Man)	Difference in-itself
Opposition of Predicates	The Union (of divine and human properties)	Positivity of (non)-being
Resemblance in Perception	The Similar (qualitatively God and Man)	Repetition for-itself

Figure 3.2

and Repetition have a dissolutive effect on all four shackles (Figure 3.2)

Traditional Christian hypotheses about the genesis of thought appeal to Christ, who in his very *identity* is purported to disclose an *analogy* between two *opposed* natures that nevertheless *resemble* one another. Although Deleuze does not thematize Christology in any detail, his attempts to loosen the shackles that bind thinking in the moral image of thought clearly have a theolytic force. Extracting these concepts and linking them to insights from the bio-cultural study of religion can create an even more productive iconoclastic theology.

The First Shackle: Analogy of Judgment

As its place near the top of Porphyry's tree (Figure 3.1) suggests, the fetter Deleuze calls "analogy of judgment" has a special theological relevance. Its function in the chain is to mediate the relation between the transcendent One beyond differentiation (in Neo-Platonism), or the eternal and immutable Father of all (in Christian doctrine), and the immanent differentiated genera and species of real experience (existing entities). This is a tricky business, because such a mediator must somehow hold these two realities together while maintaining an absolute distinction between them. Classical Christian theology was characterized by debates about the value of emanative and creationist concepts in the depiction of the causal relation between a transcendent moralistic Entity and the immanent existing entities of actual axiological engagement. However, nearly everyone in the debate assumed that the relation between divine and human being is mediated *analogically*.

Deleuze argues that analogy and judgment are tied together in the Aristotelian treatment of being. He describes the two functions of judgment as "distribution," by which concepts are partitioned, and "hierarchization," by which subjects are measured. These are correlated to the faculties of *common sense* and *good sense* respectively. The "just" proportioning of concepts to the subjects of which they are affirmed is grounded in the originary concepts, or highest genera, which Aristotle calls "categories." In relation to the latter, being simultaneously acquires a distributive and an ordinal sense. Being is distributed *through* the categories, which are said of all beings univocally. But being is also ordinated *among* the categories, insofar as they "are" the genera *of* being. Aristotle insisted, however, that the categories cannot be conceived as species of "being," understood as an overarching genus. Why? Because the *differences* between the categories also *are* (Meta, III, 3, 998^{b}27). If "being" was a genus, then it would have to be said *equivocally* of the categories (its species) and of their differences, both of which "are," but not in the same sense. To avoid this equivocation, Aristotle argued that generic difference (among the categories) must be of a different nature than specific difference; the genera must be *analogically* related to one another. This analogical ontology then serves as the basis for judgments about the hierarchical distribution of beings.

Deleuze was particularly critical of the notion of the "analogy of being" or *analogia entis,* which became bound up with(in) judgments about being in Christian theology. This idea was implicit in Aristotle, but was later developed in more detail by the Neo-Platonists and appropriated by patristic theologians. But what happens when one tries to place an infinite supernatural Agent at the top of Porphyry's tree? Most sacerdotal theologians would have insisted that, in some sense, God is beyond or transcendent to the whole chain of being. Neither the Aristotelian categories nor even "being" itself can be said of the infinite Creator in the same way (univocally) as they are said of finite creatures. How, then, is God related to beings? During this period, some theologians were tempted to link the Father to the Neo-Platonic idea of an eminent Good, the Son to the Nous (or Logos) that emanates from it, and the Spirit to the World-Soul that emanates from the Nous and animates all other entities. This linkage led to a variety of proposals that were later judged heretical, but let us not allow the details of this debate to distract from the main point: unlike Plato, Aristotle and Plotinus, sacerdotal theologians felt compelled for *religious* reasons to *represent* the absolute *infinite* as a Person who cares for a Group.

On the one hand, Christian theologians have insisted that a God comprehended is no God. On the other hand, they realize, sooner or later, that an incomprehensible God cannot bind together a religious coalition. This is why equivocity was not an option; if the divine and the human have nothing in common, and nothing can be said of God, not even that he "is," atheism begins to secrete. Moreover, such a non-existent Entity cannot be ritually engaged. And so there must be some appeal to revelation. A mediator must be detected who can tie together (while keeping apart) an infinite moralistic Entity and a plurality of finite (im)moral souls. When trying to think a supernatural Agent into the Neo-Platonic metaphysical and epistemological scheme, analogy seems to be the only option. In the thirteenth century, Thomas Aquinas would spell out the *analogia entis* in more detail, engraving it even more deeply into the thought forms of Christian theology. Thomas also clarified the distinction between two forms of analogy: the analogy of proportionality and the analogy of proportion. The former distributes being, showing the common sense of beings (e.g., *a* is to *b* as *c* is to *d*). The latter sets beings in a hierarchy, showing their relation to an eminent good (a resembles b, b resembles c, etc.). In both cases, however, we are dealing with the "mediation" between a transcendent Entity and a world of immanent causes.

The analogy of being was clearly at work in the Christological debates that shaped the formulation of the Definition of Chalcedon. As the divine Logos, Christ is the Mediator between God and Man. He is Analogans and analogatum, standing on both sides of divine and human being – as one subsistent Person. In fact, the arguments leading up to and culminating in Chalcedon were driven by attempts to utilize a particular analogy of proportionality as the basis for illuminating the ultimate analogy of proportion. In other words, the proportional relation between the eminent divine nature and the human nature of Jesus Christ was explained by an analogy of proportionality: the human nature is to the divine nature (in the Person of Christ) as the body is to the soul (in every personal subsistence). Both the Antiochene and Alexandrian schools accepted the validity and value of this analogy. However, they were strongly divided on the question of how, exactly, the relation of the body to the soul ought to be construed. The anthropology of those in the Antiochene stream was more Platonic, emphasizing the distinction between (and separability of) the body and the soul. The Alexandrians, on the other hand, preferred a more Aristotelian (hylomorphic) anthropology in which the body and the soul (as its form) cannot be so easily separated.

Following out the Platonic logic of their Antiochene anthropology, the Nestorians pressed the analogy to the point that they seemed to be suggesting the divine and human natures in Christ were only conjoined in a cooperative venture. This threatened the real union of God and Man, which was necessary, in the words of Chalcedon, "for our salvation." The Eutychians followed out the Aristotelian logic in Alexandrian anthropology, suggesting that the divine and human natures were in fact changed and fused into one nature. Not only did this run afoul of the doctrine of divine immutability, it also seemed to deny the finitude (hierarchical distribution) of Jesus' human nature, in which case that which was united to the divine Logos was not what needed saving, namely, real creaturely Man. In order to outlaw these two extremes, the framers of the Symbol of Chalcedon insisted that all with one consent teach and confess that one and the same Christ be "acknowledged in two natures, inconfusedly, unchangeably, indivisibly, inseparably." The first two adverbs condemn the Eutychians; the latter two prohibit Nestorianism. The assumption that structured the entire debate, namely, that an analogy of proportionality (*body* is to *soul* as *humanity* is to *divinity*) must guide the formulation of an analogy of proportion (humanity's lost and restored resemblance to divine Goodness), remained unchallenged for centuries.

As the Porphyrian tree (and the Neo-Platonic "chain of being") began to weaken with the rise of early modern science and philosophy, intellectuals found it increasingly difficult to accept the apparent absurdities of the "two natures" doctrine of Christ. Although it remains the orthodox position in most contemporary Christian coalitions, some late modern sacerdotal theologians have tried to develop Christologies that utilize categories other than those of the substance metaphysics and predication theories that dominated the ancient and medieval western world. Nevertheless, debates over the *analogia entis* continue to rage. Its defenders, who tend to be Neo-Thomist Roman Catholics or conservative Anglicans, insist that this is the only way to make sense of a mediation between finite creation and an infinite God. Its detractors, who tend to be neo-orthodox Reformed or relatively liberal Lutheran scholars, argue that its emphasis on a mediation of *being* compromises the transcendence of divine reality. Proposals from the latter camp include appeals for an "analogy of relations" (Barth) or an "analogy of advent" (Jüngel). Such efforts are often linked to reformulations of the doctrine of the Trinity, in which God is conceived not as the immutable One but as a dynamic Community. However creative these reactions to *analogia entis* might be, such appeals are still based on *analogy*. Creaturely relations and movements are judged in an analogy with a supernatural Agency (however relational or dynamic it might be imagined to be).

Now Deleuze's concern is to show that the analogy of being, the analogous judgment of being, still secretly shapes much of contemporary philosophy. The only way to overturn this (hidden) Platonism is with a rigorously *univocal* ontology. As we saw in Chapter 2, Deleuze gives the medieval theologian Duns Scotus a special place in the history of ontology. He even goes so far as to say: "there has only ever been one ontological proposition: Being is univocal. There has only ever been one ontology, that of Duns Scotus, which gave being a single voice" (DR, 35). Scotus' main target, of course, was Thomas Aquinas's notion of the *analogia entis*, which he found not only philosophically incoherent, but religiously problematic. It seemed to Scotus that speaking intelligibly about God required a univocal use of the term being that was indifferent to distinctions within (and between) the finite and the infinite (or created and Creator). Because of his anxiety about pantheism, however, Scotus only thought univocal being, leaving it neutral and indifferent. Spinoza and Nietzsche went further, affirming and effectively realizing the univocity of being. Deleuze's reconstruction of this univocal ontology proposes an absolutely immanent causality *of* pure differentiation *in* a complex repetition that engenders thought and animates language. Although he rejects all appeals to creative and emanative transcendent causes, we are still dealing here with a "theological" hypothesis – a retroductive argument about the conditions for axiological engagement.

In the last two pages of *Difference and Repetition*, Deleuze returns to the importance of the choice between analogy and univocity in ontology. The domain of representation, he argues, "essentially implies" an analogy of being. On this model, being is distributed in determinable forms and necessarily repartitioned among well-determined beings (DR, 303). As we will see below, this is reinforced by the other shackles of the dogmatic image of thought. For Deleuze, being is said "in all manners" with one voice, in a single "clamor of being," but it is said *of* that which differs, of difference in-itself, which is "itself always mobile and displaced within being," i.e., repetition for-itself. The only way not to betray being (by giving it only a distributive sense) and not to betray beings (by giving them only a hierarchical sense) is by insisting on the univocity of being and individuating difference. "Univocity signifies that being itself is univocal, while that of which it is said is equivocal: precisely the opposite of analogy." Deleuze contrasts the "sedentary distributions of analogy" with the "nomadic distributions or crowned anarchies in the univocal" (DR, 304). Beings are distributed across the space of univocal being, opened up by all the forms. This *opening*, which for Deleuze is an essential feature of univocity, loosens the shackle of analogy within the Chain of the dogmatic image of thought.

However enthusiastic one might be about Deleuze's revolutionary ontological proposals, it is important to understand why they can only take us so far. Clearly, Deleuze's flattening of the analogy of being produces a flow of atheist secretions. However, over the centuries sacerdotal theologians have had little difficulty stopping such flows and refastening the Chain; in fact, they have hardly needed to try. Within a religious coalition, appeals to experiences of shared imaginative engagement with supernatural agents who are detected as making ambiguous threats and promises relevant to the survival of members of the group are fueled by the hyper-activation of anthropomorphic promiscuity and sociographic prudery. It just seems more "natural" (pre-philosophical) to imagine a transcendent Person who cares for your Group. Deleuze hammers away at the analogy of being perhaps more rigorously than any philosopher before him. However, as long as Christ (or some other religious Figure) continues to function as a supernatural Logos that reveals and ritually mediates a transcendent moralistic Entity, theology will be able to carry on as usual. This is why it is so important to unveil the forces of theogonic reproduction that surreptitiously prop up Porphyry's tree or other models of transcendence in the domain of representation.

The Second Shackle: Identity in the Concept

One of the most important aspects of Deleuze's project here is creating a concept of difference in-itself that frees it from its subjection to sameness. Both Plato and Aristotle found difference difficult to deal with. The most arduous challenge for the Demiurge in Plato's *Timaeus* was forcing the different into conformity with the same. And it is precisely the fact that differences "are" that made Aristotle's task so difficult; he tried his best to constrain them within the *Categories*. Neither of these philosophers, argues Deleuze, developed a concept of difference. Instead, they inscribed difference within concepts in general, that is, into the identity of undetermined concepts (DR, 32). We can illustrate this by reference to Porphyry's tree, which maintains the domination of Identity over Disparity. Being is distributed to (and through) genera and species whose concepts are always identical. For example, the concept "body," the first of the subaltern genera in Figure 3.1, is identified (from above, so to speak) as corporeal substance by its difference from incorporeal substance. The difference between animate and inanimate things is also inscribed (from below) into the concept. However, these encounters with difference from both directions, up and down the hierarchy, do not challenge the identity of the concept. It remains the same no matter how many ways it is further divided or how many times it is repeated. Each genera is secure and all the species are fixed: difference is walled off by or imprisoned within the identity of the concept.

In other words, concepts are differentiated but difference itself is not conceptualized. Deleuze argues that the shift toward the Self or the Subject in modern philosophy did nothing to help the situation. The "thinking subject" of modernity took the place of "the Good" in Platonism (or God in Christianity), but it still functions as a grounding principle of identity for concepts in general. In the Conclusion to *Difference and Repetition*, Deleuze summarizes the four shackles, which in that context he refers to as forms of the transcendental illusion that appears in the domain of representation. There he notes that difference remains fettered in modernity insofar as it continues to be represented "through the identity of the concept and the thinking subject." Moreover, the "moral vision" of the (Platonic) world is simply extended "in this subjective identity affirmed as common sense (*cogitatio natura universalis*)," which still presupposes a naturally upright thinker (DR, 266). Difference remains fettered. Liberating it will require the inversion of the Platonist dualism still hidden within modernity; only through a "malice which challenges both the notion of the *model* and that of the *copy*" can thinking be fully freed from the "hierarchies of a *representative theology*."[11]

An obsession with Identity and Sameness was clearly operative in the debates that led up to Chalcedon over how to conceptualize "the one and the same" Christ. Perhaps the most well-known term from the Chalcedonian Definition is *homoousios*, often translated into English as "consubstantial" (*homo* = same, *ousia* = substance). It appears twice. One must confess that Christ is "consubstantial [*homoousios*] with the Father" in relation to his divine nature, and "consubstantial [*homoousios*] with us" in relation to his human nature. What often go unnoticed, in part because they usually go untranslated, are the several other terms that emphasize sameness in the identity of Christ. The phrase *ton auton* (the same) appears eight times in the Definition, although one usually finds only four (at most) in English translations. If we were to translate every appearance of this phrase, we would find that the bishops were asking us to confess "one and *the same* Son, our Lord Jesus Christ, *the same* perfect in divinity . . . *the same* perfect in humanity . . . truly God and truly human the *same* . . . *the same* for us . . . consubstantially *the same* with us . . . one and the *same* Christ, Son, Lord, only begotten . . . one and the *same* Son, and only begotten God, the Word (*logos*), the Lord Jesus Christ" (my translation, emphasis added).

If one includes the claim that Christ is "like us" (*homoion*), and the four times it is emphasized that he is "one" (*hen*), this makes fifteen references to sameness or identity in the single sentence that constitutes the Symbol of Chalcedon! As with Plato and Aristotle, difference must be conceptually tamed. In their attempts to conceptualize the identity of Christ, patristic theologians were clearly constrained by the segmentations of the Porphyrian tree. They struggled to fit both the Logos, conceived as the determining principle of the hierarchical distribution of being to and through the subaltern genera, and the man Jesus, conceived as a determined individual within a particular differentiated species, into one and the same Person. It is somewhat obvious how their attempts to represent the infinite (and the finite) within an identical concept were driven by anthropomorphic promiscuity. However, it is equally important to notice the role of sociographic prudery. Plotinus and Porphyry had no need to threaten anyone with excommunication or damnation. For the church fathers at Chalcedon, however, the Unity of the Church as a religious coalition was at stake, and so everyone in the in-group must confess One and the Same belief. When one presses too hard at the logical cracks in religious doctrine a little atheism always begins to secrete, even if one's intention is to purify or reform the tradition. As the followers of Nestorius and Eutyches learned, such tinkering cannot be tolerated.

Once again, it is important to point out how these constraints have continued to bind sacerdotal theologians, even those who explicitly reject "Platonism." During the last century, several Christian theologians have developed creative proposals for articulating the identity of Christ without appealing to the "two natures" doctrine. In part, these are fueled by recognition of the philosophical problems with the metaphysical and epistemological assumptions that saturated patristic, medieval, and early modern formulations of Christology. For example, the more relational and dynamic categories of philosophers like A. N. Whitehead, whose idea of God as a *finite* moralistic Entity is much more conducive for formulating doctrine in ways that are *religiously* relevant, have become increasingly popular among many progressive theologians. Such attempts at reforming doctrine can also be motivated by pastoral concern about the atheism that begins to secrete when the absurdity of the doctrine of the identity between the infinite Logos and finite Jesus threatens to dissolve the commitment of some members of the coalitions to which theologians belong. The key point here is that such proposals are still "Neo-Platonic" in at least two senses. First, however dynamically and relationally divinity and humanity might be conceived, the difference between them is still resolved within the conceptual *identity* of Christ. Second, they are still selecting one *image* (Christ) among many rivals as a good representation of the ideal relation between God and humanity.

Deleuze's development of a concept of *difference in-itself* is particularly useful for loosening this fetter. It is important to emphasize that he is not against concepts; indeed, in *What is Philosophy?*, he defines the task of the philosopher as the creation of concepts. His concern is *identity in* the concept, which inhibits the conceptualization *of* difference in-itself. The latter requires the inversion of the Platonic domain. Representation, Deleuze argues, has "identity as its element" and "similarity as its unity of measure." The pure presence that appears in the simulacrum, however, has the "*disparate*" as its measure and "a difference of difference as its immediate element" (DR, 69). What conditions thought? Not the identity of the generic concept in the realm of representation, but the dynamic intensity of the disparate (*dispars*) in the complex (synthetic) repetition of pure difference. In spelling out the concept of difference in-itself, Deleuze offers a philosophical interpretation of the differential calculus, which he argues provides a way of conceptualizing pure relations that do not depend on identifiable terms or *relata*.[12] For Deleuze, concepts are not grounded by the identity of God, or Man, or even the actuality of the World, but (un)grounded (and so engendered) by the reciprocal syntheses of differential relations in "ideal-virtual" multiplicities and actualized states and series, which are always different/ciating.[13] "It is always differences that resemble one another, which are analogous, opposed or identical: difference is behind everything, but behind difference there is nothing. Each difference passes through all the others . . . representation comes undone" (DR, 57). In the tortuous circle of the eternal return, sameness is said, but only *of* that which differs: difference in-itself.

Difference in-itself, the virtual, intensity: these are all clearly theological concepts. They deal with "non-existent entities" that animate language (or condition thought), and the way in which they make for it a body divided into disjunctions. In this context, Deleuze describes the virtual as "the characteristic state of Ideas: it is on the basis of its reality that *existence is produced*, in accordance with a time and a space *immanent* in the Idea."[14] Between the virtual and the actual, or along the line of their asymmetrical synthesis, Deleuze posits the operation of Disparity, that is to say, difference or intensity – or "difference of intensity," which he notes is a tautology. The "*sufficient reason* for all phenomena, the *condition* of that which appears" is not the Good (Plato), Christ as Logos (Christianity) or space and time (Kant), but the "Unequal in-itself . . . *disparateness* as it is determined and comprised in difference of intensity, in intensity as difference."[15] It is intensity, he argues, that *dramatizes* (or "animates") the process of actualization, determining the differential relations in the "ideal-virtual field" to become actualized (DR, 245). Ideas are not transcendent or identical. They are syntheses of differences immanent within the field of the virtual, which remain virtually differentiated even when they are actually differenciated. Deleuze warns against confusing the "virtual" with the "possible." The latter refers to the form of identity in the concept, but the former designates "a pure *multiplicity* in the Idea which radically *excludes the identical as a prior condition*."[16]

It is not possible (or, I should say, actualizable) in this context to present all the details of Deleuze's concept of difference. However, the main point of my analysis should be plain enough: his hypotheses about the conditions for (or genesis of) thinking do not appeal to a conceptual identity grounded in transcendence. Deleuze's iconoclastic theology unveils the extent to which philosophy has pre-supposed a dogmatic image of thought dominated by Sameness. This has a powerful theolytic force, especially when linked to the discovery of the mechanisms of theogonic reproduction. Ockham began to unhinge the notion of subaltern genera; Darwin undid the notion of the fixity of species. However, human cognitive and coalitional processes still "naturally" lead to interpretations of ambiguous phenomena that are constrained by generalizing concepts, which reinforce conceptualizations of in-group identity as "good," and of out-groups as essentially *different*, alien, threatening, dangerous. Many theologians have rejected the logical oddities that result from trying to fit Christ into the Neo-Platonic framework. Nevertheless, insofar as they still think of God as revealing his intentions *through* Christ to a coalition identifiable by its ritual engagement *in* Christ, they remain stuck in the sacerdotal trajectory of theology. Divine intentionality hierarchically distributed among beings. By challenging this fetter within the "natural" (pre-philosophical) image of thought, Deleuze loosens the hidden Platonic chain that binds thinking within religious groups, opening up and intensifying the flow of the iconoclastic trajectory.

The Third Shackle: Opposition of Predicates

Deleuze calls the next component of the quadripartite yoke the "opposition of predicates." In what sense is predication a shackle? The problem, he argues, is the way in which presuppositions about opposition, negation, and limitation are insinuated within the predicability of being (and beings). Under the constraints of the dogmatic image of thought, repetition and difference are subordinated to "the negative."[17] Being is distributed through the genera, divided into concepts that remain identical, opposed to and limited by each other. A predicate (or property) is defined in relation to others, which it is *not*. To give an example from Porphyry's tree, an animal cannot have both the property of being rational and the property of being not-rational; these mutually exclude each other. A subaltern genus must be divided into opposing predicates that make up specific differences – until one arrives at an *infima species*, below which one finds only individual members of that species. Deleuze argues that even classical mathematical set theory operates on the basis of the opposition of predicates, and so presupposes the negative distribution of being; hence his preference for the differential calculus as a philosophical resource.[18]

Where did philosophy go wrong? Deleuze argues that in Plato's aporetic dialogues, the initial Socratic form of questioning – "What is X?" – served a merely propaedeutic aim: opening up the "region of the problem." Such questions quickly gave way to more important questions like "How much, how and in what cases?" Unfortunately, beginning already with Aristotle, philosophers mistook this propaedeutic for the dialectic as a whole. Instead of the science of problems, dialectic came to be "confused with the simple movement of the negative, and of contradiction." The influence of Aristotle's predication theory is clear enough in Porphyry's tree; as the determination of species, dialectical division is merely the inverse of "generalization." Predicates are determined negatively, opposing one another. Deleuze criticizes this long tradition in philosophy, which continues with the Neo-Platonists and culminates in Hegel, for taking Socratic irony too seriously, allowing the question "What is X?" to determine Ideas as essences with exclusive predicates. This distortion, he argues, was a result of substituting negation and contradiction for the complex, positive nature of "the problematic."

As Deleuze notes, this distortion typically involved "theological prejudices" (DR, 188) in which God was postulated as the locus of the combinatory of abstract predicates, the absolute ground for any answer to "What is X?" The difficulty with this postulation, as Deleuze was well aware, is that such a ground cannot be conceived as an existing entity, as limited by or opposed to any other thing that it is *not*. Otherwise, it would be finite and relative, not the absolute combinatory ground of all predicates. Even representing the absolute infinite with predicates such as "good" or "not-sinful" would introduce negation and opposition. As Cusa realized, nothing can "oppose" an infinite God. His solution was the Logos/Son as *coincidentia oppositorum* – with an appeal to the mystery of the transcendent moralistic One/Father. Bruno, playing with theogonic fire, challenged the appeal to a personal divine Word, and got burned. In his *Ethics*, as we have seen, Spinoza would follow out the logic of the relation between infinite being and attributes in his own way, without appealing to knowledge accessible only through the revelation or rituals of a particular religious coalition.

The theologians at the council of Chalcedon were also concerned with the opposition of predicates. The Definition demands assent to a claim about the *union* of divine and human natures in a single subsistent entity (hypostasis). What about the properties of these natures, which quite obviously seem to oppose, negate, contradict, and exclude one another? The properties of the divine Logos include eternity, impassibility, omniscience, and omnipotence, and having been "begotten before all ages of the Father." The properties of Jesus' human nature include temporality, susceptibility to suffering, limited knowledge and power, and having been "born of the Virgin Mary." How can the properties predicated of two such different (indeed, infinitely different) natures be united in one Person? Chalcedon does not answer this question, but mandates confession of belief: "The distinction of natures being by no means taken away by the union, but rather the *property* [Greek, *idiotētos*, Latin, *proprietate*] of each nature being *preserved*, and concurring in one Person and one Subsistence, not parted or divided into two persons, but one and the same Son, and only begotten God, the Word (Logos), the Lord Jesus Christ." These divine and human properties must somehow be preserved in the union of natures.

The Alexandrians followed their champion Cyril, who had developed a doctrine of *communicatio idiomatum*, which taught that the properties of each nature were perfectly and permanently communicated to the other nature in the union, but without any change in either nature (God is immutable, the human species fixed). In this view, the divine Logos was united to a generic or impersonal human nature (not a particular man). The *Tome* of Leo, bishop of Rome, which was read at the council and is usually attached to the Chalcedonian Definition, affirms this view. Eutyches had pushed the Aristotelian logic too far, suggesting that a real union of natures would necessarily involve a change in properties. The Antiochenes, on the other hand, believed that the Logos indwelled a particular person, an individual instance of the *infima species* "Human." This makes more sense if one's analogy for divine:human is based on a Platonic reading of the soul:body relation in which the former term indwells the latter rather than "forming" it as a whole. The Nestorians had taken this logic too far, implying that neither the properties nor the natures were really united.

This tension between the Alexandrian and Antiochene "schools" is still evident in the debates among the Protestant Scholastics in the seventeenth century. Following their namesake, most Lutherans preferred the Alexandrian model, suggesting that *all* of the *idiomata* of the divine nature were mysteriously and completely communicated to the human nature (and vice versa) in the hypostatic union. Like Calvin, most early Reformed theologians leaned toward the Antiochene model. Many argued that some properties of the divine

Logos (such as "that which holds all things together") could not be completely communicated to the finite human nature; in some sense, part of the Logos must also be outside the man Jesus (the so-called *extra-Calvinisticum*). The logical problems with such doctrines are no secret among sacerdotal theologians; they spend much of their time arguing about them. Part of the difficulty is that they are dealing with an infinite moralistic Entity whose properties, like omniscience and omnipotence, are so abstract that they cannot get traction with the theogonic forces of anthropomorphic promiscuity and sociographic prudery. The cohesion of religious coalitions requires imaginative engagement with more accessible contingently-embodied entities with properties more like ours. Christ serves this purpose. On the one hand, splicing and grafting Christ into Porphyry's tree threatens to split it apart. It was not built to house this sort of supernatural agent. On the other hand, once Christ is woven into and around the tree, it can remain standing within Christian coalitions long after its Neo-Platonic core has rotted.

Deleuze's dissolutions, like the shackles, are all interrelated, but his concept of the *positivity of (non)-being* has a special relevance in this case. The "opposition of predicates" presupposes that the negative is a determining force in the distribution of being, whose divisions are carefully contained within exclusive, general predications. On this model, negation is determinative even in the distinction between being and non-being; the latter is understood as opposed to being, as the negation of being. For Deleuze, however, difference is being itself and so *also* non-being. Here the latter is understood not as the being of the negative but as the being of "the problematic," i.e., the virtual-ideal field of multiplicities, or differential relations that are correlated to questions as such (DR, 64). He proposes writing non-being as (non)-being, or even better as ?-being, in order to underline the *positive* relation of difference to the problematic field of Ideas, which are "made up of reciprocal relations between differential elements, completely determined by those relations which *never include any negative terms* or relation of negativity."[19] ?-being is the being *of* the problematic, in which Ideas are not opposed within dialectical predications, but expressed as forms of an "eternally positive differential multiplicity" (DR, 288). (Non)-being, or ?-being, is perfectly positive. Deleuze argues that the negations, oppositions, and limitations of predicates that appear in consciousness and language are the *effects* of the repetition for-itself of difference in-itself, effects all to easily (mis)taken as causal relations of being.

Here again we are clearly dealing with concepts that are *theological* in a Deleuzian sense. He describes problematic being as "*non-existent*," as "being implicit in those existences beyond the ground (*fondement*)." Deleuze insists on the *ens* or (non)-ens of the virtual "part" of an object, which is real "without being entirely determined or *actually existing*."[20] He is also interested in how these non-existing entities animate language, engender thought, and actualize individuations. ?-being is the "the differential element in which affirmation, as multiple affirmation, finds the principle of its *genesis*."[21] Being is not distributed negatively through the opposition of predicates but affirmatively, through the positive syntheses or multiple affirmations of differences in intensity. In his definition of theology in *Logic of Sense* Deleuze refers to the way in which non-existing entities make (for language) a glorious body divided by disjunctions. He does not use this vocabulary in *Difference and Repetition*, but this is precisely the role played by concepts like dramatization and differenciation, which refer to processes engendered by intensities that constitute the (impersonal) field of individuation and actualize the virtual (pre-individual) field of differential relations. "There is indeed, therefore, a *mē on*, which must not be confused with the *ouk on*, and which means the being of the problematic and not the being of the negative . . . This *mē on* is so called because it precedes all affirmation, but is none the less completely positive. Problems-Ideas are positive multiplicities, full and differentiated positivities . . ." (DR, 267).

Whatever one makes of the details of this aspect of Deleuze's proposal, his overall intention is relatively clear: to dissolve the fetter of negation and opposition that has bound thought within the domain of representation, in this case forcing it into the bifurcations of generalized predication. This has an obvious theolytic effect. When this shackle is loosened, Christology begins to fall apart. There is no point debating how to maintain the unity of two opposed natures in the one person of Christ if the exclusive properties by which they are distinguished are merely the effects of projections within consciousness. However, sacerdotal theologians have always found *projection* critiques relatively easy to dodge. Within their own religious traditions, they can simply appeal to their detection of a mysterious supernatural Agency that (ambiguously) promises protection for their coalition. The iconoclastic trajectory of theology can become even more productive if it brings together the resources of philosophers like Deleuze and the *detection/protection* critiques derived from the bio-cultural study of religion.

The Fourth Shackle: Resemblance in Perception

We come now to the bottom of Porphyry's tree, to the individual members of an *infima species*, repetitions of a lowest common difference. Deleuze describes the fetter that operates at this level as *The Similar*, or "resemblance in perception." In Platonic terms, the problem here is the simulacra; how can one adjudicate between perceptions of images, between false simulations and true copies of the models? In Aristotelian terms, the problem is that these smallest differences *are*; at what point do we stop repeating the division of predicates and identify the primary substance of the particular individual? At the top of the chain, Being was denied the status of common genus because generic differences *are*. Therefore, the categories, which are distributed by what Deleuze calls "common sense," are only analogically related to Being. At the bottom of the chain, further differentiation among beings is blocked because specific similarities, indivisibly equivalent qualities, *are*. In this case, individual beings are measured by their perceived resemblance to one another, guided by what Deleuze calls "good sense." Deleuze's complaint is that this shackle subordinates difference to qualitative resemblance. In the dogmatic image of thought, difference has been said only of The Same, distributed categorically through The Analogous as The Opposed. Now, at the bottom of the chain it is finally limited to the role of repeating The Similar. This shackle also forces thought to represent repetition only as variations *of* extreme equality or perfect resemblance. The dogmatic image of thought wrapped around itself like a Uroboros, strangling thinking within its coils.

Deleuze has good reasons to emphasize the role of perception here. In the famous divided line of the *Republic*, Plato placed perception at the bottom, ranking it as the lowest form of thought and the least reliable guide for distinguishing simulacra from icons. In his two volumes on *Cinema*, and in his work with Guattari in *A Thousand Plateaus*, to which we will return in Chapter 5, Deleuze emphasizes and spells out the importance of perception (and imperceptibility) in more detail. For our purposes here, the important point is the link that can be made between Deleuze's hammering away at the shackle of "resemblance in perception" and the discoveries in the bio-cultural study of religion about the role of cognitive perception in shaping coalitional practices. One could argue that this is the most *practical* of the shackles and that its dissolution is the most *productive*. Why? This is where we find the simulacra, and this, in a sense, is where Deleuze begins: the raising of the simulacra challenges not only the copies at the bottom of the chain but undoes the entire domain in which models are represented. In the Conclusion to *Difference and Repetition*, Deleuze hints at the relation between this shackle and practical motivation. There he describes the "four roots" of the principle of reason as "the identity of the concept which is reflected in a *ratio cognoscendi*; the opposition of the predicate which is developed in a *ratio fiendi*; the analogy of judgment which is distributed in a *ratio essendi*; and the resemblance of perception which determines a *ratio agendi*" (DR, 262).

Within the chain that is the dogmatic image of thought, this final shackle has a special bearing on the *ratio* (reason, order, mode) that motivates or *moves* individuals (their *agenda*, we might say). In the case of human individuals, this motivation is powerfully driven by evolutionary defaults in which cognitive and coalitional forces exert enormous pressure to conform, to assimilate, to become "like us." For Plato, of course, judging between rival images requires identifying those that truly resemble the ideal models. In the *Metaphysics*, Aristotle argues that knowledge is "of the like by the like" (1000b5). Likeness motivates and orients thought. In the *Nicomachean Ethics* he insists that the ideal friendship is between those who are "*alike* in excellence." The most constant friendships are among those who get the same thing from each other, and "from the same source, as happens between ready-witted people, not as happens between lover and beloved." Lovers stay constant in their friendship only if they learn to love each other's character, "these being *alike*" (1156b7, 1157a). Although we might have lingering suspicions about Aristotle's love life, his obsession with similarity is quite "natural." But Deleuze would argue it is pre-philosophical. Philosophy (re)commences by challenging, struggling against, breaking apart this moral image of thought that covers over and binds the powers of difference and repetition. These epistemological and ethical (Deleuze would say moral) elements of Platonic and Aristotelian philosophy, are integrated in Porphyry's tree, which is also meant as a guide for rational souls in their ascent toward participation in and true knowledge of Being.

The influence of these elements is clearly evident in the Christological debates surrounding Chalcedon, where all eyes were intent on rightly perceiving the one and the same *Christ*. The Definition stressed that Christ is "in all things *like* us," with one qualification immediately added: "without sin." Because one of the functions Christ played in the coalition was a pure and blameless sacrifice for human sin, he could not share this similarity with other members of the species. The framers of the Symbol appealed here to the book of Hebrews. The Son, through whom God "created the worlds" and has now spoken in "these last days," is described in the prologue as "the *reflection* of God's glory and the *exact imprint* of his very being." This Son was also the ultimate High Priest who, "blameless, undefiled, separated from sinners," sacrificed himself to make "purification for sins" (Heb. 1:1–3, 7:26). This qualification of the "likeness" of Christ to the rest of humanity had ontological and as well as soteriological motivation. How could the divine Logos, a perfectly moral Entity, be hypostatically united with sinful flesh? This was one of the reasons for the invention of the doctrine of the immaculate conception of Mary; the flesh that she provided for divine insemination was not corrupted by Adam's fallen human nature. But if Christ was without sin, how could he identify with us, or us with him?

Despite these problems, Chalcedon insisted that Christ resembled both God and Man perfectly: "the same, perfect in (relation to his) divinity and also perfect in (relation to his) humanity." A perfect replica of God the Father and a repetition of the first human creature – the Son of God and the Second Adam. What was perceived in him was truly God and truly Man, with all of their essential qualities (except sin). One can find the seeds of the Porphyrian tree already in the New Testament. Paul encourages the Corinthian believers: "*seeing* the glory of the Lord as though *reflected in a mirror*," they are "are being transformed into the *same image* from one *degree* of glory to another" (2 Cor. 3:18). Qualitative degrees of resemblance, reflected upward to the top of the chain of Being, toward an eminent glory. Describing his imitation of Christ, Paul tells the Philippians that he strives to "share in his sufferings" and to become "*like* him in his death" (3:10). John argues that this participation, this *imitation* of Christ, will be fulfilled and completed when he returns: "We will be *like* him for we will *see* him as he is" (1 Jn. 3:2). The final judgment will be based on a divine perception: who bears the image and likeness of Christ? Those whose simulation is false (the different) will be condemned, excluded and constrained forever.

During the last century, many sacerdotal theologians have attempted to articulate Christologies that do not rely on Neo-Platonic metaphysics, sometimes even rejecting the literal existence of the Garden of Eden or the Lake of Fire. However, this does not mean they have escaped this shackle of the dogmatic image of thought. New formulations of the doctrine are still driven by the need to explain how Christ can be perceived as the image of God and as the ideal representative of humanity, into whose likeness believers ought to be conformed. Very few theologians give up on the idea of a teleological consummation in which a group of humans will be transformed and held together by participation in an eternal coalition with a transcendent moralistic Entity. Those relatively "liberal" Christian groups that do let go of this idea usually begin to lose their cohesion as a *religious* coalition. Those "conservative" Christian groups that hold tenaciously onto this idea, and emphasize shared imaginative and *imitative* engagement with a supernatural agent as a practical way to secure one's place in an eternal coalition, are often more tightly bound (and more tightly wound). Commitment among in-group members is typically reinforced by a shared perception of divine revelation in the Bible as the "Word" of God and the practice of assimilating rituals that are intended to increase participants' similitude to Christ. In the next chapter, we will discover that the same tensions we found between the Alexandrians and Antiochenes in Christology are reflected in arguments about the sacraments.

Deleuze's battering of this final fetter at the bottom of Porphyry's tree can be helpfully illustrated by attending to his concept of *repetition for-itself*. For Deleuze, repetition is not the lowest and weakest link in a hierarchical chain of being, farthest from an eminent eternity. Rather, it is the productive force of the "eternal return" of being, that is, difference in-itself. When we consciously perceive some external repetition, we might say of two objects or events that they are similar. On the first page of *Difference and Repetition*, Deleuze suggests that this sort of repetition is only an echo of "a more secret vibration which *animates* it, a more profound, *internal* repetition within the singular."[22] In a sense, his dissolution of the whole dogmatic image of thought starts with an affirmation of individuating differences of intensity. An individual "is neither a quality nor an extension . . . no more an *infima species* than it is composed of parts" (DR, 247). Individuals do not resemble the positive differential relations of the virtual-ideal field. To be actualized is "to create divergent lines which correspond to – *without resembling* – a virtual multiplicity."[23] Repetition is not "that from which one 'draws off' a difference, nor that which includes difference as a variant." Rather, it is "the thought and the production of the 'absolutely different'; making it so that repetition, is, for itself, difference in itself" (DR, 94).

Here too we are clearly confronted with a *theological* concept. Repetition, suggests Deleuze, "is the pure fact of a concept with finite comprehension being forced to pass as such into *existence*." Individuation, he argues, is the "the act by which intensity *determines* differential relations to become actualized, along the lines of differenciation and within the qualities and extensities it *creates*."[24] In what sense does repetition for-itself create? We alluded earlier to the fact that Deleuze described repetition for-itself in relation to the three syntheses of time, past, present, and future in Chapter II of *Difference and Repetition*. It is important to note the special role of the repetition "of the future" in his construal of the eternal return. This aspect of complex repetition produces "the absolutely new itself." It is the pure and empty form of time, which undoes the ancient idea of the "circle" that repeats the same, with a more torturous, "eternally excentric circle, the decentered circle *of difference* which is re-formed uniquely in the third time of the series (the future) . . . a universal ungrounding which turns upon itself and causes *only the yet-to-come* to return."[25] This eternal returning repudiates the same and the similar, expelling them with its centrifugal force. Repetition for-itself, then, is the creation of the new; it is absolute novelty itself. In Chapter 4, we will explore Deleuze's theory of time in more detail in the context of his treatment of Chronos and Aion in *Logic of Sense*.

Deleuze's attempts to dissolve the dogmatic image of thought raise a challenge for philosophers: to begin (and begin again) by struggling against the "natural" pre-suppositions that chain thinking to Analogy, Identity, Opposition, and Resemblance. I have suggested that part of the reason that this bondage has lasted so long was the forced implantation of Christ into Porphyry's tree. This will make it all the more difficult for sacerdotal theologians, or philosophers who identify with a Christian (or other monotheistic) in-group, to loosen these constraints. This final shackle is particularly resilient because of the way in which it is fortified by the forces of theogonic reproduction that bind together individuals through the hyper-active detection of similarities and the hyper-active protection of the assimilated. The cognitive and coalitional biases that are part of our phylogenetic and cultural inheritance are extremely powerful. They contributed to the survival of our ancestors in the Late Pleistocene. Today, however, they constrain our thinking in ways that lead us to guess "supernatural agent" when confronted with ambiguous phenomena and to surround ourselves with *like*-minded individuals with whom we constantly exchange a mutual endorsement of guesses, a spiral of similarity that intensifies anxiety about defectors and out-groups.

The Liberation of Thinking

For Deleuze, thought is not a faculty by which an upright subject recognizes the common distribution of being in the world of representation grounded by the Good (or its Logos). The identities of the Self, the World, and God, presupposed by this epistemological model are phantasms that emerge in consciousness, phantasms that are elevated above empirical experience and taken as the conditions for thought, rather than as effects of that *something* which forces us to think. For Deleuze, what awakens thought every time is a "free form" of difference, the different within that difference, differenciated by an internal complex repetition. In other words, "*difference in intensity, disparity in the phantasm, dissemblance in the form of time, the differential in thought*" (DR, 145). The repetition for-itself of difference in-itself *produces* opposition, resemblance, identity, and analogy as its *effects*. These four shackles of Porphyry's tree, interpreted in classical Christian theology as created and controlled by the Logos of God, are the result of the "natural" functioning of essentialist perceptions, judgments, and negations. As we have seen, the bio-cultural study of religion illuminates why and how this "natural" mode of cognition works so well and why it is so resistant to critique within coalitions.

Thinking, argues Deleuze, is liberated by encounters with difference in thought, by the intensities engendered by the complex syntheses of the eternal return, which undoes the quadripartite yoke of representation (DR, 300). As mentioned earlier, Deleuze's reading and reconstruction of Nietzsche's concept of the eternal return, inspired in large part by Klossowski, is controversial. At several key points in *Difference and Repetition* he offers defenses of his reading.[26] However, our interest here is not in championing Deleuze's interpretation of this Nietzschean idea but in highlighting what he does with it, and emphasizing the way in which it functions for him as a *theological* concept. It takes on one of the roles traditionally played by the concept of "God" in theology and philosophy for centuries, namely, as a term that designates that reality which engenders existing things. The major difference is that, for Deleuze, conditioning realities are neither *transcendent* nor *intentional.* He postulates an *immanent* causality of endlessly synthesizing (folding and unfolding) *intensities*.

The eternal return, argues Deleuze, "concerns *only simulacra*, it causes only such phantasms to return." Simulacra are not false copies of models, but phantasms without any prior ground, "differential systems with their disparate and resonating series, their dark precursor and forced movements." This, he suggests is the "touchstone" for both understanding *and* overturning Platonism. Deleuze points to those moments within Plato's own writings where he considers the possibility that the simulacra are not secondary, but primary intensities that triumph over both icons and models. Plato quickly dismisses this idea, instead setting up an opposition between chaos and the order of "the Circle" that imprints matter with transcendent Ideas. Deleuze proposes something quite different: "the immanent identity of chaos and cosmos, being in the eternal return, a thoroughly *tortuous circle*."[27] Deleuze's literary explication of the complications within the eternal return is itself somewhat torturous. For our purposes, the most important point is the way he links it to the *affirmation* of simulacra, which undoes the Platonic domain of representation. In this conception of the eternal return, the decentered and decentering "wheel" is "at once both the production of repetition on the basis of difference and selection of difference on the basis of repetition" (DR, 42).

By "eternal return," then, Deleuze means the complex repetition of pure difference, the unlimited movement in which the Same revolves around the Different and is displaced by a Repetition that expresses the univocal being of pure becoming. The eternal return is the repetition of being, but being is difference (of intensity). Difference in-itself is the first affirmation, and the eternal return is the eternal affirmation of this affirmation of univocal being. In this sense, the eternal return is the "consequence" of a Difference that is "originary, pure, synthetic and in-itself . . . If difference is the in-itself, then repetition in the eternal return is the for-itself of difference." The same, the similar, the opposed, and the analogous are indeed said, but they are said *of* difference, which always returns precisely by *not* repeating a prior identity, quality, predicate or judgment. These become shackles when they are taken as themselves originary, or grounded by a transcendent Originator. "The eternal return has no other sense than this: the *absence* of any *assignable* origin – in other words, the assignation of difference *as the origin*, which then relates different to different in order to make it (or them) return as such."[28]

What forces us to think? Primary intensities, signals of the *confrontation* between two types of relation: "differential relations in the reciprocal synthesis of the Idea and relations of intensity in the asymmetrical synthesis of the sensible" (DR, 244). The affinity between intensive quantities (which are sensed) and differentials (which are thought) is determined by the complex repetition of pure difference (simulacra), signals of intensity "along the *broken chain* or the tortuous ring" of the eternal return, in which "we are *violently* led from the limit of sense to the limit of thought, from what can *only* be sensed to what can *only* be thought."[29] Deleuze replaces the hierarchy of being with an anarchy of beings, whose only "hierarchy" is found in their deployment of power, their degrees of intensity. Thought is not conditioned by encounters with "the gods," with ordered forms that guarantee recognition. On the contrary, "what we encounter are the *demons*, the sign-bearers: powers of the leap, the interval, the intensive and the instant."[30] The repetition of difference is a "demonic" power that both "makes us ill" and "heals us" (DR, 19). The process that engenders the liberation of thinking is *demonic* "rather than divine, since it is a peculiarity of demons to operate in the intervals between the gods' fields of action, as it is to leap over the barriers or the enclosures, thereby confounding the boundaries between properties" (DR, 37).

What are we to make of Deleuze's "demonic" imagery in his discussion of the genesis of thinking? First, it is important to note once again that these sorts of references are not limited to *Difference and Repetition*. In Chapters 4 and 5 we will examine more closely some of the devilish allusions that haunt the pages of *Logic of Sense* and the *Capitalism and Schizophrenia* project. We find this sort of diabolical vocabulary in other places in his writing as well. For example, in his last book with Guattari, *What is Philosophy?*, he rejects the use of the concept "God" as a scientific observer or as a conceptual persona in philosophy. "*Demon*," however, "is still an excellent name for indicating, in philosophy as well as in science, not something that exceeds our possibilities but a common kind of these necessary intercessors as respective 'subjects' of enunciation: the philosophical friend, the rival, the idiot, the overman . . . it is not a question of what they can or cannot do but of the way in which they are *perfectly positive*."[31]

Second, it is equally important to note that Deleuze also occasionally uses the term "God" or "gods" in a positive, or at least a neutral, sense. In his discussion of the amorous and the revolutionary aspects of Ideas, the search for fragments and the condensation of singularities, he observes that "the God of love and the God of anger are required in order to have an Idea" (DR, 191). In his analysis of the ordering of differences, he asserts that it is quite true that "God makes the world by calculating, but his calculations never work out exactly (*juste*), and this inexactitude or injustice in the result, this irreducible inequality, forms the *condition* of the world."[32] Deleuze depicts "God" as working to control differences, to fill the intervals, to regulate the rumbling of the unequal in intensity; nevertheless, God "dances upon a volcano" (DR, 334). This use of the term God anticipates the concept of the Chronos-God in *Logic of Sense* and the Lobster-God in *A Thousand Plateaus*, to which we will return below. Whatever constructive role the concepts of "gods" and "demons" play in his philosophy, however, it is quite clear that Deleuze never appeals to a transcendent moralistic Entity or any other kind of disembodied *intentional* force in his "theological" hypotheses about the conditions for real experience.

In order to begin (and begin again) loosening the chains of the dogmatic image of thought and producing iconoclastic theology, we can also take the question – *what are we to make* of Deleuze's references to the demonic genesis of thought? – in a *pragmatic* sense. What can we *do* with such forceful imagery? One thing we can do is bring them into confrontation with insights from the bio-cultural sciences on the role of the demonic in religion. How do images of the diabolical function in the bondage and liberation of *thinking* within religious groups? On the one hand, it is not hard to see how anthropomorphic promiscuity is at work. Our early ancestors would have been faced with all sorts of real dangerous entities, such as animal predators or hominid pillagers, avoidance or control of which would have been a top priority. Hyper-sensitive detection of destructive and deceitful intentional agents provided a survival advantage, and so was naturally selected and transmitted across generations. Once animal-spirits or ancestor-ghosts were postulated as the causes of ambiguous and uncontrollable phenomena, such as inexplicable noises in the forest, other intuitive and associative cognitive mechanisms would have easily linked them to other things that might be perceived as dangerous, such as disease, famine, inclement weather or frightening imagery in dreams or other states of altered consciousness.

On the other hand, imaginatively engaging such nasty supernatural agents is far from pleasant, so why do they continue to populate the religions of the world? Here is where sociographic prudery comes in.

Religious coalitions are held together, in part, by shared imaginative engagement with disembodied intentional forces that its members consider axiologically relevant. If we think we might be attacked by malicious ghosts or vindictive demons, we are all the more likely to signal our commitment to the in-group and participate in rituals designed to ward them off, or diminish their influence by constant appeals to kinder, gentler spirits. This is true not only of small-scale societies, but also of the major religions that trace their roots to the axial age. Even Daoism and Buddhism, in the actual practice of individuals who adhere to these traditions in east and south Asia, are filled with rituals for dealing with evil spirits and hellish ghosts. Judaism, Christianity, and Islam have their own devils and demons (belial, mastema, incubi, succubi, satan, jinn, etc.), as well as their own versions of a transcendent moralistic Entity. If monotheism postulated only a purely good, loving and forgiving God, who gave only blessings to his children, it would probably not survive. Religious coalitions seem to hold together better when their members are under the constant threat of deceitful and dangerous spirits.

An imaginative world full of menacing demons would make the idea of a divine Logos that can (or at least eventually will) constrain them all the more attractive. Until relatively recently, all Christian sacerdotal theologians operated within such worlds and many (perhaps most) still do. This helps to explain why grafting an all-powerful, all-knowing supernatural Agent onto Porphyry's tree was so tempting; it guaranteed (or at least promised) the final victory of the true icons over the false simulacra. Thought is protected from demonic deception by detecting a divine Logos that orders and judges all being. Deleuze's use of diabolical imagery inverts this operation. His "demons" are not supernatural intentional forces that threaten thought, but intensities of difference that break open the shackles that bind thought within a particular coalition's shared perception of a Logos that mediates a transcendent moralistic Entity. Speaking of a "demonic" genesis of thinking has a certain shock value. It shocks thought out of its dogmatic slumber within a religious Imaginary, liberating thinking into new modes of axiological engagement. It can facilitate a dissolution of analogous judgments of being, a leaping across identical concepts and opposed predicates, and an affirmation of the fabulous power of the simulacra to create new values.

Although Deleuze does not engage in detail with Christian theology in *Difference and Repetition*, he does occasionally make reference to an explicit inversion of theism. "We have too often been invited to judge the *atheist* from the view point of the belief or the faith that we suppose still drives him – in short, from the viewpoint of grace; not to be tempted by the *inverse* operation – to judge the *believer* by the violent atheist by which he is inhabited, the *Antichrist* eternally given 'once and for all' within grace."[33] In the context of a discussion of Kierkegaard and Nietzsche, he also explicitly contrasts the Christian and the atheist understandings of repetition. In the former, argues Deleuze, "it is repetition itself which takes place once and for all, whereas according to Nietzsche it operates for all times. Nor is this simply a numerical difference; it is rather, a fundamental difference between these two kinds of repetition" (DR, 295).

Anti-Christ, Anti-Oedipus. Both of these figures repress thinking. Although we already find intimations of Deleuze's use of the concept "Oedipus" as the prototype for the exclusive and negative use of disjunctive syntheses (DR, 107), it plays a relatively small role in *Difference and Repetition*. As we will see, this figure takes on more importance in *Logic of Sense*, and will become the main target of an intensified aggression in *Anti-Oedipus*. I will continue to argue that Deleuze's dissolutions of repressive Oedipalizing structures (whatever other designations he may use) can be strengthened by an equally aggressive and creative critique of religious Figures of transcendence. It is not enough to challenge the dogmatic epistemologies of the coalitions that imaginatively engage such Icons. Theological hammering not only shocks thinking into being, it also liberates acting and feeling by beginning (and beginning again) to produce new values.

4

Releasing Theological Events

Iconoclastic theology breaks religious Images that are interpreted as mediators of transcendence, clearing the field of dogmatic idols so that Friends can set out a plane of immanence. It also loosens the shackles that have imprisoned thought within sacerdotal coalitions and the philosophies bound to them, liberating thinking from the Platonic domain of representation. Although these forces clearly have a destructive effect, they are also intrinsically constructive. We turn now to a third way of using a theological hammer, which maintains the element of critique but is perhaps even more explicitly creative: extending the crack on the metaphysical surface of sense with an affirmative ethic of counter-effectuation that releases the eternal truth within events.

This new vocabulary comes from Deleuze's *Logic of Sense*, published one year after *Difference and Repetition*. Both books argue for and enact the inversion of Plato's "secret dualism," which privileges copies over simulacra (LS, 4). Just as *Difference and Repetition* insists that it is the encounter with "demons" (rather than "gods") that generates thinking, so *Logic of Sense* postulates a "diabolical" (rather than a "divine") principle that conditions the release of events (LS, 201). However, there are significant formal and material differences between them. *Logic of Sense* is not divided into traditional chapters, but into thirty-four "series," which are intertwined in complicated ways.[1] Kant's three syntheses, Spinoza's immanent expressionism, and Nietzsche's eternal return continue to play a role, but Deleuze develops them in different ways and links them to other philosophical resources, especially the Stoics, whom he praises as "the first to reverse Platonism, and to bring about a radical inversion" (LS, 9). As we will see, *Logic of Sense* also places a greater emphasis on *ethics*, and the transformational processes that condition the actor's affirmative liberation of events, whose offspring she is.

In this chapter I extract some of the iconoclastic forces that resonate within and across these interrelated series, drawing special attention to the ethical relevance of Deleuze's *theological* hypothesis about the conditions for (and genesis of) axiological engagement. Deleuze is critical of Platonic, Kantian, Husserlian, and all other hypotheses in which a transcendental condition is depicted "in the image of, and in the resemblance to, that which it is supposed to ground" (LS, 121). Supremely individuated Being or intensely personalized Form, the result is the same: the condition is construed in the *image* of the conditioned, namely human-like intentionality (the Self, consciousness, etc.). Moreover, Deleuze argues that by focusing on the conditions of all *possible* experience, such approaches still inadvertently construe them as transcend*ent* to the *actual*, and so fail to determine the conditions of *real* experience. He offers his own hypothesis: real sense-events are effectuated by the immanent causality of the transcendent*al* field of singularities, which bear no resemblance to individual actors. "The idea of singularities, and thus of anti-generalities, which are however impersonal and pre-individual, must now serve as our *hypothesis* for the determination of this domain and its *genetic* power."[2]

I will outline Deleuze's hypothesis by tracing the contours of a point-line-surface motif that he develops throughout *Logic of Sense*. He argues that the conditions for real experience are the emission of singularities on the metaphysical *surface* that is engendered by the endless movement of the two-sided aleatory *point* in both directions (past and future) along the unlimited *line* of the Aion. In the last few series, Deleuze utilizes this motif in a discussion of the psychoanalytic idea of the production and metamorphosis of Oedipus (with all of his pious intentions). All of this emerges out of a creative engagement with the Stoics (and Lewis Carroll), whose treatment of nonsense and paradoxes of becoming are read by Deleuze as opening up a new way of describing the donation of sense and the immanent genesis of events, which entails an entire ethic of counter-effectuation. This will require some explanation. As in earlier chapters, my goal is not to offer a full analysis of Deleuze's arguments,[3] but to flesh them out sufficiently to indicate their iconoclastic force. Here too, we will see that the force of his "theology" is both destructive (dissolving the anthropomorphic Images of transcendence that order and orient sacerdotal hypotheses) and constructive (affirming the always fragmented, infinitely divided events of *eventum tantum* or the great Event).

Logic of Sense and the Christian doctrine of the Incarnation are both concerned with the relation between ideality and corporeality, language and bodies (or Word and flesh). I will argue that the Deleuzian hypothesis about the pure becoming that constitutes this relation, and the roles of paradox, incarnation and "the actor" in making sense of events, is the reverse – or inverse – of the Christian hypothesis. Deleuze warns against permutations of God-Man and Man-God but, as usual, does not treat Christian theology in any detail. In the latter, the Incarnation is interpreted as *the event* that reveals *the sense* of the divine Plan for human actors. It denotes a (paradoxical) transcendent truth and manifests the ultimate significance of creation: the intention of an immaterial moralistic Entity to redeem (some) human persons from material decay and into an everlasting pleasurable coalition. Deleuze's atheist critique is powerful, but so are the forces of theogonic reproduction that render such doctrines so resilient. This is why here too I will link his philosophical concepts to insights extracted from the bio-cultural study of religion, demonstrating how together they help to drive a wedge between the sacerdotal and iconoclastic trajectories, releasing the latter to produce an immanent ethics of joy as it is liberated from moral philosophies that depend on *Christ* (or other ideal Signifiers) that mediate the transcendence of a supernatural Agent.

It is within an appendix to *Logic of Sense* that we find Deleuze's description of theology as "the science of non-existing entities, the manner in which these entities – divine or anti-divine, Christ or Antichrist – animate language and make for it this glorious body which is divided into disjunctions" (LS, 322). As we will see, the series that make up the main text of the book are populated (without being filled) by his analysis of such non-existent entities. For example, sense is "not of being . . . sense *does not exist*," and events are not things but have the "minimum of being" appropriate to a "*non-existing entity*."[4] Deleuzian ethics depicts the metamorphosis of the actor who releases the "eternal truth" within events; "the *liberation* of the *non-existent entity* for each state of affairs."[5] If we clearly distinguish between the sacerdotal and iconoclastic trajectories, we can begin to see that all events are theological, although not all theologies release events, and that sense is always theological even if all theologies do not make sense. All of this sounds "paradoxical" indeed. In any event, in every sense, it is.

Paradox and Becoming

As we might expect from his critique in *Difference and Repetition* of the fetters of the moral image of thought, Deleuze's affirmative use of the term "paradox" does not refer to a "contradiction" in which opposed predicates (such as divine and human) are attributed to substances (or sublated within subjects) whose perceived identities are judged analogically. Rather, for Deleuze, paradox (or nonsense) is that which is opposed to *doxa*. In the first series of *Logic of Sense* (Of the Paradoxes of Pure Becoming), Deleuze announces that paradox is initially that which destroys good sense and common sense, which are grounded in *doxa*. By the thirty-fourth and final series (Of Primary Order and Secondary Organization), it is clear that this destructive "opposition" between paradox and doxa is not a negation or an exclusion, but a positive, inclusive disjunctive synthesis, engendered by a two-sided aleatory point whose endless movement in both directions (past and future) along the unlimited line of the Aion constitutes a metaphysical surface on (or as) the frontier between the heterogeneous series of bodies and propositions.

This movement of "nonsense" or "the paradoxical agency" distributes *sense* to both series, as the extra-being attributed to bodily states of affairs and as the to-be-expressed that inheres in propositions, without merging with the terms of either series. This pure becoming along the frontier between them produces a "secondary" organization that is "proper to language." This secondary organization is the effect of the mixtures of bodies (the depths), the production of what Deleuze calls the metaphysical surface. Rather than appealing to the Platonic *heights* (the realm of the Ideas or Forms) to tame the *depths*, Deleuze finds inspiration in the Stoics for the development of a concept of the *surface* engendered by the immanent (co-present) asymmetric disjunctive synthesis of bodies (existing things) and "incorporeals." At (or on) this metaphysical surface, good sense and common sense are finally deployed in a "tertiary" organization when the terms of both series are determined by the conditions of signification, manifestation, and denotation.

What is this "nonsense?" Beginning with a treatment of the Stoic's use of paradoxes may not seem like a serious, much less a promising, way to start a philosophical discussion on the "logic" of sense. As is so often the case with Deleuze, we have to recognize that his creative use of the concepts *nonsense* and *paradox* is an attempt to disrupt us from our Platonic slumber, to force us to think and to free us to act. He argues that the Stoics use paradox in a completely different manner, inverting the Platonic Eidetic domain. For them, "paradox appears as a dismissal of depth, a display of events at the surface, and a deployment of language along this limit" (LS, 11). Deleuze is not asking us to affirm contradictory propositions that do not make sense. In fact, by nonsense he means *that which* actually *makes* or produces sense, that which *gives* or bestows sense to bodies and propositions. What we must understand as nonsense, Deleuze suggests, is "that which has no sense, and that which, as such and as it enacts the *donation* of sense, is *opposed to the absence* of sense."[6] As that which is expressed in the event, sense "emanates from *non-sense*, as from the always displaced paradoxical instance and from the eternally decentered ex-centric center" (LS, 200). Nonsense is not negative, but the positivity of the immanent principle of disjunctive synthesis that produces or bestows sense upon both series as they converge toward a "paradoxical element," which is their "differentiator" (LS, 60).

It feels more natural to begin with good sense, which moves in one direction, determining a sedentary distribution from the most to the least differentiated, and common sense, which identifies and subsumes diversity under the form of the Same. Together these seal the alliance between the Self, the World, and God, who is conceived as "the final outcome of directions and the supreme principle of identities" (LS, 90). We can tell that Deleuze's concern with the great chain of analogous being is still in the background. In *Logic of Sense*, his attempts to invert this "pre-philosophical" Platonic domain will utilize a point-line-surface system, which we will explore in more detail below. At this stage, it is important to emphasize the function of what Deleuze calls the "paradoxical agency,"[7] which moves in *both directions* at once (the paradox of regress, or indefinite proliferation) and conditions sense-events *without resembling* them (the paradox of sterile division, or dry reiteration). This *genetic* element of pure becoming, for which he uses a variety of names (paradoxical instance, nonsense, aleatory point), endlessly moves along the line of the Aion (the pure, empty form of time) in both directions animating the metaphysical surface.

It also feels natural to begin with essences and divide them into two types, material and immaterial, and then reflect on the ways in which they causally impact one another. Research in the bio-cultural study of religion suggests that these cognitive biases toward "intuitive dualism" and attributing causality to unseen intentional forces are part of our evolved phylogenetic inheritance.[8] Plato's arguments about the causal relation between Ideas and matter followed out the logic of these biases, as did most western philosophers and theologians after him – even when they disagreed materially with his ideas. Deleuze reads the Stoics as offering a very different kind of hypothesis, which starts with *events* rather than essences and *splits causes from effects* rather than distinguishing types of causality.

First, following the Stoics, Deleuze insists that "to reverse Platonism is first and foremost to remove essences and to substitute *events* in their place, as jets of *singularities*." Singularities are "veritable events," or to put it the other way, "events are ideational singularities," that communicate in "one and the same Event which endlessly redistributes them." Singularities-events are "displaced, redistributed, transformed into one another, and change sets" as the series of bodies (existing things) and the series of propositions (or sayables) are traversed by the paradoxical agency (LS, 64). Notice how this maintains the univocity of *being*. For the Stoics, "states of affairs, quantities, and qualities are no less *beings* (or bodies) than substance is." But all of these "bodies" are "contrasted with an *extra-Being* which constitutes the incorporeal as a *non-existing entity*. The highest term therefore is not Being, but Something (*aliquid*), insofar as it subsumes being and non-being, existence and inherence."[9] Sense, argues Deleuze, was discovered by the Stoics as the "pure event" that insists in propositions (the expressed *of* the proposition) but is never reducible to them, and as the incorporeal "extra-being" that is attributed *to* states of affairs (actual bodies and qualities) but is never merged with them (LS, 23).

This brings us, second, to the Stoic cleavage of the causal relation. For Plato, the causal relation moves from eternal ideality to temporal corporeality; the former is the constitutive and regulative condition for the latter. Similarly, Aristotle's Unmoved Mover (thought thinking itself) is the final cause of all corporeal movement. The Stoics, on the other hand, characterized states of affairs, quantities and qualities, along with bodies, as substances and (therefore) as *causes*, thereby relegating Ideas to the other side, "that is to this impassive extra-Being which is sterile, inefficacious, and on the surface of things: *the ideational or the incorporeal can no longer be anything other than an 'effect'*" (LS, 10). Corporeal somethings enter into causal relations with one another, the effects of which are incorporeal somethings. The latter are not beings but, so to speak, ways or modes of being. Bodies are causes, ideas are effects. This is clearly a reversal of Platonism, but it is also an *inversion* in which the causal relation itself is split by the operation of the affirmative disjunctive synthesis of the paradoxical agency, freeing incorporeal effects to enjoy their own "quasi-causality." The Stoics can affirm destiny while denying necessity because "the event, that is, sense" is referred "to a paradoxical element, intervening as *nonsense* or as an aleatory point, and operating as a quasi-cause assuring the *full autonomy* of the effect."[10]

Deleuze's hypothesis replaces transcendence and resemblance with immanence and differentiation. The paradoxical agency (nonsense) is a "two-sided entity" whose *immanent* movement along the frontier between bodies and propositions constitutes the "communication" between these two *heterogeneous* series. How can such divergent series be connected to each other without reference to an originary intentional Being that determines their relations? For Deleuze, singularities-events are affirmative disjunctive syntheses at the frontier between these two irreducible yet reciprocally determined "sides" of reality: bodies and propositions, depth and surface, Chronos and Aion, etc. The emission of singularities has an "immanent principle of auto-unification, always mobile and displaced," as a paradoxical agency "traverses the series and makes them resonate" (LS, 118). As an always mobile vacancy and always vacating mobility, this entity does not, properly speaking, "exist." It simultaneously constitutes one series as signifying and the other as signified; always displaced in the two series in relation to itself, it is excess in relation to one (mobile empty place) and lacking in relation to the other (occupant without a place).[11]

This has serious implications for theology. Traditional sacerdotal theology has followed the "natural" Platonic/Aristotelian model, prioritizing the infinite divine Word over finite flesh. In Christian doctrine, infinite *intentionality* is the cause (origin, order, and orientation) of all corporeality. Deleuze's iconoclastic theology argues the reverse: all intentionality is the effect of corporeality. But also the inverse: it is the emission of singularities along the frontier between bodies and propositions that generates and asymmetrically synthesizes the movements of the mixtures of bodies (causes) and the communication of sense-events (effects) on the two sides of the metaphysical surface along the unlimited line of the Aion. The paradoxical agency is the "productive nonsense" that "*animates* the ideal game and the impersonal transcendental field."[12] The movement of sense, which is determined as the eternal return, and whose true subject is "intensity and singularity," is *from the infinity of intensities to intentionality*, not from divine (or human) intentionality to finite intensities. As the principle of the emission of singularities, "the eternal return is the *nonsense* which distributes sense into divergent series over the entire circumference of the decentered circle."[13]

No doubt this will strike most people as an astonishingly odd and speculative hypothesis. Indeed. But the speculative and the practical moments of Deleuze's philosophy are more closely linked than they initially appear, as they were for his heroes Spinoza and Nietzsche. And it seems less odd as one unpacks the way in which his proposal makes use of complex theories in other disciplines, such as physics, biology, psychology, and meta-mathematics. We will explore some of these links below, but my main concern is to show the relevance of his hypothesis for *iconoclastic* theology. My initial point here is that it does little good for atheists to point out the logical absurdities and internal contradictions within the Christian doctrine of the Incarnation; these are no secret even, or especially, among sacerdotal theologians. Deleuze offers a hypothesis that challenges the doctrine at a different level, criticizing the (Platonic) presuppositions that surreptitiously support it. He argues that the conditions of real experience do not *resemble* human actors or provide a *transcendent* teleological orientation for a human coalition. In what follows, I try to show how we can enhance the theolytic force of Deleuze's anthropomorphic prudery and sociographic promiscuity by more explicitly attending to the mechanisms of theogonic reproduction unveiled by the bio-cultural study of religion.

Logic of Sense is a contribution to the science of non-existing entities that animate language and make for it a glorious body divided into disjunctions – a theological tome of the *Anti-Christ* sort. Deleuze's Stoic-inspired theology is fabulously iconoclastic, chasing away the "order of God," in which the disjunctive syllogism is used negatively to secure identities (e.g., the Self, the World, and even God) by exclusive predication, and affirming the "order of the Anti-Christ," the system of simulacra in which the fragments themselves rise to the surface and form mobile figures of intensity. Here we have a positive and inclusive disjunctive synthesis in which "each thing is opened up to the infinity of predicates through which it passes" (LS, 336). The context of these comments is the appended essay on "Klossowski or Bodies-Language," whence I have derived Deleuze's broad definition of theology.[14] The non-existing entities that engender language and enact disjunctions may be conceived in the manner of Christ or Anti-Christ, whose uses of this synthesis make all the difference in the world. As we will see in Chapter 5, Deleuze's insistence that it is not God, but the Anti-Christ who is master of the disjunctive syllogism, continues to motivate his theological argumentation in the *Capitalism and Schizophrenia* project.

Despite his appreciation of the Stoics, Deleuze acknowledges that they did not go far enough. He draws on a variety of other resources, including Leibniz, whom he elsewhere calls the first important theoretician of the event.[15] In *Logic of Sense*, Deleuze praises Leibniz's theory of (in)compossibility for making events originary and anterior to predicates. "Convergence and divergence are entirely *original* relations which cover the rich domain of alogical compatibilities and incompatibilities."[16] The problem, however, was that Leibniz was hindered by "theological exigencies," and still made a negative and exclusive use of disjunction, through which events were already "grasped under the hypothesis of a God who calculates and chooses, and from the point of view of their actualization in distinct worlds and individuals" (LS, 197). Leibniz did not go far enough either. Like Nietzsche, Deleuze was not hindered by such (sacerdotal) theological exigencies. When confronted with a contradiction, he will not rely on "Hail Mary" appeals to the mysterious reproductive activities of a supernatural Agent. As we will see, Deleuze develops a quasi-incarnational ethics that liberates acting through an "immaculate conception" of an entirely different sort.

Christ as the Incarnation of God

"And the Word became flesh (*logos sarx egeneto*) and dwelled among us" (John 1:18). This is the most common biblical text to which Christian formulations of the doctrine of the Incarnation appeal. The Johannine prologue begins by asserting that "the Word (Logos) was with God and the Word was God" (1:1), and ends by announcing the domestication of this same divine Word within the human *sarx* of Jesus of Nazareth. The term *incarnatio* was used by later Latin-speaking Christian theologians to gloss this claim about the relation between divine Ideality and human carnality. In Chapter 3 I explored the way in which the religious notion of Christ as *Logos*, the eternal ground and ordering principle of analogy, identity, opposition, and resemblance, constrained human thinking. In this chapter, I focus on how the notion of a divine act, in which this ideal Logos became (*egeneto*) material flesh, binds human acting. As we will see, Deleuze's theory of "pure becoming" releases events from their imaginative imprisonment between the identities of God and Man in the World.

There are several points of (dis)connection between the complex series of concepts that resonate throughout *Logic of Sense* and the sacerdotal representation of Christ as the Incarnation of God. First, the latter struggles to make sense of how the Eternal (unchanging) nature of the Logos could *become* related in some way to the temporal (changing) nature of flesh. Deleuze offers a novel theory of time (and space-matter-energy) within the context of a univocal ontology of pure becoming. Second, Christian theologians have typically been rather suspicious about *flesh*, whose concupiscent tendencies must be restrained by reason (Logos). Deleuze, on the other hand, celebrates the affects and passions of bodies. In fact, he argues that perversion (what can a body do, and how are its movements related to sense?) and theology (as the science of non-existing entities) have been discovered together in our epoch, and praises their unification in Klossowski's "superior pornology."[17] Third, classical Christian attempts to explain how the *Word* as incorporeal (divine) substance could be related to the corporeal (human) substance of the man Jesus were saturated in Platonic and Aristotelian categories. The latter are inverted by Deleuze's appropriation of Stoic theories about the relation between bodies-causes and incorporeals-effects.

As we saw in the last chapter, the Christological debates that led to (and continued after) the council of Chalcedon were shaped by the tension between two general streams of thought, which I referred to generally as Antiochene and Alexandrian. In both "schools" assertions about the relation between Word and flesh in Christ were judged according to an analogy with the relation between the soul and the body in the identity of human persons. They differed in their understanding of what it meant for a *human* (rational) soul to become embodied. This anthropological disagreement affected their interpretation of what the divine Logos would need to *become* in order to be truly human. Are persons in their current fleshy state a result of immortal souls having fallen into human bodies (Plato) or of entelechies orienting psychically formed individual bodies, efficiently caused by seminal potentialities (Aristotle)? Antiochenes and Alexandrians leaned toward one or the other of these answers, although they modified them in various ways for diverse reasons.

Those with more Platonic anthropologies developed doctrines of the Incarnation in which the *distinction* between the Logos and the flesh of Jesus was emphasized. Following through the logic of this model, one might be tempted to say that the Logos simply could not be immutable in the same sense as the Father, else it could not "become" joined to a human nature (Arius) or that, like a soul and a body in a person, the divine and human natures interacted but remained separable in Christ (Nestorius). Those with strongly

Aristotelian tendencies preferred formulations of the Incarnation in which the *union* between the natures was emphasized. On this model, the logic of the analogy would have made it tempting to say that the Logos took the place of the human rational soul in the forming of the individual body of Jesus (Apollinaris) or that a union of the divine and human natures in one person would require a fusion in which both substances are changed (Eutyches). For those within the religious coalition, these heresies were problematic for *soteriological* as well logical reasons: real salvation requires a real mediation between God and humanity. Christ must be truly God because only God can save, and Christ must be truly human because humanity is what needs saving.

When the doctrine of the Incarnation is driven under the influence of Platonic and Aristotelian categories it tends to veer in one heretical direction or the other. Chalcedon set up rigid guardrails in an attempt to protect coalition members from straying too far off the path. Some late modern theologians have tried to sober up, using other categories derived from more relational, dynamic, holistic anthropologies. This abstemious attitude toward ancient substance metaphysics is admirable, but even becoming essentialist teetotalers will not do any good if the plan is to continue driving straight ahead on the same intoxicating road of theogonic reproduction. The result will still be a conceptual dead end, at which point sacerdotal chauffeurs must simply appeal to the shared imaginative engagement of those willing to live in the cul-de-sac. Theology really needs to get hammered in a completely different way.

Christian theologians familiar with the scholarly literature on these debates might complain that my brief summary does not capture all of the nuances of the arguments, or that I have not included a proposed theological solution favored by their coalition. But my simplification of the process should not distract from the main point, which can in fact be made quite simply: no matter what kind of philosophical and anthropological categories are used in a formulation of the doctrine of Christ as the Incarnation of God, such arguments are still attempts to identify one religious Image among others as a true mediator of a transcendental moralistic Entity. The problem with sacerdotal theology is not that its adherents are unaware of the logical absurdities and contradictions from which and to which their arguments lead. The problem is that the premises and conclusions in formulations guided by this trajectory, which more or less explicitly appeal to a transcendent condition that resembles the conditioned (coalition-favoring human-like intentionality), are covertly driven by the hidden dualism of Plato's Eidetic framework, which is fueled by the even more deeply hidden evolved tendencies toward anthropomorphic promiscuity and sociographic prudery.

This is why complementing iconoclastic philosophical arguments such as Deleuze's with the insights about theogonic forces derived from the bio-cultural study of religion is so important. Otherwise, creative and concerned sacerdotal theologians, especially those who are logicians, egalitarians or contemplatives, may be tempted to try to appropriate even Deleuze's own concepts for the task of clarifying the revelation and ritual mediation of the supernatural Agent detected by their coalition, despite the fact that throughout his work Deleuze himself consistently hammers any and all appeals to Figures of *transcendence* that human selves are called upon to *resemble*.

On the other hand, atheist critiques derived from the bio-cultural (and other) sciences must also be complemented with plausible philosophical ("theological") hypotheses about that which conditions finite axiological engagement. Humans feel the need to make sense of their real experience of valuing and being-valued, and automatically make abductive "guesses" that shape their engagements. Simply making empirical observations about cognitive and coalitional tendencies does not help satisfy this need. Without alternative retroductive hypotheses, it is all too easy to fall back onto the default guess: supernatural agents are watching our group. Or, a version of this guess complicated by the emergencies of the west Asian axial age: an infinite supernatural Agent has revealed a Plan that affects all human groups, enjoyable participation in which requires ritual engagement with Christ.

In any version, the doctrine of the Incarnation is anthropomorphically promiscuous. It identifies the "cause" of the ambiguous phenomena we call "the world" as an Entity that is *intentional* in some sense. The idea that the Word becomes flesh presupposes the priority of intentionality (Logos) over flesh. The Incarnation postulates an ideal divine origin, ordering, and orientation of bodily intensities. On this model, carnal knowledge is always unlawful; knowledge can only penetrate bodies from without. The Christ-event is interpreted as the ultimate revelation of a supernatural Agent, ostensibly overcoming human ignorance about divine intentions. Insofar as this divine intentionality is represented as *infinite*, however, ambiguity remains: how can we know for sure what such an Agent meant? What exactly does God mean for us to do?

We are back to the problem of impotence. An absolutely infinite Agent has no obvious, immediate relevance to the everyday life of members of a coalition. This is why they need access to supernatural agents who bear more resemblance to real social actors, whom they can engage in rituals that incarnate the transcendent within some material element (e.g., the water of Baptism, the bread of the Eucharist). The Christian sacraments, along with other religious activities like communal worship and Bible study, perform this function by incorporating individuals into the "Body" of Christ, binding them together as an in-group. No matter how permeable the imaginative boundaries of this group may be, the doctrine of the Incarnation is still sociographically prudish, construing an ideal human coalition in accordance with the normative inscription of a transcendent moralistic Entity. The remainder of this chapter will explore ways in which Deleuze's overturning of the (hidden) Platonism within moral philosophy, presupposed in the Christian doctrine of Christ as the Incarnation of God, opens up new possibilities for actively making sense of events without any appeals to religious Figures of transcendence.

The Aleatory Point

As we saw above, Deleuze uses several terms to refer to the two-sided, infinitely mobile, impassibly neutral "entity" that traverses the heterogeneous series of bodies and propositions, endlessly moving in both directions (past and future) along the frontier between them as a principle of asymmetric disjunctive synthesis. He most often calls it the paradoxical agent, nonsense or the aleatory point. I want to focus on this latter term because of its connection to the point-line-surface system that he uses throughout the book as a new way of conceptualizing the eternal return: not as "a theory of qualities and their circular transformations, but rather the theory of pure events and their linear and superficial condensation" (LS, 204). The adjective *aleatory* is used by Deleuze to link this "point" to his reflections on chance, the dice roll, the ideal game, etc., which are important in his reading of the Stoics as affirming destiny but denying necessity, as well as in his reading of Nietzsche's eternal return as the repetition of (and only of) the essentially accidental. The *punctuality* of this entity is unique. It is "the Instant," the infinitely divided moment that is never present, but whose movement across and between the series determines their dissymmetrical correspondence precisely by not allowing them to converge. The aleatory point appears in one series as empty square, lack, or place without occupant, and in the other series as supernumerary object, excess, or place without occupant, thereby allowing the determination of one as signifying and the other as signified.

This two-sided *point* runs through the two series at the *surface*, tracing the straight *line* of the Aion along the frontier between them (LS, 92). We will return below to the linearity and superficiality of this complex motif and its implications for the philosophy of time and the emergence of consciousness. Our focus here is on the determinative role of the aleatory point in the emission of singularities-events on the surface as it traces the line. Sense is made by the infinite mobility and impassible neutrality of the aleatory point. The latter is the genetic element that donates *sense* to the terms of each series, which insists in propositions as that which they can express and appears as the attributes (extra-being) of bodily affairs, without being reducible to either. The endless movement of this aleatory principle of pure becoming is what makes everything happen "at the boundary between things and propositions" (LS, 11). Here it is crucial to keep in mind the Stoic splitting of the causal relation. Causality is limited to bodies (in the broad sense, including states of affairs, quantities and qualities), which are variously active and passive. Their mixtures have an effect of a different kind – incorporeal entities that are neutral, neither active nor passive and therefore not causal like existing things (bodies). Nevertheless, these non-existing entities are real, and do have their own "quasi-causality" in relation to one another.

The affirmative synthetic *differentiation* between body-causes and events-effects is engendered by the aleatory point (nonsense, paradoxical agency), which is itself an incorporeal quasi-cause that assures the full autonomy of the effects at the "surface." The aleatory point is neither transcendent nor similar to that which it conditions. As the fourteenth series on "double causality" makes clear, it is an *immanent* quasi-cause that effectuates a *neutral* genesis by disjunctively tracing the endless "line" at the boundary between the series of bodies and propositions. The difficult problem is describing the passage from neutrality to productivity, impassibility to genesis, which seems to require a kind of "immaculate conception" (LS, 110). As we will see below, Deleuze's solution involves the proposal of a "static" genesis with ontological and logical elements. For our purposes at this stage, the most relevant aspect of his hypothesis is its attempt to explain the genesis of events and sense without appealing to *transcendent* conditions to which the conditioned bear some *resemblance*.

The neutral aleatory point is the immanent principle of the emission of singularities-events. "Only when the world, teaming with anonymous and nomadic, impersonal and pre-individual singularities, *opens up*, do we tread at last on the *field of the transcendental*."[18] Because Deleuze so consistently calls for clearing the field of transcendence, and celebrates the vertigo of immanence, it may be surprising to find a concept like "the transcendental field" playing a significant role in *Logic of Sense*. Here it is of crucial importance to distinguish once again between the transcend*ental*, on the one hand, and the transcend*ent* or transcend*ence*, on the other. Deleuze consistently rejects both of the latter, but this does not stop him from exploring the "transcendental" conditions for (or genetic elements of) real experience, which he insists are wholly *immanent*.

He argues that these conditions are pre-individual and impersonal singularities, which distribute sense to things and propositions on the two sides of the frontier between them. "This frontier does not mingle or reunite them (for there is no more *monism* here than *dualism*); it is rather something along the line of an articulation of their *difference*: body/language."[19] The immanent process of auto-unification that envelops the singular points is the single aleatory point, which "circulates without end" in both series, guaranteeing their convergence but "precisely on the condition that it makes them endlessly diverge" (LS, 48). Connective syntheses operate in the construction of a single series (if, then), while convergent series are constructed by the conjunctive synthesis (and). The disjunctive synthesis (or) distributes the divergent series. Instead of negatively relating the series through an exclusion of predicates, however, Deleuze argues that the aleatory point, with its two uneven faces, *affirms* the disjunction as it "traverses the divergent series as divergent and causes them to resonate through their distance and in their distance" (LS, 199).

Deleuze spells this out in relation to the concept of "the problematic," which we have already met in our discussion of *Difference and Repetition* in the last chapter. In this context, he relates it to sense and the emission of singularities-events. "The mode of the event is the *problematic*." The world of sense has a "*problematic* status: singularities are distributed in a properly problematic field and crop up in this field as topological events to which no direction is attached."[20] Events are "singularities deployed in a problematic field" (LS, 66). Adopting and adapting Lautman's meta-mathematical interpretation of the theory of differential equations, Deleuze argues that the problematic field itself is not transcend*ent* to, but rather determined by the distributed singularities, which bear no likeness to the problems or the questions they condition. Moreover, the singularities preside over the genesis of the solutions as well.

The true problem "bears *no resemblance* to the propositions it subsumes under it; it rather *engenders* them as it *determines its own conditions* and assigns the individual order of permutation of the engendered propositions with the framework of general signification and personal manifestation."[21] As the reality of the *genetic* element, "the problem" in itself is a complex *theme* that cannot be reduced to a propositional *thesis*. Along with "the question," it is produced and determined by the movement of the aleatory point, which distributes the singularities. Although it inheres in propositions and blends with the extra-being of states of affairs, Deleuze insists that, properly speaking, the problem "*is not.*" This non-being is not negative, but the being *of* the problematic, which he prefers to write as (non)-being or ?-being (LS, 139–40), just as he did in *Difference and Repetition*.

Deleuze's hypothesis is clearly theological, in his own (Klossowskian) sense of the word. The aleatory point, singularities-events and the sense of the problematic fields they generate: all of these are "non-existing entities." The paradoxical agency or doubling nonsense of the aleatory point animates language and makes for it a body divided by disjunctions. "The problem" is the great animator of questions (*animal tantum*, LS, 140). Language "is *animated* by the paradoxical element or *aleatory point* to which we have given various double names."[22] However, this animating, affirmatively synthesizing disjunctive entity does not resemble or transcend what it conditions.

Deleuze is aware of how easily consciousness is deceived by the movement of simulacra, interpreting some combination of images as standing for an object, representing some entity beyond itself. This is especially true, he notes, of erotic, oneiric, and theological phantasms. His analysis of the latter occurs in the context of a treatment of the Epicurean theory of the clinamen, in which a "swerve" that conditions the movements of the smallest bodies occurs in a time smaller than the minimum of continuous, thinkable time. When this infinite movement is forced into the categories of thought, the result is an illusion that arises from the desire for infinite pleasure and the fear of infinite punishment. This is why Lucretius depicted the two aspects of "the religious man" as "avidity and anguish, covetousness and culpability – a strange complex that generates crimes" (LS, 310).

There are surely many reasons for the suppression of Stoicism and Epicureanism in the centuries that followed the death of Jesus of Nazareth, but we should not downplay the role of the theogonic forces that fueled the sacerdotal trajectory during the patristic period of Christian theology. As Deleuze notes, these "two great ancient systems . . . attempted to locate *in things* that which renders language possible."[23] Evolved cognitive and coalitional defaults would have contributed to patristic theologians' resistance to these philosophical schools, whose explanatory systems had less room for "gods" and religious rituals than those of the Academicians and the Peripatetics. Insofar as they were locked into explanations that would make sense of their detection of a transcendent moralistic Entity that protected their in-group, it makes sense that sacerdotal theologians would have resisted the psychological and political implications of Stoicism and Epicureanism. The pragmatic ethical programs of Chrysippus and Lucretius (for example) resisted appeals to shared imaginative engagement with supernatural agents who could provide moral regulation and eschatological security for particular coalitions. The fathers of the Church would "naturally" have found Platonism or Aristotelianism more attractive, which helps to explain why doctrinal formulations so quickly and easily became entwined within and reinforced the philosophical dominance of Neo-Platonic categories.

The doctrine of the Incarnation asserts that the *Word*, through whom all things were made, became *flesh*, revealing the divine intentions for humanity. The genetic element in Christianity is the transcendent Logos, whose embodiment in the life, death, and resurrection of Jesus discloses the Plan of God for the regulation and redemption of bodies in pleasurable community (or exclusion in painful isolation). As the ultimate condition for axiological engagement, Christ represents both God and Man and manifests the ideal resemblance between them. However, revelation alone is not enough to hold together a religious coalition. Supernatural agents must also be imaginatively engaged in rituals that provide opportunities for members to signal their own commitment to protecting the group by enthusiastically engaging in activities in which such agents are ambiguously detected.

Declarations of detection reinforce dedication to protection, and vice versa. Research in the bio-cultural study of religion suggests that coalitional cohesion requires that at least some of the group's rituals represent the active presence of a supernatural agent in a way that can be materially engaged by its participants.[24] As we will see below, the same tensions that we observed above between Platonic and Aristotelian tendencies in the doctrine of the Incarnation of the Logos in the flesh of Jesus are reflected in the debates among sacerdotal theologians over the real presence of the eternal, resurrected Christ in the bread of the Eucharist.

Deleuze's iconoclastic theology is anthropomorphically prudish and sociographically promiscuous. The aleatory point is a transcendent*al* condition for the real experience of intentionality and axiological engagement, but it bears no resemblance to them. It does not transcend individuals or persons. Its pure becoming is the immanent quasi-cause that conditions their effectuation on the surface by its endless movement in both directions, emitting singularities as it traces the line of the Aion on the frontier between heterogeneous series that are asymmetrically co-present to one another. The emission of pre-individual and impersonal singularities constitutes a transcendental field in which the genesis of individuals and persons can be witnessed as surface-effects of the mixtures of bodies. It is not that singularities are imprisoned in individuals or persons (coherent identities) to keep them from falling into an undifferentiated abyss. Rather, those "identities" are produced by the nonsense or paradoxical agency that circulates throughout singularities, raising the simulacra into surface-effects whose coherence consists only in their communication with other events in the "Instant."

The circulation of the aleatory point "does not allow God to subsist" (LS, 201). In fact, it does not allow the World or the Self to subsist either. This leads to a very different sort of theological ethics, as we will see. Through the process of *counter*-effectuation, the dissolved Self and the cracked I can begin to "liberate the singularities of the surface" (LS, 159). The humor-actor can release the eternal truth of the event, as it communicates with all other events in the univocal being of the great Event.

The Line of the Aion

Bodies move, sense is expressed, events happen. How are we to account for our real experience of this temporal becoming? Philosophers and theologians have typically used the term eternity to refer to that which conditions temporality itself, and Deleuze is no exception – although his creative use of the concept is exceptional indeed. For Plato, time was the moving *image* of a *transcendent* eternity. For Aristotle, the final cause of all becoming was the Unmoved Mover, the perfect being that *transcends* temporal change but *resembles* that which it conditions ("thought thinking itself"). Deleuze follows a minority tradition he finds emergent in Stoicism, and flowing through Nietzsche, which rejects these presuppositions about eternity. For him, the determining source of the real experience of flowing intentions (past, present, future) is an immanent quasi-causality that bears no similarity to that which it conditions. It is the "eternal return." As we have seen, Deleuze argues that the eternal return is not a circular repetition of the Same, not "a theory of qualities and their circular transformations, but rather the theory of pure events and their *linear* and superficial condensation."[25] This linearity is neither teleologically oriented (by good sense toward an ideal) nor identically distributed (by common sense forming general continuities).

The "eternity" of the line of the Aion, the great Event (*eventum tantum*) in which all events communicate and have their "eternal truth," is far more tortuous than an everlasting circularity, not because it goes on forever but because it endlessly subdivides singularities-events in both directions (past and future). The Aion is the two-sided straight *line* traced by the aleatory *point*, which is endlessly displaced over it. As the frontier between bodies and propositions, the line of the Aion brings to both series "the instantaneous aleatory point which traverses it and the singular points which are distributed in it" (LS, 190). It separates the series, but through an affirmative disjunctive synthesis, so the Aion should also be understood as "the flat *surface* that articulates them, an impenetrable window or glass."[26] As the Aion "circulates" throughout the series, its two "faces" engender the two corresponding dissymmetrical aspects of sense-events. Sense is produced along the line of the Aion, which makes a singular event both "the expressed of propositions and the attribute of things" (LS, 75).

The Aion is a non-existing (incorporeal) entity that animates language and makes for it a body divided by disjunctions. To understand how it does this, however, we must clarify its relation to another reading of time, which Deleuze designates as Chronos. He finds both of these readings of time in the Stoics. The real experience of temporality is conditioned by the tension between them. Deleuze argues that time should not be conceived as having three modes: past, present, and future. Rather, there are two times, "*one of which is composed only of interlocking presents; the other is constantly decomposed into elongated pasts and futures*" (LS, 73). The former has a special relation to "God." Chronos is "an encasement, a coiling up of relative presents, with God as the extreme circle or the external envelope . . . the regulated movement of vast and profound presents" (LS, 186–7). Chronos measures the actions and passions of bodies-causes and their mixtures in depth; it is the always limiting present. Aion gathers incorporeal events-effects at the surface; it is essentially unlimited past and future.

The present is always moving, slipping out from under us. It seems that "becoming" cannot be "present," for then it would "be" and no longer become. Yet, insofar as it is now becoming, it also appears that becoming is present in this "now." Chronos tries to measure the mixtures of bodies (existing things) in the present. The Stoics distinguished between good mixtures, which conserve and spread, and bad mixtures, which alter and escape regulation. In the latter, the order of qualified bodies is threatened by the measureless becoming of qualities from within. "Bodies have lost their measure and are now but *simulacra*."[27] In this reading of time, the unleashed forces of past and future threaten all that exists *in* the present. So, Chronos is split: the good Chronos of the living present is opposed by the bad Chronos of the "becoming-mad of the depths." Chronos represents both aspects of the adventures of the chronic present: the good, measured present and the terrifying subversion of the present by the measureless past and future. Chronos attempts to evade the present with "all the force of a 'now' which opposes *its* panic-stricken present to the wise present of measure."

The Aion of surfaces, on the other hand, is the pure, empty form of time that evades the present with "all the power of the 'instant,' which distinguishes its occurrence from any assignable present subject to division and redivision" (LS, 189). The Aion is opposed to Chronos as a whole, including the becoming-mad of the depths. It is no longer the time of Zeus or Saturn, who "rumbles deep within Zeus," but the time of Hercules, who climbs to the surface. The Aion is pure becoming, freed from the circularity of corporeal presents, unwinding its own circle and stretching out limitlessly in either direction. The Aion is not bound by the actions and passions of bodies and the corporeal qualities that fill the present, and not threatened by the "bad" mixtures that alter the present. It is the unlimited time of incorporeal events, always already passed and yet to come. It is populated, but never filled, by the expressed of propositions and the attributes of states of affairs, which inhere or subsist but never "exist" in the series of bodies-causes that fill up the present (good *or* bad Chronos).

Chronos measures the temporal realization of the event, its "*incarnation* in the depth of acting bodies and its incorporation in a state of affairs."[28] But the incorporeal aspect of the event has no embodied "present." The paradoxical "Instant," which runs through the entire straight line, gives to the event "the present of the pure *operation*, *not* of the *incorporation*."[29] The present of Chronos subverts and effectuates the event. The only "present" of the Aion, however, is that of a "counter-effectuation" that keeps the event from being fully incarnated in the depths of bodies. The affirmative disjunctive synthesis of the series along the frontier of the Aion frees the incorporeal aspect of the event, the past and future of the event considered in itself (its "eternal truth"), from the limitations of states of affairs. The two sides of the aleatory point, lack and excess, empty square and supernumerary object, endlessly divide the event into past and future. This allows it to enjoy its own quasi-causality. As we will see below, this has important implications for Deleuze's theological ethics.

Christian formulations of the doctrine of the Incarnation must also employ retroductive hypotheses about the relation between time and its "eternal" conditions. How does an immutable Creator relate to mutating creatures? How can an unchanging transcendent Logos *become* changing immanent flesh? Debates over these sorts of questions during the medieval period were increasingly shaped by the philosophy of Aristotle, as his thought came to dominate the broader discourse among Christian theologians in dialogue with their Muslim and Jewish counterparts. As we have seen, neither Aristotle nor Plato had to deal with the problems that emerge when the absolute infinite is represented as a transcendent Person whose "Word" is revealed in corporeal form. The cohesion of sacerdotal coalitions, however, depends on shared imaginative engagement with axiologically relevant supernatural agents. The notion of an Incarnation seems to presuppose that God acts intentionally, that is, uses *some* of his power to *achieve* a good that he does not *yet* have. However, it also seems that the very idea of a *perfectly* Good, *infinitely* powerful, and *timeless* Intentionality who "acts" is internally incoherent. Christian theologians struggled to combine their appreciation for the Aristotelian concept of an impassible, Unmoved Mover with their detection of a passionate movement by a Fatherly God toward the world in the revelation of Christ his Son. Some of Aristotle's views, such as his somewhat compelling arguments about the eternity of the world, simply had to be rejected in order to maintain the idea of divine transcendence over distributed creaturely identities, and of the eschatological orientation of time toward the restoration of the human resemblance to God.

As we have seen, anthropomorphic promiscuity alone is not enough to hold together a religious coalition. The supernatural agents who are detected must somehow be imaginatively engaged in ways that lead to the protection of the group, regulating its axiological engagement (with promises and/or threats). Rituals play an important role in the reinforcement of sociographic prudery. One of the most important of these rituals in Christianity is the Eucharist. In a hymn still often used today in the Roman Catholic mass, Thomas Aquinas referred to it as *sacramentum tantum* (the great sacrament).[30] The verse in which this phrase appears also offers a prayer for a faith that will supplement the failure of the senses (*sensuum defectui*) to detect the real presence of the resurrected body of Christ in the bread of communion distributed by the priest. The tension between Antiochene and Alexandrian inclinations in the doctrine of the Incarnation was reflected in the debates among medieval theologians about the presence of the heavenly Christ in the earthly bread. How is the eternal substance of the divine Logos related to the temporal substance of the wafer? Is there a true *becoming* here?

Thomas's Aristotelianism led to his somewhat Alexandrian doctrine of the trans-substantiation of the ritual element, which won the day doctrinally. Christians ingest their supernatural Agent and sing his praises. Bodies and propositions all mixed up in the oral zone of religiosity. Of course, most medieval peasants attending mass had little interest in these debates. They needed access to the sacrament in order to secure their place within the coalition now, and to avoid the torture of Hell later. Even if the Latin terms spoken by the priest as he waved his hand over the sacred Host (*hoc est corpus meum*) sounded like "hocus pocus," the social pressure and emotional arousal associated with regular repetition of the ritual would have stirred the imagination and encouraged more or less costly signals of commitment, thereby reinforcing in-group cohesion.

Chronos eats his children. The personal God of Christianity *incorporates* (some) of his children; those who confess rightly are brought into the "Body of Christ." The offspring of the Aion, however, are opened up and released to communicate with all other event-effects along its unlimited line. The consumption of the *sacramentum tantum* binds individual persons together, orienting their distributed identities toward a teleological consummation; it measures their commitment to the moral regulations that secure their own "presence." *Eventum tantum* is the endless release of pre-individual and impersonal singularities-events in both directions, forming problematic fields in which questions are generated in an ideal game that only "the actor" can play.

Deleuze is clearly offering a *theological ethics* – of the Antichrist sort. God and the actor are opposed in their readings of time. The actor is "an anti-God (*contradieu*)," who "belongs to the Aion." The divine present of Chronos is the measuring circle of regulation in its entirety. The "present" of the actor, on the contrary, "is the most narrow, the most contracted, the most instantaneous, and the most punctual. It is the point on a straight line which divides the line endlessly, and is itself divided into past-future" (LS, 171). Singularities-events are not reducible to the individuals or persons in which they are effectuated. As we will see, this is what makes possible the release of their "eternal truth" in the counter-effectuation of the actor, the Stoic sage who is a creature of the surface.

The Metaphysical Surface

In the eighteenth series of the *Logic of Sense*, Deleuze distinguishes between three different ways in which philosophers are oriented in thought. The Platonic philosophical orientation is toward the heights, an ascent or conversion to the highest principle. The pre-Socratics, on the other hand, did not want to leave the cave; they were oriented toward the depths, a descent toward the foundational element (water?, fire?). This subversion was a way of philosophizing with a hammer, "the hammer of the geologist and speleologist" (LS, 146), which is what endeared them to Nietzsche. However, even more endearing was what happened after Plato. A third orientation is one of "perversion," the extraordinary art of surfaces in which there is no longer depth or height, but a rising to the surface.

For the Stoics, the incorporeal is not high above but at the surface, "the superficial effect par excellence . . . not Essence but event" (LS, 148). Here the hammer flattens outward, stretches across the surface and releases sense-effects, fragmentations and fabulations that are irreducible to lofty ideas or deep bodies. The Stoic sage replaces Socratic irony, which ascends to the heights to repress the depths, with the adventure of humor on the surface, which dismisses both height and depth. As we will see below, she wills the effectuation of the event in bodies but also its *counter*-effectuation, affirming the pure event, its eternal truth independent of its incorporation. The sage "sets up shop at the *surface*, on the straight *line* which traverses it, or at the aleatory *point* which traces or travels this line."[31]

Deleuze uses the phrase *metaphysical surface* to designate the "frontier established, on the one hand, between bodies taken together as a whole and inside the limits which envelop them, and on the other, propositions in general." This is *the transcendental field* itself. At the surface, sense is formed and deployed, distributed on both sides "as the expressed which subsists in propositions and as the event which occurs in states of bodies" (LS, 142–3). And so we have the whole organization in three abstract moments, running "from the point to the straight line, and from the straight line to the surface: the point which traces the line; the line which forms the frontier; and the surface which is developed and unfolded from both sides" (LS, 191). This is not dualism or monism but a punctual, linear, and superficial holism in which pure becoming engenders the affirmative disjunctive synthesis of corporeal and ideal series. The point-line-surface system is also *theological*, in the sense that it *animates* the secondary (verbal) organization of language and determines the conditions for a tertiary arrangement in which the "objects" of sense-events (nouns) are subjected in everyday language to the rules of good sense and common sense, including "the analogy of significations, the equivocity of denotations, and the eminence of the one who manifests himself – the whole comparative play of self, world and God" (LS, 284).

The production of (and at) the metaphysical surface is wholly *immanent*. It does not transcend either series, but is their "doubling up," as they are traversed by the aleatory point that traces the line of the Aion. This doubling is not a reflection in which one series *resembles* the other, or in which both resemble something that transcends them, but the pure operation of an unlimited affirmative disjunctive synthesis. Deleuze argues that the sense deployed at the surface "produces even the states of affairs in which it is embodied" (LS, 141). However, it is also the "product of the actions and passions of mixed bodies" (LS, 142). How can he maintain both its genetic power and its sterility? His answer is an "immaculate conception" that he calls the *static* genesis. The first and second elements of this genesis are *ontological*, and have to do with the way in which individuals and persons are derived out of the transcendental field of pre-individual and impersonal nomadic singularities. The third element, however, has to do with "the problem," which we discussed above – the genetic element in what Deleuze calls the static *logical* genesis. The causality of the bodily series and the quasi-causality of the incorporeal series are both engendered by the emission of singularities-events on the neutral frontier that separates and articulates them.

The ontological productivity of beings and the logical productivity of the problematic field are "doubled up" without either transcending or resembling the other. Deleuze maintains "that *sense is a doubling up*, and that *the neutrality of sense is inseparable from its status as a double*."[32] On the one hand, the surface-effects of sense are "produced" by the mixtures of bodies. This production is not the result of already individuated bodies, however, but of the emission of pre-individual singularities. The measureless pulsation of bodies taken in their undifferentiated depth "acts in an original way, *by means of its power to organize surfaces and to envelop itself within surfaces*." On the other hand, the states of affairs that may be attributed to bodies are "produced" by the quasi-causality of the metaphysical surface itself, distributed by the same impersonal singularities that constitute the transcendental field. Impassibility and productivity, indifference and efficacy: the two characteristics of the static genesis, "the *immaculate conception* which now characterizes the Stoic sage."[33]

Deleuze's concept of the metaphysical surface corresponds to what he calls the pure physics of surfaces. He notes, for example, that "the events of a liquid surface refer to the inter-molecular modifications on which they depend as their real cause, but also to the variations of a surface tension on which they depend as their (ideational or 'fictive') quasi-cause" (LS, 108). The productivity of surfaces is also illustrated in the formation of crystals, which develop "only at the edges." He also refers here to the work of Simondon on the topological surface of membranes, whose biological value to organisms is related to the way in which they carry potentials and regenerate polarities. Deleuze draws a parallel to the way in which events frequent the surface, but do not *occupy* it, and the way in which superficial energy is "not *localized* at the surface, but is rather bound to its formation and reformation" (LS, 119).

Metaphysically speaking, "everything happens at the *boundary* between things and propositions."[34] The metaphysical surface does not emanate from, nor is it created by, something transcendent to it and to which it bears some resemblance. The true "transcendental field" is immanently produced and immanently productive as the pure becoming of the point-line-surface system. Deleuze is careful to emphasize the extreme fragility of the surface. Sense is deployed as long as the frontier between bodies and language holds, but the incorporeal play of the silent *crack* of thought can all too easily lose its superficial energy and collapse into the noisy blows of corporeal mixtures, becoming *incarnated* in the depths of bodies (LS, 177). Stoic ethics requires an affirmative, yet cautious, use of the hammer.

The theologians of the Reformation who smashed the physical images (literally) and allegorical interpretations (figuratively) of the Roman Catholic and Eastern Orthodox traditions were not "iconoclastic" in the sense I have been developing here. They were still selecting among rival claims about the true mediator of transcendence, and remained firmly within Plato's Eidetic framework. One of the prominent characteristics of early Protestant theology was its strong emphasis on "the Word." *Sola verbi.* The Bible itself became an icon. *Sola scriptura.* Revelation is not mediated by the Church; each individual has direct access to the Word. *Sola Christi.* Salvation is effectuated not by bodily regulation or rational effort, but by divinely given belief. *Sola fidei, sola gratia.* Still, one is left with the task of making sense of the relation between human logic and the human body. Reformation theologians conceptualized this relation in a variety of ways. Luther famously called reason the devil's whore (and Deleuze might have agreed, but in a sense more inspired by Klossowski's *Roberte*). Calvin preferred to think of reason as the handmaiden of theology (and Deleuze might have agreed, but in a sense more inspired by Carroll's *Alice*). Our focus here, however, is on the relation between the divine *Logos* and the human *flesh* of Jesus. Luther's doctrine of the Incarnation was more Alexandrian, emphasizing the union of the natures, while Calvin preferred the Antiochene model, emphasizing their distinctiveness.

This is reflected in their attitudes toward the real presence of Christ in the bread of the Eucharist. On the one hand, the resurrected body of Christ is in the heights, sitting at the right hand of God in heaven. What is the nature of its journey into the sacramental loaf? On the other hand, when the wafer is ingested it follows the usual alimentary path, descending to the depths. What happens to the divine Logos during *this* journey? Scatology and Eschatology were all mixed together in these debates. Although he rejected the doctrine of *trans*-substantiation, the Alexandrian-leaning Luther insisted Christ was really present in and with the substance of the bread (*con*-substantiation). Calvin's Antiochene tendencies shaped his emphasis on the *symbolic* nature of the sacrament, which mediated the presence of Christ through a mysterious union that incorporated him into the life of the believer, and vice versa. Zwingli went even further, insisting on a real *absence* of Christ from the bread. The table of communion is only a reminder of what Christ did for believers on the cross and an anticipation of a fulfillment of divine promises. It may well be that the rediscovery of and renewed attention to Stoic and Epicurean sources in the Renaissance influenced his resistance to notions of "magical" transformations of supernatural agents in material rituals. At any rate, Zwingli's position won the day in practice. In many, if not most, Protestant churches today the practice of the Lord's Supper is primarily about obedience and remembrance.

From the point of view of the sacerdotal trajectory, however, the intuitions of Calvin and Luther were right. A religious coalition cannot live by god-free bread alone. Regular participation in regulated rituals is only sociographically prudish if it is reinforced by anthropomorphic promiscuity. During the patristic and medieval periods, most theologians insisted not only on the real presence of a *transcendent* agent in the bread, but also on the latter's *resemblance* to that which it signifies. From Augustine to Hugh of St. Victor and beyond, a sacrament was defined in part by its *likeness* to what it represents (e.g., the water of Baptism washes the body like the Spirit cleans the soul). This emphasis on similitude fits easily into cognitive and coalitional defaults, making it easier to remember and transmit ritual practices across generations. In early human and contemporary small-scale societies, ritual imaginative engagement is typically with supernatural agents who are explicitly perceived as similar to members of the group. For example, the qualities of a totem animal-spirit might reflect the values of the coalition. Resemblance is even more obvious in the case of ancestor-ghosts who are part of the same familial lineage as their progeny, who now "feed" them with sacrifices or imaginatively engage them in other ways that mimic the way one treats natural agents.

Things are more complicated with a transcendent moralistic Entity of the sort that emerged in the mental and social fields of the monotheistic traditions that trace their roots to the west Asian axial age. An infinite supernatural Agent is hard to relate to, and so a religious coalition needs rituals that activate and satiate the forces of theogonic reproduction; it needs sacred rites and communal practices in which its members can imaginatively engage contingently-embodied entities that are more like them and whose power is more directly relevant for everyday axiological engagement. The relative unimportance of "communion" in so many Christian congregations today is not unrelated to the ease with which religious people flow from one denomination to another in their ongoing consumption of religious commodities. We will return to this in our discussion of the capitalist socius in Chapter 5.

It is not hard to understand why people react to threats to their religious beliefs and behaviors by over-protecting their in-groups and over-detecting disembodied agents. This is the natural result of evolved cognitive mechanisms and social entrainment practices. Deleuze's "superficial" theology is anthropomorphically prudish and sociographically promiscuous. His flattening of the metaphysical surface secretes atheism. Of course this is frightening: it challenges the ways in which we hold together the fragile psychological and social surfaces that organize our lives. Christian theology has traditionally encouraged, and sometimes even enforced, the holding together of these surfaces by holding down sexual (and other bodily) desire, which intensifies anxiety about gender. Deleuze's iconoclastic theological proposals suggest another way of relating to and experimenting on the surface. Instead of obscuring or excluding the role of sexuality in articulating the relation between word and flesh, Deleuze explicitly links the process of sexual development to the dynamic genesis that effectuates a quasi-incarnation of sense in bodies.

Sexuality and Pious Intentions

In the last eight series of *Logic of Sense*, Deleuze begins to spell out in more detail the ethics he finds entailed in Stoic physics and philosophy. He does this through a critical and creative engagement with some key themes within psychoanalysis, which he here calls the "science of events" (LS, 242). Deleuze builds on insights from Freud, Klein, and Lacan as he applies his complex point-line-surface system to the process of Oedipalization and its metamorphosis.[35] Up to this point in the book he has been treating the *static* genesis, outlining his hypothesis about the neutral productivity of the aleatory point that endlessly moves in both directions along the line of the Aion as it traces the frontier of the metaphysical surface, emitting singularities whose problematic status effectuates the extra-being of the event in states of affairs and donates sense to propositions. Now, he examines what he calls the *dynamic* genesis, the "history which liberates sounds and makes them independent of bodies," the movement from states of affairs to events, "*from depth to the production of surfaces*." Deleuze goes out of his way to emphasize that the one genesis does "not implicate at all the other genesis" (LS, 214). *Implication*, it should be remembered from our last chapter, was the term used by Nicholas of Cusa to describe the function of Christ as the Logos, who makes the opposites of the finite and the infinite coincide.

Our main interest here, however, is Deleuze's understanding of the release of "intention as an ethical category" (LS, 237) and its relation to the psychoanalytic concept of the Oedipal complex. When he wrote *Logic of Sense* he had not yet met Guattari, and Deleuze's treatment of Oedipus is less antagonistic than it will be just three years later in *Anti-Oedipus*. Nevertheless, we can already see evidence in the former of many of the concerns that become more explicit in the latter, such as the link between Oedipus, the negative use of the disjunctive synthesis, and "morality" (as opposed to ethics). It is easy to get distracted by Deleuze's constant references to penises and little girls, but let us bracket concerns about phallocentrism for the moment, and focus on his philosophical argument. He correlates the first two psychoanalytic "positions" to the first two philosophical "orientations" he had outlined earlier: the paranoid-schizoid position (the pre-Socratics) is followed by the manic-depressive position (Platonism). In the latter, the child (or the philosopher) selects a "good object," and extracts a "Voice" from above, distinguishing it from all the internal sounds of the depths. Deleuze uses the phrase "sexual-perverse" to designate the third position, in which the superficial energy of the liberated libido produces the partial zones, which are "facts of the surface," in its pre-genital phase. In its Oedipal-phallic phase, the ego coordinates them around the genital zone, as the child pursues on his or her "own body the constitution of a surface and the integration of the zones" (LS, 230). Although Deleuze refers to Oedipus as a Herculean hero of the surface, he does not identify him with the Stoic philosophical orientation. Despite, or perhaps because of, his "good intentions," things end badly for Oedipus. Why?

First, it is important to notice that sexual organization has its own point-line-surface system. Deleuze explicitly describes the phallus, which is not an organ but an agency operative at the surface, as "the *paradoxical element* or object = x, missing always its own equilibrium, at once excess and deficiency, never equal, missing its own resemblance, its own identity, its own origin, its own *place*, and always displaced in relation to itself."[36] It plays the role of *nonsense*, distributing sense to the heterogeneous pre-genital and Oedipal sexual series (LS, 279). The line that the phallus traces at the frontier of these series is threatened by two kinds of "castration" (being devoured by the depths or deprived by the heights). A third "castration," the resolution of the "Oedipal complex" proper, involves a desexualization of the libidinal urges through sublimation and symbolization, through which "the intention – the moral notion par excellence is born" (LS, 235). The trace of this castration becomes the "crack of thought," opening up "the pure line of the Aion and the death instinct in its speculative form" (LS, 239). From the child's perspective, this is the creation of a total surface for the benefit of the parental images; like Hercules, he believes that he can now act morally along the surface of the world because he has "warded of the monsters of the depth" and is now allied "with the powers from on high" (LS, 236).

The problem is that Oedipal intentions are all "still located within the *domain of Images* – with the narcissistic libido and the phallus as a surface projection."[37] Here it is important to note the distinctions Deleuze makes between images, idols, simulacra, and the phantasm. He uses the term *simulacra* to designate what Klein called "partial objects," the fragmented objects of the depth. *Idol* refers to the idealized object of the heights. In this context, *image* designates "that which pertains to partial, *corporeal surfaces*, including the initial problem of their phallic coordination (*good intention*)."[38] The Oedipal ego has formed on the surface, but its intentions are formed in relation to a mother *image* and a father *image*, which it wants to subsume under a single good object that it *idolizes*.

Oedipus plays with images whose origin is the idol of the heights, already selected on the basis of an imposed choice between modeling itself on the good object or identifying with bad objects. In other words, he selects some images as *icons* (in the sense in which I have been using the term). This alternative is forced on the ego by a negative, exclusive use of the disjunctive synthesis. Deleuze relates the three syntheses to the three moments of the organization of the sexual surface. The connective synthesis bears on a single homogeneous series in an erogenous zone. In the phallic coordination of these zones, the conjunctive synthesis bears on these heterogeneous (yet, continuous and convergent) series. During the evolution of Oedipus, the phallic line is transformed into the trace of castration through a disjunctive synthesis that bears on divergent and resonating series (namely, the pre-genital and the phallic). But this negative use of the disjunction traps Oedipus in the domain of "action in general," which is designated by the "very notion of Image" (LS, 237).

The *phantasm*, on the other hand, is not an action or passion but a pure event, an *effect* of the causal mixtures of bodies at the physical-sexual surface. The Oedipal situation makes possible the disengagement of the event from its causes in the depths of bodies, so that it can spread out on the metaphysical surface and connect to its quasi-cause. For Deleuze, the sexual organization is a prefiguration of the secondary organization of language, and serves as "intermediary between physical depth and metaphysical surface." From the point of view of the dynamic genesis, the phantasm is "the movement by which the ego opens itself" to the metaphysical surface and "liberates the a-cosmic, impersonal and pre-individual singularities which it had imprisoned" (LS, 244). From the point of view of the static genesis, the phantasm-event is "the process of the constitution of the incorporeal." As that which brings into contact the incorporeal and the corporeal at the metaphysical surface through an *affirmative* use of the disjunctive synthesis, the phantasm is "the site of the *eternal return*." Within the crack of thought, the phantasm liberates sense, which "hovers over bodies," and distributes a "difference of potential at the edges of the crack," making possible "the liberation of the *non-existent entity* for each state of affairs."[39] This non-existent entity is the pure event that communicates with all other events on the line of the Aion, *eventum tantum*. As we will see, the Stoic sage – the actor – accomplishes the liberation of this "eternal part" of the event through what Deleuze calls *counter*-effectuation.

The Oedipal transformation is from an orientation in depth (noise) to an orientation toward the heights (voice) to an orientation on the surface (speech). What happens next? The tertiary organization of language depends on the superficial energy of the physical-sexual surface, but all sorts of regressions and repressions can occur. Deleuze associates *satire* with a pre-Socratic regression into the depths. *Irony*, on the other hand, appears when language utilizes eminence, analogy, and equivocity as figures of speech – a Socratic repression of simulacra that appeals to a disembodied Voice of the heights, which somehow already deploys these figures although it has no physical principle of organization corresponding to them. Sacerdotal theology utilizes this ironic speech about its supernatural

Agent, selecting among rival images that claim to mediate between Man and God in an attempt to regulate the depths of bodies with the help of imagined voices from an idealized height. Deleuze argues that *humor* is the *art of surfaces* "and of the complex relation between the two surfaces" (LS, 285). The Stoic sage, or iconoclastic theologian, sets up shop on the metaphysical surface, selecting pure events in their asymmetric relation to bodily states of affairs. She is a "humor-actor" who affirms the effectuation of events in bodies, but also counter-effectuates each event, *not* allowing the incorporeal surface-effects to crack irremediably and become fully incarnated in the mixture of bodies. In this way, she becomes the "comedian" of her own events.[40]

When it comes to carnal knowledge ("unlawful" or not), most sacerdotal theologians have little tolerance for funny business. General discussions about "flesh," and the importance of its being domesticated by the "Word," are awkward enough. The discomfiture increases exponentially when one begins to inquire into the role of particular body parts in reproduction – human or divine. Sex is usually high on the list of activities that must be regulated by the fostering of pious intentions within sacerdotal coalitions. But what about *divine* reproduction? The doctrine of the Incarnation is about the becoming-flesh of the only begotten Son of the heavenly Father. How precisely was the earthly womb of the Virgin Mary inseminated in accordance with the words of the angel Gabriel (Luke 1), who foretold that the Holy Spirit would "come upon her" and the "power" of the Lord God would "overshadow" her, leading to the conception of the "Son of God?"

This mystery is one of the best kept secrets in Christianity, kept best in the open where it is confessed as a mystery to block further inquiry. However Christ is conceived, the mystery of the Incarnation presents him as a supernatural Oedipus. He unfailingly does the will of God, attempting to please a withdrawn heavenly Father. In the Gospel account, Jesus' relationship to Mary is somewhat ambiguous, but the patristic invention of the doctrines of her immaculate conception and perpetual virginity depict her as a restored mother beyond wounding. We will examine the relation between Oedipus and Christ in more detail in our exploration of *Anti-Oedipus* in the next chapter.

The important point to make at this stage is that most attempts among late modern Christian theologians to articulate the doctrine of the Incarnation in ways that escape patriarchal and other forms of oppression within the tradition are still susceptible to the critiques implicit in Deleuzian philosophy and the bio-cultural study of religion. Egalitarians within sacerdotal coalitions often resist doctrinal formulations that privilege some members of the religious group and exclude others from power on the basis of gender, class or race, or even from membership on the basis of sexual preference. Some propose, for example, speaking of Christ as Lover instead of Son, or emphasizing his role as Servant instead of King. Such suggestions are usually intended to transform piety and moral behavior within the coalition, opening its members up to new inclusive practices.

Unfortunately, the very sociographic prudery that is the target of these proposals is reinforced by the anthropomorphic promiscuity inherent within them. Encouraging the detection of a supernatural Agent whose knowledge and power are axiologically relevant for the in-group, and resemblance to whom is a condition for participation in an eternally protected coalition, will automatically activate anxiety about defectors and out-groups. Moreover, even when they use less ancient philosophical categories, such proposals still operate within Plato's Eidetic framework insofar as they select one Image among others as mediating a transcendent Entity who intentionally determines the regulative ideals for human morality "once and for all."

In Deleuze's iconoclastic theology, on the other hand, the conditions for the real experience of axiological engagement are neither intentional (like us) nor transcendent (beyond us). For Deleuze, it is the pure becoming of the infinity of intensities or singularities-events, emitted at the metaphysical surface by the endless movement of the aleatory point in both directions along the unlimited line of the Aion that engenders intentionality. The latter is doubly caused, caused by the doubling up of bodily causes and the incorporeal quasi-causes in the static genesis, which constitutes the metaphysical surface to which the simulacra rise in the dynamic genesis of the sexual-physical surface. Flesh, in a sense, becomes word. Corporeal intensity becomes spoken intentionality. As Deleuze puts it in his discussion of Klossowski, "the simulacrum becomes phantasm, intensity becomes intentionality to the extent that it takes as its object another intensity which it comprehends and is itself comprehended . . . on to the infinity of intensities through which it passes" (LS, 338). If intentionality is the result of the crack of thought engendered by the rising of *simulacra-events* on the metaphysical surface, then action – the act of the Stoic sage – is the affirmation of the eternal return, which quasi-incorporates them (as the states of affairs of bodies) and releases their eternal truth "for all time."

The Liberation of Acting

In *Difference and Repetition*, Deleuze argued that there has only ever been one ontology: the univocity of being. In *Logic of Sense*, he asserts that there has only ever been one ethics: the *amor fati* of the Stoics. When it comes to ethics, Deleuze insists:

> Nothing more can be said, and no more has ever been said: to become worthy of what happens to us, and thus to *will and release the event*, to become the offspring of one's own events, and thereby to be *reborn*, to have one more birth, and to break with one's carnal birth – to *become the offspring* of one's events and not of one's actions, for the action is itself produced by the offspring of the event.[41]

You must be born again?! Yes indeed, but this rebirth has nothing to do with conforming to the image of a transcendent religious Figure or joining a supernatural Family.

In his later work with Guattari on the *Capitalism and Schizophrenia* project, Deleuze invents yet another vocabulary set but, as we will see in Chapter 5, he remains committed to an immanent ethics of surface-events. The vocabulary of *Logic of Sense* returns in his last book with Guattari in 1994, *What is Philosophy?*: "There is a dignity of the event that has always been inseparable from philosophy as *amor fati*: being equal to the event, or *becoming the offspring* of one's own events . . . there is *no other ethic* than the *amor fati* of philosophy."[42] In contrast to the popular stereotype, Deleuze does not portray the Stoic sage as passively resigned, accepting as inevitable whatever has already been fatalistically pre-determined. On the contrary, she *loves* "fate," joyfully *affirming* the endless movement of the aleatory point in the ideal game that makes possible the liberation of the incorporeal within all events as they communicate with all other events along the line of the Aion traced on the metaphysical surface.

Another common stereotype, sometimes applied to Deleuze himself in the secondary literature, is that the indifference of Stoic ethics entails a mystical escape from this world.[43] The language of "counter-effectuation," which we have already met several times in our analysis in the preceding pages, is easily interpreted in this way if one presupposes that there is something that transcends this world, from which escape is possible. For Deleuze, however, the incorporeal "side" of the metaphysical surface is not "outside" the real world (or chaosmos), although it is indeed extra-being. As he makes clear at several points, counter-effectuation cannot occur apart from the effectuation of events in bodies. Nevertheless as an affirmative use of the disjunctive synthesis, it opens us up for "our greatest freedom," a transmutation of events by which we "finally become *masters of effectuations and causes*."[44]

Far from a mystical escape driven by slave morality, counter-effectuation is a masterful intensification of intentional engagement in the world. The metamorphosis of the event involved in *counter*-effectuation liberates the non-existent entity in each state of affairs, the sense that hovers over bodies, the *aliquid* that can be expressed in propositions, precisely in a way that gives the actor "*the strength to orient its effectuation*." By doubling the physical effectuation of the event with an incorporeal counter-effectuation, it is "*properly* inscribed in the flesh" without becoming fully incarnated in the depth of bodies. This occurs through the freedom that befits "the patient thinker," and only in virtue of the incorporeal part or extra-being of the event.[45]

Nevertheless, Deleuze is calling for a real *counter*-effectuation. This concept arises at a crucial point in his argument. In the twenty-fifth series (of Univocity), he notes how the problem has changed in the course of the investigation as a result of his clarification of the *positive* use of the disjunctive synthesis. Now we can see that all singularities-events are compatible in the affirmation of their divergence, as endlessly divisible emissions in the point-line-surface system. Incompatibilities (logical contradictions and linguistic paradoxes) only appear at the level of individuals and persons in which events are effectuated, in the *negative* use of the disjunctive synthesis in the "order of God."

In order to free herself from the individuation and personhood that binds up events in the depths of bodies, the individual must "grasp herself as event . . . grasp the event effectuated within her as another individual grafted onto her."[46] The individual is "born of that which comes to pass," engendered by events, but she can be *reborn* (and keep having "one more birth") by affirming her disjunction from every other event, thereby extracting the pure event that communicates with the others in the universal freedom of the eternal return, and affirming all chance in a single instant. Opening up onto the line of the Aion, she becomes "the humor-actor" of her own events, counter-effectuating or doubling them in her own way, liberating the "immaculate portion" of singularities from their incarnation in individuals and persons (LS, 171–2).

Counter-effectuation does not mean affirming or willing an event as distinct from *what might have happened*, but doubling the effectuation of *what effectively occurs*. To be more precise, it is the affirmation of "something *in* that which occurs, something yet to come which would be consistent with what occurs, in accordance with the laws of an obscure, humorous conformity: the Event" (LS, 170). For Deleuze, each event is not an accident, that is, something that might not occur in some other incompatible world, but rather the purely expressed of what effectively happens. "Nothing other than the Event subsists, the Event alone, *Eventum tantum* for all contraries, which communicates with itself through its own distance and resonates across all of its disjuncts" (LS, 201). *Amor fati* is the universal freedom in which one affirms the eternal truth of one's events, liberating the non-existing entity within them to communicate with all other events in the great Event. Eternal truth? Here "eternity" must be understood as the unlimited line of the Aion, and "truth" must be understood not as that which is opposed to the false but as the *sense* of the verbal "infinitive" (to love, to die, etc.) as opposed to the *sense* of the verbal "present" (as it bears on all the tenses and moods) effectuated in the bodies of Chronos.

In the twenty-second series (Porcelain and Volcano), Deleuze refers to a phrase in Fitzgerald's *The Crack Up*, which resonates like a "hammer blow" in our heads: "Of course all life is a process of breaking down . . ." (LS, 176). Of course . . . The cracks on the surface of life are always in danger of collapsing into the depths of bodies, which helps to explain why we so desperately listen for voices from the heights to save us. Deleuze distinguishes between the incorporeal crack itself, which extends silently on the straight line of the Aion at the surface, and the noisy internal pressures of bodies that threaten to deepen the crack so that it becomes fully effectuated in a corporeal mixture. Hammering on the surface can all too easily become a "demolition job." The task of the Stoic sage or "the actor" is to maintain and even extend the inherence of the incorporeal crack "while taking care not to bring it into *existence*, and not to *incarnate* it in the depth of the body."[47] How does one go about this? Deleuze notes that there are no general rules for preventing the crack from being fully incarnated or effectuated in the noisy mixture of paranoid-schizoid depths. Religious "morality" is guided by a pious intention to keep individual persons safe and healthy, protecting the everlasting presence of the group by a manic-depressive detection of an eminent supernatural Regulator.

Stoic (or Spinozist) ethics, on the other hand, is dangerous. Anything great in humanity, argues Deleuze, enters and exits through the crack. "Better death than the health which we are given" (LS, 182). We must take risks, and not lose sight of a great Health. All life is a process of breaking down, of course, but through counter-effectuation "a life" is constructed in which each event is affirmed *in* its own disjunction from all other events, thereby affirming their eternal truth as well as its own. Counter-effectuation lets the crack "fly over" its own incorporeal surface area "without stopping at the bursting within each body." It gives us "the chance to go *farther than we would have believed possible*. To the extent that the pure event is each time imprisoned forever in its effectuation, counter-effectuation *liberates* it, always for other times."[48]

As she extracts the pure event, moves from the physical surface to the metaphysical surface, "becomes worthy" of what happens to her, the actor's *amor fati* frees her to become the offspring of her events rather than of her actions and passions, and so "master" *of the effectuations* of bodies and their causes. This might not initially seem to be a very pragmatic ethics. However, what could be more practical than actively fostering the liberation of individual persons from binding anxiety, from the anxiety that binds them to over-protect their embodied coalitional "present" and over-detect idealized supernatural voices that promise to secure their in-group "once and for all" in a final judgment that excludes defectors and out-groups?

It might also seem impractical to promote an ethics based upon the "diabolical principle" of the affirmative disjunctive synthesis (LS, 201). As in *Difference and Repetition*, we find several references to the demonic and the anti-divine in *Logic of Sense*. We have already seen that Deleuze describes the actor as an "anti-god" (*contradieu*) and the positive use of disjunction as a function of "Anti-Christ." In the appendix on Klossowski, Deleuze gives an account of some of his novels, in which the spirits of ill-will resist the order of God, "sufflating" multiple bodies in diverse ways. The order of the Anti-Christ is "an order of perversity" that explodes the "divine order of integrity" (LS, 333). Sacerdotal theologians who wish to appropriate Deleuze's occasional use of terms like the "spiritual will" (LS, 170) should keep this in mind. But why does Deleuze use this perverse language? Of course, the etymology of the term *perversion* itself suggests "overturning," which reinforces his overall concern for reversing and inverting Platonism. His references to the *diabolical* also have a certain rhetorical force, a shock effect that wakes us from our moral slumber. Whatever he was up to, it is quite clear that he was *not* affirming the existence of evil supernatural agents who are attempting to disrupt a good supernatural Agent's plan for a human coalition.

In light of the discovery of the forces of theogonic reproduction in the bio-cultural study of religion, however, Deleuze's humorous depictions of the disjunctive affirmations of spirits in the order of the Anti-Christ can serve another function. They can draw attention to our "natural" reaction to such images. The environment of our ancestors was a dangerous place, filled with deceitful predators they had to avoid; indeed, they were deceitful predators too, which also contributed to their survival. Hyper-sensitive cognitive detection of deceit and predation granted a significant survival advantage, despite the many false positives. These sorts of detections also reinforced hyper-sensitive coalitional protection, since a certain level of heightened anxiety about ambiguous forces that might destroy a support system increases in-group cohesion.

These detections also would have stimulated participation in shared rituals that engage *good* ambiguous forces that can protect the group from predators. Moreover, this sociographic prudery creates a feedback loop that reinforces the anthropomorphically promiscuous detection of evil spirits. Members who are truly committed to the group will be on the lookout for discarnate deceitful predators with bad intentions. Signaling their detection of such spirits, especially during high arousal rituals in the presence of the group, produces an emotional contagion that amplifies the tendency among other members to detect these empirically obscure yet apparently dangerous entities. And so it goes. Shared imaginative engagement with supernatural agents is self-reproducing.

No doubt the forces of theogonic reproduction helped our early ancestors survive. During the axial age, these cognitive and coalitional tendencies were transmuted in new environments that required bigger gods to protect bigger groups. Eventually, an infinite supernatural Agent was born(e) in the west Asian monotheistic religious traditions. In Christianity, it is the religious Figure of Christ who mediates this transcendent moralistic Entity. Anthropomorphic promiscuity and sociographic prudery did not evolve to engage such an Entity, and so minds and groups naturally default to imaginative engagements with supernatural agents who are more like them and more relevant to their immanent axiological practices. However, even Christ (as a transcendent Lord) is sometimes an inadequate mediator when it comes to figuring out exactly what God wants one to do today, in this situation, with these people.

And so cognitive mechanisms scan for even more proximate contingently-embodied mediators, such as angelic messengers or even spirit-filled human souls who can provide pastoral comfort and guidance in the fight against demons, atheists or other forces that are perceived as narratively immediate threats in everyday life. Coalitional mechanisms reinforce such detections, as well as biases against out-groups and defectors, and on it goes. Instead of leaving these fears boxed up in religious coalitions, where they are nurtured and foster superstition and hostility, let us bring them into the open and ask: how is this evolved strategy working for us as we try to live together on the increasingly fragile surface of a globalized social field?

In this brief chapter, I have not been able to do justice to the complexity of Deleuze's proposals in *Logic of Sense*. The reader will have to come to her own decision about the plausibility of his hypotheses. My task has not been to defend the details of his argument, but to demonstrate its relevance as an iconoclastic contribution to *theological* ethics. Like all sciences, the science of non-existing entities is motivated by ongoing critique and construction. One way to extend the discussion would be to bring Deleuze's philosophical reworking of Stoic and Epicurean physics into more explicit dialogue with contemporary physical cosmological proposals about the expansion of a finite yet unbounded, "flat" universe that arises from "nothing" (virtual universes, non-zero energy in empty space, quantum gravity, etc.).

In this context, however, I have focused on ethics. What can atheist bodies do? What happens to ethics in an environment in which there is no need to detect supernatural agents behind ambiguous natural phenomena and no transcendent idealized *telos* for the coalitions that imaginatively engage them? At the very least, Deleuze's Anti-Christ ethics get us moving. His diabolical literary corpus disrupts our manic-depressive imprisonment between the depths and the heights, liberating thinking and acting into a newfound freedom at the surface. As we will see in the next chapter, Deleuze's oeuvre is also characterized by a passion for the liberation of feeling, for the production of machinic assemblages that overturn the priestly curse on desire in all its forms.

5

Assembling Theological Machines

In the previous three chapters, we have focused for the most part on the iconoclastic force of Deleuze's solo authorship prior to his collaboration with Félix Guattari. We drew attention to some of the "theological" aspects of his early works of philosophical portraiture and the two major monographs produced in the late 1960s. As we have seen, Deleuze uses a theological hammer to flatten religious Icons of transcendence, to crack open the chains of the dogmatic image of thought, and to free the actor for an unlimited affirmation of events. This chapter explores his major project with Félix Guattari, *Capitalism and Schizophrenia,* which is composed of *Anti-Oedipus* and *A Thousand Plateaus*, published in French in 1972 and 1980, respectively. This project introduces a whole new array of ways to theologize with a hammer, such as constructing a Body without Organs and connecting rhizomic multiplicities on the plane of consistency.[1] However, I will concentrate on Deleuze's treatment of the territorial, despotic, capitalist and war machines and the relation of these *social*-machines to *desiring*-machines. This constellation of concepts provides us with an opportunity to clarify the difference between sacerdotal and iconoclastic *theological* machines, whose ongoing (dis)assemblage either casts or dispels the priestly curse on desire.

Once again we are faced with a new, complex, and somewhat strange vocabulary. As we go along, we will notice several points of continuity with Deleuze's earlier work. For example, he remains focused on the inversion of Platonism. The "whole task" of schizoanalysis is to "overturn the theater of representation into the order of desiring-production" (AO, 294). When thought becomes a "war machine" it does not set up another image to oppose the image of the State apparatus but "destroys both the image *and* its copies, the model *and* its reproductions" (TP, 416).[2] The "schizzes" of desiring-production will remind us in some ways of the intensities of difference and emissions of singularities we have already met in *Difference and Repetition* and *Logic of Sense.* As the latter two books depicted that which conditions thinking and acting as "diabolical," so the *Capitalism and Schizophrenia* project will occasionally refer to "demoniacal" processes and "pacts with the Devil" as genetic elements in the becomings of desire. However, we also meet several new characters, such as the schizophrenic God and the Lobster God, neither of which is the God of monotheistic religion. Instead of downplaying these references, I want to highlight them as part of my ongoing assemblage of an iconoclastic machine that couples Deleuzian concepts with insights from the bio-cultural study of religion, producing the secretion of a creative atheism.

Both *Anti-Oedipus* and *A Thousand Plateaus* make it clear that "schizoanalysis" (or pragmatics) has both negative and positive tasks. Schizoanalysis overturns the Platonic theater of representation *and* affirms the eternal return as the deterritorialized circuit of all cycles of desire (AO, 294, 364). Rhizomic pragmatics dissolves repressive psychic and social planes of organization *and* constructs planes of consistency that mobilize and connect desires (TP, 179, 280). Deleuze unveils presuppositions about the status and function of the molarized consciousness of Oedipus *and* experiments with new ways of analyzing and liberating the schizzes and break-flows of the molecular unconscious. He challenges the sedentary formations of the despotic State *and* creates his own revolutionary nomadic distributions. In each case, critique and creation are intertwined. Stratification and destratification, the striated and the smooth, the molar and the molecular – each of these dissymmetrical forces is necessary for life, and creative critique happens precisely in the tension between them. I will not be able to treat all of these complex concepts in this short chapter. Instead I do a little experimentation of my own, engaging in a kind of theological schizoanalysis or iconoclastic pragmatics that also intends to be at least as constructive as it is destructive.

The first page of *Anti-Oedipus* tells us that machines shit and fuck (AO, 1). In what sense, then, can we call such assemblages *theological*? As the reader may have come to expect, Deleuze's hypotheses about the conditions for the real experience of the relation between desiring-machines and social-machines will rely heavily on concepts of non-existing entities that animate language and make for it a body divided into disjunctions. Moreover, his theology will remain resolutely Anti-Christ. In his collaboration with Guattari and in other single-author works from this later period, Deleuze often discusses the connection between monotheism (especially Christianity) and the despotic and colonializing forces associated with "Oedipus," a term that now carries a more negative connotation than it did in *Difference and Repetition* or *Logic of Sense*. He also enters more explicitly into combat with what he calls "the judgment of God" and the "priestly curse on desire." However, he does not deal in any detail with the *religious* use of the image of Christ as the High Priest who mediates the Judgment of God, or its repressive function within sacerdotal coalitions. In *A Thousand Plateaus* Deleuze emphasizes the importance of maintaining a "meticulous relation" with the strata when freeing lines of light and flows of intensities in the construction of a plane of immanence. In what follows, I begin the process of relating more meticulously to the doctrinal stratifications of Christology erected by sacerdotal machines in order to find precisely where to insert the cutting edges of iconoclastic machines, to open up the secretion of atheism that Deleuze suggests flows from Christianity more than any other religion.

In his preface to *Anti-Oedipus*, Foucault called it "an introduction to the non-fascist life." Indeed, one of Deleuze's main concerns is explaining why people so easily embrace their own repression and Oedipal subjugation, and sometimes even seem to desire fascism (AO, 31). As we will see, his hypothesis is that social-production "falls back on" desiring-production, repressing the productive schizz-flows of desire with inscriptive processes of coding, decoding, and recoding surplus value. These inscriptions mediate the signifying subjectivity of individuals within the socius, so that their desire becomes "represented" in consciousness in a way that fuels the reproduction of the social-machinic assemblage. Schizoanalysis analyzes these inscriptions, discovers the desiring-machines beneath these social representations and seeks to liberate them from the exclusive disjunctions that characterize reactionary and paranoid social investments of desire. In this sense, as Foucault also commented in his preface, *Anti-Oedipus* is a "book of ethics."

However, it is also chock full of *ontological* assertions. "Everything is a machine . . . Everything is production" (AO, 2, 4). "There is only desire and the social, and nothing else" (AO, 31). Acting and thinking are analyzed in their relation to revolutionary and schizoid investments of desire, but all within the context of an understanding of "the Real" as "the objective *being* of desire."[3] Deleuze's robustly aesthetic ontology helps us understand why we so easily accept our own despotic bundles (*fasciculi*). Connecting it to insights from the bio-cultural study of religion can help us understand why we also desire our own coalitional binding (*religatio*) through shared imaginative engagement with supernatural agents.

Desiring-Machines

Deleuze insists that his use of the term "machine" is not metaphorical. Machines are systems of interruptions or break-flows, processes inseparable from the continual material flow of reality. It is important to keep in mind that Deleuze is not proposing a "mechanistic" – as opposed to a "vitalistic" – ontology. In fact, his development of the concept of *desiring-production* is explicitly intended to overcome a simple dualism between the living and the machinic (AO, 314), to undo such dichotomies by passing through them (TP, 23). In *Anti-Oedipus*, Deleuze maintains that *everything* is animated by break-flows. In contrast to Plato's treatment of desire as acquisition, he argues that desire *is* production, the production of *production*, which is always and already a production of *recording* and a production of *consumption* (or consummation) as well.

A desiring-machine is that which interrupts and is interrupted in accordance with these three modes, which Deleuze correlates with the three syntheses we have met in his earlier work. The connective synthesis produces production itself, the infinite continual material flux of break-flows by which machines are connected to other machines. The disjunctive synthesis is a recording process that cuts into the flows of heterogeneous chains, producing continual detachments or "schizzes" (*schizein*: to split, divide). These are not detachments that exclude or "slice off" machinic flows from one another, but indifferent signs that engineer a polyvocal inscription "on the very surface of the Real" (AO, 42). Finally, the conjunctive synthesis is related to a third type of interruption that Deleuze calls a residual break, which produces a residuum, a "subject" that is born anew as it consumes and consummates each of the states through which it passes (AO, 44).

As we will see below, social-machines "fall back on" desiring-machines, forming inscribing surfaces that repress desire and fix the identity of subjects through different regimes of signs. This does not mean they are not real, or not really productive; the reality of social-production is a folding or rotating effect in which desiring-production is represented and repressed. Social-production "*is purely and simply desiring-production itself under determinate conditions*" (AO, 31). These are the two types of machine, or the two sides of reality. "There is only desire and the social" (AO, 200). These machinic distinctions are still present in *A Thousand Plateaus*, but are spelled out in more detail in relation to the concept of *assemblages*. There we read that "all we know are assemblages," and discover a new distinction between "machinic assemblages of desire" and "collective assemblages of enunciation" (TP, 25). We are reminded of the distinction in *Logic of Sense* between series of bodies and series of propositions, folded or doubled up on the metaphysical surface. *A Thousand Plateaus* also introduces the concept of the rhizomic extension of multiplicities in the formation of "plateaus," which are constructed within a complex relation between stratification on the plane of organization and destratification on the plane of consistency. In that context, a machine is described as "a set of cutting edges that insert themselves into the assemblage undergoing deterritorialization, and draw variations and mutations of it" (TP, 367).

The task of clarifying and correlating the diverse vocabularies within and across Deleuze's oeuvre is as interesting as it is important, but this is not our current task. We will focus on drawing attention to the *theological* dimension of some of his key concepts in *Capitalism and Schizophrenia* as part of an ongoing attempt to liberate the productive break-flows of the *iconoclastic* machine by "detaching" it from the *sacerdotal* machine – not slicing them off from one another, but coupling them in a such a way that the former dissolves the arboreal, molar, sedentary, and despotic regimes of the latter. It is important to keep in mind that theology is not another social-machine, in the technical sense to be outlined below. It is a machine for generating and appraising retroductive hypotheses about the conditions for axiological engagement. In a broader sense, however, we can say that concepts like the machinic assemblage and desiring-production are already *theological*. We will continue to take Deleuze's provocative description of theology in his essay on Klossowski in *Logic of Sense* as our starting point. In the remaining sections of this chapter, we will have ample opportunity to demonstrate the Anti-Christ flow of Deleuze's theology, but let us begin by briefly indicating how these two volumes with Guattari contribute to the "science of non-existing entities," and clarify "the way in which they animate language and make for it this glorious body that is divided into disjunctions" (LS, 322).

The concept of the *disjunctive synthesis*, taken from Kant and rendered inclusive and affirmative through Nietzsche, played a major role in Deleuze's early philosophical works, as we have seen. This idea continues to function theologically in *Anti-Oedipus*. In the first chapter, Deleuze describes as "divine" the energy of disjunctions that sweeps through the Body without Organs (to which we will return below) and attracts to itself the entire connective process of production, creating a miraculate, enchanted surface that it inscribes in each and every one of its disjunctions. What counts for Deleuze is not designations (parental, racial, or divine) but the *uses* that are made of them. He is willing to use the designation "God" for the "the energy of recording," but this has nothing to do with the idea of a transcendent, moralistic Entity. "To anyone who asks: 'Do you believe in God?' we should reply in strictly Kantian or Schreberian terms: 'Of course, but only as the master of the disjunctive syllogism, or as its a priori principle.'" God is depicted here in relation to what Kant called *omnitudo realitatis*, that from which all "secondary realities are derived by a process of division" (AO, 14).

The key question is what *use* is made of this disjunctive synthesis. Most forms of social-machinic inscription make exclusive disjunctions that fix subjects and striate groups so that they represent and reproduce its inscriptions. The affirmative, inclusive disjunction of intensities (or simulacra), on the other hand, decenters the Self, as well as God as a "being above man and nature," as that which motivates and orients desire. Now the center is "the desiring-machine, the celibate machine of the Eternal Return" (AO, 22).

It is important to distinguish clearly between three different uses of the term *God* in these two volumes. First, there is the schizophrenic God, whose divine energy flows through all *affirmative* disjunctive syntheses. Throughout *Capitalism and Schizophrenia*, the latter term in the title designates *not* a psychoanalytic judgment about a clinical subject, but the *process* of break-flows and the schizzes of desiring-production. Although they are related to the same syllogism, the "*schizophrenic* God" must not be confused with "the God of *religion*."[4] The former is the "God" in whom Deleuze confessed belief above. This has nothing to do with a divine Subject with more or less stable psychological states, a supernatural Agent interested in holding together a particular social-machinic inscription. In *A Thousand Plateaus*, Deleuze's Professor Challenger claims that "God is a Lobster, a double pincer, a double bind" (AO, 45). This *crustacean* God forms the strata through a "double articulation." The first articulation imposes a statistical order on particle-flows and molecular units ("sedimentation") and the second constructs molar compounds in which structures are established ("folding").

Deleuze calls these strata "the judgments of God," but here too we are clearly not dealing with the God of religion, but with a natural process of physical (and metaphysical) stratification. The Lobster God reminds us of the God who dances on a volcano in *Difference and Repetition* and the Chronos-God of *Logic of Sense*. For Deleuze, the flows and articulations of the first two "Gods" are conditions for life; desiring-production lives and moves and has its being (which is becoming) in the tension between them. As we will see, the "God of religion" plays a relatively small role in this project. Deleuze is critical of monotheism, but uses the term in a rather vague way. I hope to intensify his critique by focusing more concretely on the way in which desiring-production is repressed through shared imaginative engagement with an infinite supernatural Agent who promises eternal protection for an in-group. Throughout the rest of the chapter, we will clarify this distinction between the schizophrenic God, the crustacean God, and the monotheistic God of Christianity.

Another theological concept that appears in both volumes is the Body without Organs (BwO). Deleuze uses this term in a variety of ways, sometimes referring to *the* BwO as the field of immanence, the surface upon which all disjunctive syntheses are recorded, and sometimes to the construction of *a* BwO made up of plateaus. For our purposes, the important point is that all of his uses of the term are theological. The BwO, properly speaking, does not *exist*; it is "what remains when you take everything away." Insofar as it "causes intensities to pass," it animates language and its regimes of signs. The BwO is not space, nor is it "in" space; it "occupies" space as "intensity = 0." But there is "nothing negative about that zero." As the matrix of intensity, the BwO is the "production of the real as an intensive magnitude starting at zero."[5]

As the "full body" upon which all (partial) bodily productions occur, it is "the unproductive, the sterile, the unengendered, the unconsummable." Everything – each existent producing/product – happens on the *surface* of the BwO, which belongs to the realm of "anti-production" and exerts its own special force in relation to the syntheses of production.[6] The full body of the BwO is a "naked body," which functions as "the limit" and "tangent of deterritorialization" of the socius. As we will see below, when social-machines make a *transcendent* use of the disjunctive (and other) syntheses, their surface inscriptions are recorded on a "clothed" body – the full body of the earth, the despot or capital.[7] Schizoanalysis works to restore the syntheses to their positive, inclusive and *immanent* use in desiring-production (AO, 123).

The criteria for constructing *a* BwO are entirely immanent. In *A Thousand Plateaus*, Deleuze spells this out in relation to the concept of the plane of consistency. A BwO "swings between two poles, the surface of stratification into which it is recoiled, on which it submits to the judgment, and the plane of consistency in which it unfurls and opens to experimentation" (TP, 176). Deleuze calls for combat with the "judgments" of the Lobster God, which threaten to confine us within a "plane of organization." Desire is tested not by finding the right object of desire or by denouncing "false" desires, but by "distinguishing *within desire* between that which pertains to stratic proliferation, or else too-violent destratifications, and that which pertains to the construction of the plane of consistency."[8] Although the immanent criteria for constructing a BwO or plane of consistency are "Anti-Christ," in the sense that they resist the order of God (crustacean and religious), they are still clearly *theological* insofar as they have to do with non-existing entities that animate language and make for it a body divided into disjunctions.

Another significant theological concept introduced in *A Thousand Plateaus* is the "abstract machine." An assemblage has two inseparable sides, one that formalizes expression, and another that formalizes content. On one side it is an enunciative assemblage, on the other side it is a machinic assemblage or "an assemblage of bodies." The two formalizations are reciprocally presupposed, but what is it in the assemblage that accounts for the relation between the regimes of signs and the regimes of bodies? It is the *abstract machine*, which "constitutes and conjugates all of the assemblage's cutting edges of deterritorialization" (TP, 155). In other words, it synthesizes. An abstract machine "does not function to *represent*, even something real, but rather *constructs a real* that is yet to come, a new type of reality."[9] It is neither corporeal nor semiotic, but "diagrammatic."

Here Deleuze distinguishes *diagrams* from *indexes*, *icons*, and *symbols*, which pertain to territorial signs, reterritorialization, and relative deterritorialization respectively (TP, 157). These latter three aspects of the assemblage are oriented toward the strata on a plane of organization. The abstract machine enables a conjunction of the most deterritorialized elements of the assemblage's contents and expressions, creating a shared acceleration of absolute deterritorialization on the plane of consistency. We will return to this new terminology about "territories" below, but the important point at this stage is the theological function of these concepts. Notice, for example, how the *diagram* is related to indexes, icons, and symbols on a "plane" in much the same way that the *phantasm* was related to simulacra, icons, and images on a "surface" in *Logic of Sense.*

In assemblages, content becomes a pragmatic system and expression becomes a semiotic system; what is done (actions and passions) and what is said (regimes of signs) are articulated simultaneously and inseparably, but distinctively and irreducibly (TP, 555). As in *Logic of Sense*, Deleuze is not here proposing a new dualism (or monism) but an affirmative disjunctive synthesis that constitutes the two asymmetric sides of a metaphysical surface. Moreover, the abstract machine "*constructs continuums of intensity . . . emits and combines particle-signs . . . performs conjunctions of flows of deterritorialization*" (TP, 78). This is much like the function of the "paradoxical agent" or "aleatory point" discussed in the previous chapter, which also constituted and traversed a two-sided frontier.

Abstract machines are "*effectuated* in forms and substances" within the dimension of two-sided assemblages, but they are not reducible to this effectuation; they are already self-composed along with the planes of consistency they draw, "real yet nonconcrete, actual yet *non-effectuated*."[10] The abstract machine is an Absolute; however, it is "neither undifferentiated nor transcendent" (TP, 157). Because the abstract machine is singular and immanent, it proceeds by way of synthesizing *relative* deterritorializations on the plane of organization, but its movement is one of *absolute* deterritorialization, drawing a plane of consistency that creates a "new earth" by connecting "lines of flight" and raising them to the power of an "abstract vital line" (TP, 561).

Finally, the *Capitalism and Schizophrenia* project is also theological in the broader sense of the term I introduced in the first chapter. It develops retroductive hypotheses about the conditions for axiological engagement. For Deleuze, these conditions neither transcend nor resemble that which is conditioned. Our conscious lives are characterized by all sorts of pragmatic evaluations, shaped by the inscriptions of the social fields in (or on) which we live. These inscriptions produce representations, molar formations, and arboreal images that we interpret as *genetic* elements of value, which makes it all too easy to submit to their regulation and embrace our own repression. For Deleuze, however, it is the schizzes that are "valuable in themselves" (AO, 43). Schizoanalysis finds the conditions for lively engagement and the creation of new values in the complex relations among desiring-machines, which are always producing, registering, and consuming on the surface. Perhaps even more than in his earlier writings, Deleuze makes explicit the connection between the speculative and the practical moments of philosophy. "Schizoanalysis, or pragmatics, has no other meaning. Make a rhizome" (TP, 277).

The bulk of this chapter explores the relation between what I have called the sacerdotal and iconoclastic trajectories and the four main social-machines Deleuze describes in these two volumes. First, however, we need to clarify one more function played by the Figure of Christ in the religious coalition that he believed secreted atheism more than any other.

Christ as the Judgment of God

In previous chapters we have seen how Christ is represented in Christian doctrine as the Image, the Logos, and the Incarnation of God. Christ is imaginatively engaged as the representation – the eternal reflection, the creative regulation, and the true revelation – of a transcendent moralistic Entity. In this chapter, we attend to the way in which Christ is also represented as the mediator of providential redemption – at least for members of the in-group. For defectors or out-group members, the final inscription of divine intentionality within the social field will be experienced as everlasting torment or (at best) annihilation. To those who harden their hearts, Paul warns "you are storing up wrath for yourself on the day of wrath, when God's righteous *judgment* will be revealed." On that day, God will "*judge* people's secrets through Jesus Christ" (Romans 2:5, 16). The author of Hebrews writes that "the adversaries" of Christ should fear the judgment of a "fury of fire" (10:7). The Apocalypse of John envisions Christ as holding the keys to "Death and Hades" and meting out punishment on those whose names are not written in the "Book of Life."

And so on. This sort of language works quite well *within* a religious coalition, protecting its cohesion by activating the detection of supernatural agents who are allegedly watching and judging human behavior. This helps to explain the anxiety that arises within the group when a daring sacerdotal theologian suggests that perhaps all will be saved. In practice, belief in an all-powerful *and* all-loving, all-forgiving supernatural Agent makes for a much harder motivational row to hoe.

We will return below to the tensions between some of the major theories of atonement (or salvation) in Christianity, tensions due in part to the internal struggle between sacerdotal and iconoclastic machines within this tradition. The main goal of this section, however, is to emphasize the significant difference between the ongoing "judgment" of Deleuze's *crustacean* God, whose organization of the strata of consciousness can all too easily repress the energetic flows of the *schizophrenic* God within the desiring-production of the unconscious, and the final judgment of the *monotheistic* God whose ultimate organization of human subjects is an exclusive disjunction between two eternal states of consciousness – infinite pleasure or infinite pain.

The complex, natural processes of social-machines fall back on desiring-machines, producing little Oedipuses everywhere, anxiously trying to fit into the various exclusive disjunctions inscribed on the socius, embracing their subjectification and subjugation. As we will see, Deleuze is quite aware of the role of religion (broadly conceived) in these processes, and pays special attention to an inherent link he identifies between Oedipus, the despotic machine, and monotheism. However, he was writing before the discovery of the forces of theogonic reproduction within the bio-cultural study of religion. His hypotheses can be strengthened by more careful attention to the intensification of anthropomorphic promiscuity and sociographic prudery in shared imaginative engagement with axiologically relevant supernatural agents. A qualitatively different sort of repression results when sacerdotal machines represent God as an all-powerful Father who eternally determines to reproduce and judge little images of Himself. Little Christs everywhere, anxiously judging desire (other's and their own) with a transcendent criterion: ideal resemblance to a perfect Son, who always does the will of an ambivalently distant Father, and whose mother (Mary) and true bride (the Church) are unwounded, pure and holy.

In *A Thousand Plateaus*, the "judgment of God" primarily has to do with the articulation of the strata, the sedimentations and foldings that organize the flows of intensities; in other words, the "work" of the Lobster God. The strata that most directly bind us, Deleuze argues, are the organism, signifiance and subjectification. "You will be an organism, you will articulate your body – otherwise you're just depraved. You will be signifier and signified . . . otherwise you're just a deviant. You will be a subject, nailed down as one . . . otherwise you're just a tramp" (TP, 177). All of these are the judgments of God, that is, bonds, pincers and articulations, which uproot the immanence of the Body without Organs (BwO). The BwO or plane of consistency is in "perpetual and violent combat" with the judgment of God or plane of organization. Constructing one's own BwO does not mean emptying the body of organs; the enemy is not the organs (or partial bodies) but *organizations* that constrain desires, flows, and intensities by forcing exclusive disjunctions between subjective identities and signifying interpretations.

Deleuze notes the "particularly important case" of Christianity, which "invents a new assemblage" (TP, 139) in which representation of the infinite becomes the necessary starting point for subjectification and signifiance, and desire becomes trapped within interpretations of a sacred Book. In a related single-authored essay "To Have Done with Judgment," he also singles out Christianity as playing a special role. In its infancy, Deleuze argues, the doctrine of judgment separated value and debt from existing bodies, presuming "that the gods give *lots* to men, and that men, depending on their lots, are fit for some particular *form*, for some particular organic *end*" (ECC, 128). One is always at risk of making false judgments in the attempt to discover and evaluate one's lot.

In Christianity, however, the debt is inscribed not on bodies in finite blocks that circulate in a territory but in an autonomous book that renders the debt infinite. Now judgment takes over existence, because we "have become in our *entire being* the infinite debtors of a single God." There are no longer lots that are judged but judgment is "our only lot."[11] All that is left is judgment, every judgment bearing on another judgment – judgment, so to speak, all the way down. In such a situation, asks Deleuze, what can be distinguished from judgment? Like Nietzsche, he suggests one can evoke an anti-judicative, "understood as *Antichrist* – less a ground than a collapse, a landslide, a loss of horizons" in which "existing beings confront each other, and obtain redress by means of *finite* relations that merely constitute the *course* of time."[12]

In *The Antichrist*, Nietzsche had distinguished, as had Spinoza and others before him, between the amorous person of Jesus and the mortuary enterprise of Christianity. He blamed the shift on "Paul's invention, his method of priestly tyranny, of forming the herds, the belief in immortality – *which is to say the doctrine of the 'judgment.*'"[13] In another chapter in *Essays Critical and Clinical*, Deleuze examines D. H. Lawrence's treatment of the Apocalypse of John, whom he blames for inventing "*a completely new image of power:* the system of Judgment" (ECC, 39). Like Deleuze, Lawrence is no more optimistic about the pacifist Jesus than he is about militant Christianity, for the one is wrapped up in the other: the carnivorous lamb who roars like a lion and presents itself as a sacrificial victim but who slays "mankind by the million," destroying all powers to take all power for its own.

Unintentionally, the Apocalypse convinces us that "what is most terrifying is not the *Antichrist*," but the descent upon the "sulfureous torture-lake" of the New Jerusalem, "the demented installation of an ultimate judiciary and moral power."[14] For our purposes, the main point here is Deleuze's understanding of the special function of Christian monotheism in the production of a judgment that organizes to infinity, inscribing infinite judgment upon existence itself. There is nowhere to hide from this judgment: you will turn or you will burn, otherwise you're just nothing.

Another important concept related to the judgment of God, which appears in both volumes of *Capitalism and Schizophrenia*, is the *priestly* curse on desire. "Every time desire is betrayed, cursed, uprooted from its field of immanence, a priest is behind it. The priest cast the triple curse of desire: the negative law, the extrinsic rule, and the transcendent ideal." Deleuze suggests that the most recent figure of the priest is the psychoanalyst, who invents "new ways of inscribing in desire the negative law of lack, the external rule of pleasure, and the transcendent ideal of phantasy" (TP, 171). In *Anti-Oedipus* as well, he accuses psychoanalysis of reinforcing the priestly way of seeing things. In that context, he describes the three errors related to desire as lack, law, and signifier, all based on an "idealism" that inscribes a pious intentionality upon the unconscious. The priestly curse on desire is brought into psychoanalysis, but "these notions cannot be prevented from dragging their *theological* cortege behind – insufficiency of being, guilt, signification . . . but what water will cleanse these concepts of their background, their previous existences – *religiosity*?"[15] This cortege is clearly religious and does in fact emerge out of the dominant trajectory within theology. The tragic journey of Oedipus – from Sophocles to Freud and beyond – does indeed have more to do with Christian theology than most people think.

There is no doubt that loss, guilt, and idealization (the stuff of traditional Christian interpretations of human desire) are related to castration, incest, and fantasy (the stuff of psychoanalysis in late modern capitalist societies). Like the classical interpretation of the Genesis myth as a "Fall," some models of the Oedipal conflict articulate their understanding of human desire with privative, punitive, and palliative categories: anxiety, prohibition, and displacement from a desexualized familial paradise. In Christianity, however, the religious inscription of desire was reinforced by appeals to a transcendent moralist Entity who judged all of humanity for the transgression of the first parents. Augustine, for example, argued that when Adam and Eve disobeyed the divine rule about eating fruit in the Garden of Eden and "fell" from their original state of holiness, this corrupted the very nature of human desire itself. The deficiency, brokenness, and guilt associated with inordinate concupiscence were then passed on to each new individual soul through sexual procreation.

For Augustine, the problem with humanity is its bad desire – a sexually transmitted disease for which there is no earthly cure. The heavenly solution is the Creator's provision of a new Adam (Christ), the transcendent Son of God who provides a model for holiness, mediates the (ritual) means for cleansing and healing, pays the just penalty for (at least some of) Eve's offspring, and defeats the powers of worldly temptation. This material link between "fallen" human desire and sexuality has clearly registered its effect on the Christian understanding of salvation as a future ideal. Those who acknowledge their lack, confess their guilt, and repress their physical desires are promised idealized, spiritual pleasures in a renewed paradise.

The Christian sacerdotal machine does indeed cast a priestly curse on desire, but Deleuze's broad application of terms like "priest" and "judgment" to a wide variety of social-machines and stratifications can obscure the unique features of *religious* assemblages. The complex operation of the Oedipus machine, for example, in its various couplings and conjugations with psychoanalytic (and other) machines, does not necessarily involve shared imaginative engagement with axiologically relevant supernatural agents. Like the Oedipus machine, the Christ machine of Christian monotheism has been and continues to be hooked up in different ways to all four of the social-machines we will explore below. However, it is important to distinguish it (and other *religious* machines) from social assemblages that do not appeal to special revelations and rituals sanctioned by gods. For reasons we have been describing throughout the book, humans have evolved with a high sensitivity to the judgment of other human beings in their coalition, and it makes sense that this would lead to the ascription of judgmental tendencies to the supernatural agents that populate the religious imagination.

Sacerdotal machines press this anthropomorphic promiscuity to infinity. It is not enough for God to have, for example, an intellect and a will: as an infinite transcendent moralistic Entity, God must fore-know and fore-ordain *everything*. It is difficult to know how to relate to such a deity, whose maximally counter-intuitive features seem irrelevant for the sorts of practical decision-making necessary for everyday life. Affirming these features also leads to the so-called "problem of evil," which in turn has led to all sorts of debates among sacerdotal theologians about the precise nature and limits of divine knowledge and power. Professing belief in such a God does not come naturally, and so coalitional doctrines must be carefully coded and extensively policed by priests and other religious leaders.

However, these intramural hermeneutical rivalries should not distract us from the main point: in whatever way it deals with the concept of an infinite supernatural Agent, sacerdotal theology involves an appeal to Christ as the mediator of divine judgment. In the epistle to the Hebrews, Christ is described as the ultimate "High Priest," who offered himself as a sacrifice once and for all. "Holy, blameless, undefiled, separated from sinners, and exalted above the heavens" (7:26), he entered once and for all into the "holy place" obtaining *eternal* redemption through his own blood (8:12). However, belief in this kind of "once and for all" event is not sufficient for holding together a religious coalition. Keeping up the supernatural agent detection that helps to protect in-group cohesion requires the regular repetition of rituals in which such agents are imaginatively engaged as actively present, and mediating (or promising) some sort of *temporal* redemption from earthly problems while waiting for the ultimate separation of saints from sinners. In this sense, sacerdotal machines also press sociographic prudery to eternity.

I have suggested that the iconoclastic trajectory of theology evolved in the wake of the west Asian axial age alongside the sacerdotal trajectory, but has consistently been domesticated by the latter. How are these *theological* machines related to the various *social*-machines Deleuze describes in the *Capitalism and Schizophrenia* project?

Theology and the Territorial Machine

In *Anti-Oedipus*, the territorial machine is described as "the first form of socius, the machine of primitive inscription." It is the production of a social field by a "megamachine" with human beings as its parts (AO, 155). A socius is produced when some coding (inscription) of stock (consumption) falls back upon the flow (production) of desire.

As we will see, the other two main forms of social inscription treated in that context – despotic and capitalist machines – are characterized by an overcoding and a decoding of flows respectively. It is important to keep in mind that Deleuze is creating concepts, describing abstract (or virtual) machines that are effectuated within, without being reducible to, actual empirically observable cultural mechanisms in a particular context.

In *A Thousand Plateaus* the concept of territorialization is spelled out in more detail and applied to assemblages in general. "The territory is the first assemblage, the first thing to constitute an assemblage; the assemblage is fundamentally territorial" (TP, 356). While the first volume used the term *territorial* primarily for the primitive or "savage"[16] mode of inscribing the (human) socius, the second volume expanded its semantic field to include all sorts of other assemblages, including music, painting, and animal "territories." In addition to the first three social-machines, *Anti-Oedipus* also alludes to a "revolutionary machine," which produces a "new earth."[17] In *A Thousand Plateaus*, Deleuze distinguishes nomadic societies, which are defined by "war machines," from primitive, State, and urban societies. Even between these two books, Deleuze's vocabulary is not always consistent.

However, the broad contours of the four basic social-machinic assemblages are clear enough for our purpose: exploring how their inscriptions are reinforced or weakened by the theogonic forces of the sacerdotal machine and the theolytic forces of the iconoclastic machine. When considering the distinction between *social*-machines, it is important to keep in mind that Deleuze's concern is not with establishing a historical ordering of societal forms, but with demonstrating the sense in which each of these "abstract" machines is operative in complex ways in *every* human society, even if only as assemblages that are (for example) prevented, overcoded, or captured. When considering the distinction between the *theological* machines, it is important to keep in mind that we are not dealing with new social assemblages in Deleuze's technical sense, but with integrated cognitive and coalitional tendencies that drive two significantly different ways of machining hypotheses about the conditions for axiological engagement.

Ever since it was assembled during the axial age, "theology" has been adopted within and adapted to the different modes of social inscription in a variety of complex ways. As we will see, however, the sacerdotal theological machine seems to function best within a monotheistic despotic machine that overcodes the finite flow of gods in a primitive machine, while the iconoclastic theological machine is borne along by a war machine that escapes even the axiomatic reterritorializations of the capitalist socius.

In *Anti-Oedipus*, each of the first three types of social-production is described as a machine that constitutes a "recording surface," which "falls back on" (*se rabat sur*) desiring-production. The "full body" of each socius (earth, despot, or capital) not only establishes an inscribing surface but also "arrogates to itself" all the forces of production, as though it were their origin and destination rather than their "quasi-cause."[18] This falling-back (or rotating-on, or reducing-to) involves a *representation* of desiring-production; the latter is inscribed with lack, law, and idealization as it becomes reduced (*rabattue*) to the representational space of social-production (AO, 337). Representation, Deleuze argues, "is always a social and psychic repression of desiring-production," but this repression "is exercised in very diverse ways, according to the social formation considered" (AO, 201). In the *primitive* machine, the desiring-production of bodies, which are part of the earth, is represented by means of alliance-debt, which represses the intensive germinal filiation of human bodies. The unit of alliance is debt and "*alliance is representation* itself."[19] Territorial representation organizes itself at the surface through a coding of flows, a debt system involving "a voice that speaks or intones, a sign marked in bare flesh, an eye that extracts enjoyment from the pain." This mode of representation introduces an element of transcendence, but it is still "quite close to a desiring machine of eye-hand-voice" (AO, 207). Deleuze makes occasional allusions to "the gods," but does not focus on the concrete role they play in the primitive socius.

In *A Thousand Plateaus*, Deleuze argues that the two most notable effects of territorialization are the reorganization of functions and the regrouping of forces. He explicitly relates the latter to "rites and religions," which he argues are "common to human beings and animals" (TP, 354). For our purposes, this use of the term religion is too *broad*. Other animals do indeed regroup forces within a milieu as they set up territories, but their territorializations are not characterized by shared imaginative ritual engagement with axiologically relevant supernatural agents. Even if there are intimations of this behavior among some primates, it does not make sense to ascribe it to the birds and the bees (for example).

Later Deleuze suggests that a general characteristic of religion is converting the absolute, or "making the absolute appear in a particular place." In that context, he is describing the tension between nomads and monotheistic religions. Religion, he argues, essentially includes *both* the monotheist dream of an absolute spiritual State *and* a turning-against the State-form that mobilizes the absolute deterritorialization of nomadic war machines, as when a prophetic personality is motivated by the idea of "holy war" (TP, 423). For our purposes, this use of the term religion is too *narrow*. Monotheistic coalitions may indeed fuel "holy" wars against defectors or outgroups and be obsessed with global domination of the ecumenon but, as Deleuze knows full well, archaeological and ethnographic research is filled with examples of small-scale societies that are not. The biocultural definition I have been utilizing picks out features that are common to all of the "religions" that function on the organized surfaces inscribed by primitive, despotic, and capitalist machines.

In the context of the *Capitalism and Schizophrenia* project, the term *Oedipus* designates the effect of the "priestly" curse on desire. Oedipus is the result of the social-machines' *transcendent* use of the syntheses (global and specific connections, restrictive and exclusive disjunctions, and segregative and biunivocal conjunctions), which represents and represses the desiring-machines' *immanent* use of the syntheses (local and non-specific connections, inclusive disjunctions, and nomadic and polyvocal conjunctions). As we will see below, Oedipus (the King) has a special relation to the despotic machine in which it functions as the repressing representation, and is fully installed in the capitalist machine where it becomes represented (by means of the familial triangulation of desire) as the displaced representative. However, Oedipus also plays a role in the primitive socius, as that which is anticipated and prevented. This first *territorial* machine is marked by a representation (coding of the flows through alliances) that represses the representative of desire (the germinal influx of intensity), displacing and reducing it to what is blocked in the system (filiation through incest).

Deleuze's main target here is psychoanalysis and the way it can fuel the repressive Oedipal machine in the capitalist socius, so he focuses on the representations within "the Imaginary" of Oedipus: castration, incest, and fantasy. Our target is the sacerdotal machine, whose theological representations are fueled by imaginative engagement with a supernatural agent who reveals the intentions of an infinitely transcendent moralistic Entity, which requires a (real) priestly ritual mediation of "the Imaginary" of Christ: loss, guilt, and idealization. Of course cognitive and coalitional defaults are at work in both the Oedipus machine and the Christ machine, but the repressive power of representations of the "judgment" of the monotheistic God is far more intense than that of psychoanalytic (or other nonreligious) representations that submit to the stratifying "judgments" of the crustacean God, whose foldings and articulations organize us into signified and signifying subjects.

Deleuze describes the primitive organization of the socius as a "system of cruelty," a surface inscription of "eye-hand-voice" that is marked directly on bodies, coding the flow of desire by signifying alliances that segment filiations. As we will see below, he draws attention to the role played by Christian monotheism in the "system of terror" inscribed by the despotic machine, wherein judgment is rendered infinite and all debt-alliance is ultimately oriented toward the despot-God. However, it is also important to note the way in which the theogonic forces of the sacerdotal machine make it so easy to participate in these cruel and terrorizing systems. All of the major theories of atonement (or doctrines of salvation) in Christian theology revolve around an anthropomorphically promiscuous hypothesis about the conditions for the restoration or fulfillment of an idealized mode of axiological engagement.

The *sacrificial* motif, for example, presents Christ as a heavenly High Priest who offers himself as a final sacrifice that takes away the sins of the world, making possible a reconciliation between impure sinners and a holy God. The early Christian theologians detected an infinite divine eye-hand-voice, a transcendent moralistic Entity represented as a Father who watches the torture of his Son, whom he put forward himself as a sacrifice of atonement by his blood, and through whom he proclaims his judgment of the whole world "once and for all" (see, e.g., Romans 3:25, Hebrews 9:26, I John 4:10).

The problem is that a "once and for all" sacrifice will not hold a religious in-group together. It does seem to follow from the Christian attempt to represent God as an infinite Person that divine judgments would be eternal and incontrovertible, but this sort of abstraction does not come naturally and has little pragmatic value. Ongoing ritual engagement with supernatural agents who are imagined as watching quotidian behavior and whose judgments can immediately impact the fortunes of the coalition, on the other hand, powerfully reinforce sociographic prudery. Such rituals also need to be relatively frequent, memorable, and emotionally arousing in order to provoke ongoing costly signals of commitment among group members.

Deleuze's formal analysis of modes of social inscription can be complemented by more careful attention to the theogonic mechanisms by which religious coalitions reproduce. In the case of Christianity, this has always involved participation in a ritual that celebrates the "body and blood" of a human-like, coalition-favoring supernatural agent.

Paul's warnings to the Corinthians about their practice of the "Lord's Supper" are illuminative in this regard (1 Cor. 11:17–32). He is not surprised at the factions among them, since such exclusive disjunctions are necessary to determine who among them is "genuine." Participation in the ritual is a proclamation of "the Lord's death until he comes." Because they have not been examining themselves adequately before participating, they are eating and drinking "*judgment* against themselves; for this reason, many of you are weak and ill, and some have died." He argues that "if we *judged* ourselves we would not be *judged*, but when we are *judged* by the Lord we are disciplined so that we may not be condemned along with the world." In other words, early Christians were warned that their weakness and illness were the result of their failure to detect the real presence of a judgmental supernatural agent who was returning soon to reveal who was genuinely part of the in-group and who would be eternally condemned. Although it promotes anxious self-judgment and antipathy toward out-groups, this is just the sort of ritual that holds a religious coalition together.

The iconoclastic theological machine, on the other hand, is fueled by the theolytic forces of anthropomorphic prudery and sociographic promiscuity. It resists appeals to contingently-embodied intentional entities as causal explanations for weakness or disease, and interpretations of tsunamis or the toppling of towers as divine judgments of human behavior. It resists appeals to divine revelation as the basis for establishing territories (a promised Land, one nation under God, etc.), and segregations of bodies based on their similarity to and conformity to a particular religious Figure. Like schizoanalysis and rhizomic pragmatics, the iconoclastic machine is constructive as well as destructive. In earlier chapters, we have already noted some of Deleuze's creative theological hypotheses about the immanent conditions for real axiological engagement. His productive iconoclasm continues in the *Capitalism and Schizophrenia* project. The energy-flows of the schizophrenic God are conditions for the molecular liberation of schizzes from their molar Oedipal formations, and the stratifications of the crustacean

God are conditions for the construction of deterritorialized plateaus and planes of consistency.

Every territorial assemblage (in the broader sense) releases lines of flight or deterritorializations, which in turn always involve a "special reterritorialization" (TP, 334). As Deleuze notes elsewhere, even philosophy reterritorializes – on the always mobile "concept" (WP, 101). Religions, however, reterritorialize on transcendent "figures." By focusing on the distinctive nature of a *monotheistic* Figure, which falls back on desiring-production with the force of an *infinite* representation, we can better understand how and why hammering theology secretes a productive atheism.

Theology and the Despotic Machine

This excessive secretion is a result, in part, of the unbearable pressure exerted upon cognitive and coalitional defaults as Christianity took over the empire and overcoded the mental and social space of medieval Europe with a representation of an *infinite* supernatural Agent, while simultaneously denying the possibility of such a representation. As we will see below, the compulsion of vows toward – together with the insistent disavowal of the possibility of – a concrete representation of a transcendent moralistic Entity, contributed to a decoding of flows in the Renaissance that would eventually lead to the inscriptive dominance of the capitalist machine. Understanding why and how this promoted the secretion of atheism requires us to attend to the unique way in which Christian theology evolved within, accommodated to, and eventually assimilated the *despotic* machine.

It is important to remind ourselves again that social-machines are not particular, historical formations of the socius but abstract machines that are actualized in a wide variety of ways. The despotic State, Deleuze insists, is an abstraction that is realized only as an abstraction (AO, 240). This allows him to conceive it as "the common horizon" to what comes "before" and what comes "after," that is, as a complex of syntheses that can overcode the primitive machine's coding of break-flows and, in turn, becomes relativized and incorporated within the capitalist machine's axiomatization of decoded break-flows. This *overcoding* of the despotic machine (or imperial barbarian formation) is characterized by the mobilization of the categories of *new* alliance and *direct* filiation.

The primitive machine is declined on the full body of the earth through lateral alliances and extended filiations. But the despotic machine appears with the force of a "projection that defines paranoia," in which a "subject leaps outside the intersections of alliance-filiation, installs himself at the limit, at the horizon, in the desert, the subject of a deterritorialized knowledge that links him directly to God and connects him to the people" (AO, 211). This is the first principle of a paranoiac knowledge that withdraws from life and from the earth, producing a judgment of both from on high. The socius will now be inscribed on a new surface, not the earth, but the full body of the despot (or his god). The voice is no longer one of alliance across filiations, but "a fictitious voice from on high." The eyes watching the hands' inscription of bodies are replaced by the Eye and the Hand of the despot, who watches everyone through the eyes of his bureaucrats, officials, and priests, and subordinates graphism to the Voice that "no longer expresses itself except through the writing signs that it emits (revelation)." Now, interpretation becomes all important: "The emperor, the god – what did he mean?" (AO, 224).

Having claimed a direct and transcendent filiation, the despot appropriates all the forces of production; all alliances are organized around and oriented toward him. Instead of blocks of mobile and finite debt coded by horizontal alliances, the despot extracts taxes for a vertical tribute that feeds a constantly expanding glorious expenditure. "The infinite creditor and infinite credit have replaced the blocks of mobile and finite debts" (AO, 242). The savage system of *cruelty* has been replaced by the barbarian system of *terror*.

Deleuze often notes a special relation between the despotic machine and *monotheism*. When the coding of flows in the primitive socius are overcoded by the despotic socius, then "the *ancestor* – the master of the mobile and finite blocks – finds himself dismissed by the *deity*, the immobile organizer of the bricks and their infinite circuit."[20] For Deleuze, the main role of the deity seems to be the inscription of debt into the very existence of the despot's subjects; they owe their being to the despot-god. "There is always a monotheism on the horizon of despotism: the debt becomes a *debt of existence*, a debt of the existence of the subjects themselves" (AO, 215). Deleuze is well aware of the special impact of Christianity when it took over the empire, and his analysis has been tremendously fruitful for other critics of capitalism and colonialism.[21]

Here too, however, Deleuze is working with rather broad definitions of monotheism and religion. He suggests, for example, that it does not matter whether the despotic enterprise is military or religious, motivated by conquest or converted into an internal asceticism. The same figures of a "paranoiac and his perverts" are discovered in each case, whether as "the conqueror and his elite troops, the despot and his bureaucrats, the holy man and his disciplines, the anchorite and his monks, Christ and his Saint Paul" (AO, 211). For our purposes, however, it is important to distinguish between *religious* or *theogonic* machines, which always reproduce shared imaginative engagement with axiologically relevant supernatural agents, and *social*-machines, whose inscription of surfaces may or may not involve such reproduction.

In *A Thousand Plateaus*, the overcoding inscription of the despotic machine is spelled out in more detail, and in relation to a new set of concepts, such as the abstract machine of macropolitics, whose rigid segmentarity is linked to the State as an "apparatus of capture." It is also connected to what Deleuze calls the *faciality* machine. His use of the term Face in this context is not a reference to a particular part of the body located at the front of the head any more than his use of the term Phallus refers to the presence (or absence) of an actual penis. Facialization overcodes the whole body, rendering it a signified and signifying subject, subjected to the judgment of the despot-god. Faciality is always correlated to a "landscapacity" (*paysagaéité*), a "landscapification" of territory into which the subject is placed and given significance (TP, 191).

The Face, argues Deleuze, is "in fact *Christ*, in other words, your average ordinary White Man." The faciality machine computes normalities and functions as a deviance detector. It takes a concrete face and "*judges* whether it passes or not."[22] Facialization is the overcoding wrought by the signifying despotic Face, which irradiates a surveillance that reproduces paranoid faces. It is "the *Icon* proper to the signifying regime," the reterritorialization internal to the despotic system of terror. "Look, his expression changed." The Face of the despot is always open to interpretation. His subjects anxiously make judgments about his and one another's facial expressions, and *interpretosis*, which is "humankind's fundamental neurosis," spreads like a virus. As one of the despot's bureaucrats, the priest plays a special role, administering the face of the god. "A new aspect of deception arises, the deception of the priest: interpretation is carried to infinity and never encounters anything to interpret that is not already itself an interpretation."[23]

In *Anti-Oedipus*, the imperial representation of the despotic machine is also distinguished from the savage representation of the territorial machine in terms of the role played by "Oedipus." Here we do not yet have the Oedipal *complex*, which will emerge only with the installation of the capitalist machine and which, with the help of psychoanalysis and the "holy family," makes Oedipus the representative of desire itself: Oh, that's what I wanted! However, in the barbarian social inscription, the Oedipal "cell" moves from its status as an after-effect of social inscription, the displaced represented of desire in the savage socius, and becomes the "*repressing representation.*" The limit that had been unoccupied in the primitive machine is now occupied by the despot. Although there is often actual incest within despotic families, Deleuze's point is that "incest" is *symbolically* occupied in the despotic machine (AO, 289).

The despot enjoys desires he prohibits to others. Deleuze describes this symbolic filling as the breaking of lateral alliances through marriage with "the sister," and the creation of a direct filiation through marriage with "the mother." All filiation and alliance now falls back on the full body of the despot, whose system of subordination-disjunction overcodes the territorial system of connotation-connection. Desire becomes desire for the desire of the despot. "Yet it is still *as the displaced represented* that incest now comes to occupy the position of the repressing representation . . . The royal barbarian incest is merely the means to *overcode* the flows of desire, certainly not a means to liberate them."[24] Flows are not permitted to escape; even the flight of the excommunicated scapegoat is overcoded *as* the exclusion of that which cannot be tolerated: absolute deterritorialization (TP, 129).

But what happens when monotheism attempts to represent the despot-God as an *infinite* supernatural Agent, from whose all-seeing Eye, all-powerful Hand, and all-judging Voice absolutely nothing can escape? On the one hand, such a representation is both logically incoherent and doxologically forbidden: an infinitely mysterious Entity cannot and should not be reduced to a finite image, for this leads to absurdity in thought and (material or semiotic) idolatry in practice. On the other hand, a religious coalition cannot survive without ritually engaging and interpreting the revelation of its supernatural agents, whose judgments help to code the flow of desiring-production. It is hard to engage an infinite despot whose immutable judgment eternally determines all things. "Christ" was born(e) in the imagination of early Christian theologians who postulated a mysterious supernatural agent who was somehow both finite *and* infinite. Such an agent could mediate between an absolute divine despot and everything else. Paul, for example, writes that God, as the invisible

Father of glory, places all things under the feet of his Son (Christ) and makes "him the head over *all things* for the church, which is his body, the fullness of him who *fills all in all*" (Eph. 1:22–3). Everything falls back on the "full body" of Christ; all things are brought under domination "for the church."

However, the monotheistic despot-machine would dissolve if those who subjected themselves to this infinitely repressing representation began to imitate Christ by taking his Lordship as their model. The *moral exemplar* theory of atonement helps to resolve this problem. Believers should not (yet) imitate Christ in his role as cosmic King, but rather conform themselves to his role as Servant – the submissive Son who represses his own desire and does only the will of the Father. One of the pleasures reserved for the divine despot is *not* forgiving his enemies, but placing them under his feet; his followers, on the other hand, must emulate only the kindness of the despotic Son.

But where is the Mother? In another context, Deleuze wonders why Christology is an all-pervasive theme in the work of Masoch.[25] The pious intentions of the perfect Child lead to an abandonment by the Father; the Son suffers the punishing afflictions that will make possible the formation of a new Body, an everlasting pleasurable union with his purified Bride, the Mother Church. The sacerdotal theological machine intensifies the bundling power of the despotic machine as it binds the social Imaginary together by policing the interpretation of revelation and the practice of rituals that regulate the production (and especially the sexual reproduction) of the members of its coalitions, replicating spiritualized Oedipuses who internalize their infinite guilt.

Several Christian rites explicitly celebrate the value of sexual repression. The celibate priesthood is reserved for those who model an idealized Christ. Those who find this regulation of filial flows too onerous may enter a special alliance authorized and consummated by God, effecting a union between "man and wife" that no one should set asunder. The criteria that guide such rituals may change over time but, insofar as they are driven by sacerdotal machines, they always regulate desire in reaction to an interpretation of an alleged divine revelation. An infinite despot is hard to think and impossible to live with. As a more human-like, coalition-favoring supernatural agent, Christ is cognitively and coalitionally easier to handle; naturally defaulting into small-scale groups, believers can bracket their monotheistic belief and get on with life.

The putative presence of an *infinite* white elephant in the room, however, becomes increasingly hard to ignore, and the absurdity and irrelevance of such a belief begins to secrete. The "mystery" of monotheism becomes an open secret. This casts suspicion on the relevance of all the *finite* white elephants (animal-spirits, ancestors-ghosts, saints or other limited "gods") that are allegedly watching and judging what is happening in the room. Iconoclastic theology challenges the plausibility of appeals to supernatural agents in attempts to explain events in the natural world or to orient behavior in the social world.

Deleuze has helped to unveil the way in which the repressive representations of despotic social-machines work, thereby weakening their power and opening up new lines of revolutionary flight. The assemblage of iconoclastic theological machines, linked to the insights of the bio-cultural study of religion, can help to unveil the repressive representations of shared imaginative engagement within monotheistic and other religious coalitions. One of the main negative tasks of *theological* schizoanalysis (or pragmatics) is criticizing the social-ecclesial reproduction of these representations. One of its main positive tasks is participating in the machining of new assemblages that are inclusive and nonrestrictive, immediately connected to social investments of desire. In our contemporary context, this requires special attention to a third mode of social inscription, which displaces the full body of the despot and intensifies the decoding of flows, but reterritorializes the flows in a new way that complicates matters for both kinds of theological machine.

Theology and the Capitalist Machine

Throughout the *Capitalism and Schizophrenia* project Deleuze is critical of the way in which the capitalist (or "civilized") social-machine organizes and represses desiring-production, especially its colonization of the self (the Oedipal complex) and subjugated groups (those effaced by the White Man). However, he also consistently emphasizes a positive feature of capitalism, which it shares with the schizophrenic process: it *decodes* the break-flows of desiring-production that had been coded in savagery and overcoded in barbarism. It is important to remember that in this context schizophrenia refers not to the "artificial" schizophrenic in a mental institution, but to universal primary production, "the universe of productive and reproductive desiring-machines" (AO, 5).

The social-production of capitalism creates an "awesome schizophrenic accumulation of energy or charge," deterritorializing the other modes of social inscription and releasing the break-flows of desiring-production. This sounds promising, at least from a Deleuzian perspective. The problem, however, is that this deterritorialization is only relative, and the capitalist machine immediately brings a new and even more pitiless power of repression to bear on the decoded flows, reterritorializing them on the "full body" of Capital. The surplus value of production had been coded through *kinship* or *tribute*, but now the qualities of alliances are decoded, rendered quantitative and relativized in relation to the surplus flux of the *market*, which bestows worth based on the potential for earning wages or generating profit. "It is no longer the age of cruelty or the age of terror, but the age of cynicism, accompanied by a strange piety . . ." (AO, 245).

Deleuze's critique of capitalism is complex and controversial, but for our purposes the most relevant aspect of his analysis is the tension between cynicism and piety within this surface inscription of the socius, which has important implications for *theological* machines. The "civilized" mode of social inscription engenders cynicism because of the way it decodes the flows that had been coded in the other modes. Whether primarily through connotative-*connections* (savagery) or subordinative-*disjunctions* (imperialism), surplus value had been managed through a qualitative coding of filiation and alliance. The capitalist machine, on the other hand, is characterized by a special use of *conjunction* – a coordination or conjugation of decoded flows.[26] The most important case for Deleuze is the conjugation of two flows that were deterritorialized after the collapse of feudalism in Europe; the free worker who must sell his labor capacity and the decoded money of finance-capital that is capable of buying it. "Capitalism forms when the flow of unqualified wealth encounters the flow of unqualified labor and conjugates with it" (TP, 500).

As Deleuze puts it in *Anti-Oedipus*, the capitalist machine is installed when capital ceases to be based on alliance and becomes filiative, when "money begets money" (AO, 247). Unlike the flow of payments in the exchange of impotent money signs that are relative to consumer goods, the flows of financing are signs of the power of capital to accumulate and multiply through the circulation of drafts of credit. This profound dissimulation between payment and financing "expresses the capitalist *field of immanence*."[27] The capitalist machine decodes local, qualitative flows of exchange and reterritorializes them on the full body of Capital, which renders all social valuation in terms of abstract quantities (Money). Capitalism endlessly expands as it creates new "axioms" that *conjoin* quantified flows of surplus value, extracting profit from the differential relations of labor power and capital itself.[28] Capitalism "axiomatizes with one hand what it decodes with the other" (AO, 267).

This leads not only to cynicism but also to anxiety, oppression, resentment, and fear of exclusion from the capitalist system, which appears to be consuming everything. Yet, everyone keeps buying into it. Why? Here is where the strange *piety* comes in. "Cynicism is capital as the means of extracting surplus labor, but piety is this same capital as *God*-capital, *from which* all the forces of labor seem to emanate."[29] We are reminded of one of the most well-knowing sayings attributed to Jesus: "you cannot serve God and mammon" (Luke 16:13). In the system of the capitalist machine, however, everyone serves God-Mammon. There are no more masters, only slaves. On the other hand, the "invisible hand" of the market is not transcendent; it does not care what you "believe." Like the other "full bodies" on which the surface of the socius is inscribed, Capital-Money, properly speaking, does not exist.

It is an axiomatic differential mass that does not "exist" anywhere, an Imaginary in which monetary social-production is *represented* as the origin, condition, and goal of desiring-production. The capitalist machine produces one *idealized* image after another, installing *lack* into desire even – or especially – where there is excess. But what about *law*? How is desire regulated so that it comes to embrace its own repression within this inscribed surface? Deleuze argues that the capitalist machine utilizes auxiliary apparatuses, such as the State, to regulate and colonize the desire it simultaneously stimulates. Just as the despotic machine preserved primitive territorialities within its overcoding, capitalist piety resuscitates the despotic State but maintains it as a "spiritualized Urstaat" (AO, 289, 409).

Perhaps the most important agent of psychic repression, however, is the "holy family," to which capitalism delegates the function of inscribing the recording surface of desire so that social repression itself becomes the *representative* of desire (AO, 131). Deleuze argues that psychoanalysis plays a special role in reinforcing a piety toward the familial triangle (mommy-daddy-me), finding or inserting the "Oedipal complex" everywhere. The capitalist machine uses the "intimate colonial formation" of the privatized family to maintain a hold on the productions of the unconscious. In this sense, Oedipus is an effect of the capitalist inscription of the socius, the production of little consumers whose desire is cursed by lack, law, and idealization. Production and reproduction no longer pass directly through the coding of the flows of filiation and alliance, but through an "axiomatic of decoded flows" (AO, 195).

Fully Oedipalized agents are the *result* of this mode of social-production; the capitalist socius produces docile neurotics who internalize their guilt and fantasize about what they lack. The Oedipal cell had passed from its position as the displaced represented in the primitive machine to the position of repressing representation in the despotic machine. In the capitalist machine, the unoccupied limit that had been symbolically filled in despotism is now inhabited and lived as "the social images produced by the decoded flows actually fall back on restricted familial images invested by desire."[30] Oedipus becomes the representative of desire itself. Incest and patricide – that's what I wanted! The dirty little secret of sexuality is brought into the open by psychoanalysis, but *as* a secret, as the repressed representative of desire.

Deleuze is well aware of the Christian "theological cortege" that is dragged along into the "priestly psychology" he attributes to bad psychoanalysis (AO, 121). He chips away at the familial triangulation by which desiring-production is repressed in the capitalist socius, and constructs schizoanalytic machinic assemblages that liberate the creative break-flows of desire without reterritorializing them through Oedipal signifiance and subjectification. Deleuze occasionally (and indirectly) notes parallels between Oedipus and Christ. "It will hardly come as a surprise to learn that Oedipus as a structure is the *Christian Trinity*, whereas Oedipus as a crisis is a *familial trinity* . . ."[31] He also alludes to the special role of Christianity in the inscription of infinite debt into modern consciousness, first through the extreme spiritualization of the despotic State in Catholicism and then through the extreme internalization of the capitalist field in the Reformation.

Together, these define "bad conscience," whose cynical tactics (*ressentiment*, judgment, etc.) flow out of an obsession with "a transcendent object that is more and more spiritualized, for a field of forces that is more and more immanent, more and more internalized" (AO, 291). This creative critique can be enhanced by attending more carefully to the repressed representative of desire in monotheistic religion. Within the capitalist machine, one can still find individual expressions of theogonic forces (e.g., faith in the "invisible hand" of the market, patriotic piety toward one's nation-State). Within the sacerdotal (priestly) machines of Christianity, however, the activation of anthropomorphic promiscuity and sociographic prudery is reinforced and intensified, leading to an even more secretive and more powerful form of repression.

One of the most important motifs in the Christian doctrine of salvation is the *satisfaction of infinite debt.* It is taken for granted that such a debt exists; if personal alliances and filiations are managed through debt, it is quite natural to assume that any relation to an infinite Person would involve an infinite debt. Hypotheses about the cause of this debt, and the mode of payment that resolves it, however, have varied significantly over the centuries. Until the nineteenth century, all versions of this motif traced the debt back to Adam and Eve, whose sin placed them in bondage to Satan, the "ruler of this world." One popular approach during the patristic period was to depict God as paying a ransom (Christ) to Satan, as a Roman general might do to buy back captives after a war.

Perhaps the most well-known version is Anselm's satisfaction theory of atonement, which depicted the relation between God and humanity in a way that reflected the social structure of England at the turn of the twelfth century, wherein disobedient serfs who dishonored their lords would be required to pay some kind of satisfaction in order to restore and maintain the social order. Adam and Eve had been granted a plot of land to tend (Eden), but they dishonored God by their disobedience. Because the honor of the Lord of the universe was infinite, so was the debt. Neither the first parents nor any of their finite offspring could pay; only an infinite being could satisfy such a debt. As the God-Man, Christ could represent both parties in a single transaction. Protestant versions of this atonement motif have taken a variety of forms, from the early modern European penal substitution theory to the late modern American prosperity gospel, each mirroring the legal or financial values of its context. In each case, however, the problem is debt and the answer is provided by a transcendent moralistic Entity.

Here again, however, we can see that ideas like the full payment of an infinite debt are impotent when it comes to holding together a religious coalition. If the debt of humanity really has been satisfied, and filiative alliance with the divine has been eternally secured by an infinite payment, this seems to diminish the importance of attending to the finite debts that organize everyday temporal alliances and filiations. The ritual of infant baptism has traditionally been interpreted as cleansing the soul of the original sin and guilt that automatically accrues to it as a member of Adam's race. However, even properly baptized Christian infants grow up and commit their own sins; clearly, inordinate desire is inadequately repressed by this sacrament. What is to stop cheating, freeloading, and defecting to out-groups?

The ritual of penance takes over. The new debts accrued by the soul in its childhood and adult years must be paid by confessing guilt to a priest, demonstrating real remorse and making new payments (monetary or behavioral) that signal commitment to the in-group's belief in a judgmental supernatural Agent. Not all sacerdotal coalitions practice these rituals in these particular forms, but in one way or another they exert pressure on their members to repress their desiring-production by internalizing the social-production of a religiously engendered repressed representative. Christ resists the temptation to escape the penalty of an eternal Father and abstains from all but spiritual relations with his siblings, his pure Bride, Mother Church. Oh, that's what I wanted!

The sacerdotal machine has a strong investment in maintaining the piety of the capitalist machine, which is always willing to allow the revival of a spiritualized Urstaat or the internalization of anxiety about fitting into a heavenly Family . . . as long as these do not interfere with the decoding of flows that keep falling back on the immanent field of Capital. The cynicism engendered on this field, however, weakens the binding power of appeals to a supernatural Agent who has revealed a normative mode of axiological engagement. Why should the religious consumer accept *this* coding (or overcoding) of surplus value? Might as well shop around.

Perhaps because of the way in which it emerged within and eventually took over the Roman Empire, Christian monotheism seems to work best when coupled to the despotic machine. However, Deleuze argues that the despot has now become relativized as just one of capitalism's images, namely, the paranoiac-fascist pole of its axiomatic, in contrast to its schizophrenic-revolutionary pole. Capitalism axiomatizes even religious codes, folding them back into the surplus flow of Money. In this mode of social-machinic inscription, values are no longer primarily regulated by overcoding despots – human or divine. The system of cynicism "works" no matter what you believe. Atheism begins to secrete more rapidly.

By hammering away at Oedipus and Christ (and other Figures of transcendence) the iconoclastic theological machine can intensify the continuous flows of desiring-production. What is the revolutionary path? Deleuze suggests that new institutional regulations alone cannot solve the problem, for the capitalist machine will only generate new axioms that consume them within its apparently limitless power to reduce all codes to Money. Trying to escape the world market by reviving one of the other two social-machines is not likely to help either. Might the solution be "to go in the opposite direction? To go still further, that is, in the movement of the market, of decoding and deterritorialization? For perhaps the flows are not yet deterritorialized enough, not decoded enough . . . not to withdraw from the process, but to go further . . . the truth is that we haven't seen anything yet" (AO, 260).

Theology and the War Machine

The fourth basic type of social assemblage is perhaps the most controversial. As though terms like "savages, barbarians, and civilized men" were not problematic enough, Deleuze uses the phrase *war machine* to designate the revolutionary path. As with his use of other startling terminology (e.g., the "diabolical," or even the "divine"), Deleuze is trying to get our attention. To what does he want us to attend? Despite its name, this machine in itself does *not* have war for its object (TP, 463). Only when it is appropriated by the State apparatus of capture does war necessarily becomes its object. In contrast to the State's power of appropriation, the war machine has a power of *metamorphosis* (TP, 483).

It may sometimes be destructive, but in its essence the war machine is creative; it is "the *constitutive* element of smooth space, the occupation of this space, displacement within this space, and the corresponding composition of people: this is its sole and veritable *positive* object (*nomos*)."[32] Like the territorial machine, its operation is not limited to human beings; every creation is brought about by a war machine. In terms of social-production, the aim of the war machine is "revolutionary movement." Once the capitalist machine has relativized the Urstaat's overcoding of the primitive machine and taken hold of the socius, every struggle involves an opposition between "*revolutionary connections*" and "*conjugations of the axiomatic*" (TP, 522).

Deleuze argues that it was the nomads who invented the war machine. Here again it is important to remember that his main point is not historical, but philosophical. Deleuze is developing a political (and psychological) philosophical hypothesis *about* axiological engagement. What are the forces at work in the social-psychic repression of desiring-production and what are the conditions *for* its liberation? Although Deleuze does not use the phrase "war machine" in *Anti-Oedipus*, he sometimes refers to a "revolutionary machine" that converts schizophrenia as a *process* into an "effectively revolutionary force," which is opposed to the fascisizing investments of the reactionary, paranoiac pole of the capitalist socius.[33] He also contrasts the hunter in nomadic space, who "follows the flows and escapes the sway of the full body of the earth," from the primitive form of the socius that codes the flows and segments the earth (AO, 163).

In the other social-machines, surplus value is dealt with through kinship, tribute or the market, but the nomads form itinerant, ambulant societies that invent, mutate, and relay valuables. Instead of money, the nomad prefers jewelry, tools, and weapons, which can be used on the move. "A schizophrenic taste for the weapon that turns it into a means for peace" (TP, 444). Yet another productive use for theological hammers.

Each of the other social-machines was defined by the way in which its *representations* fell back on desiring-production. The war machine Deleuze discovers through nomadology, however, operates by inverting the Platonic domain of representation. As a "nomad" propelled through continuous variations in the passage of the war machine, "one *does not represent*, one engenders and traverses."[34] In *Difference and Repetition*, Deleuze had challenged the dogmatic image of thought; here, he explores its special relation to the State-form, which helps to explain the role of "public philosophers" in the latter. The "private thinker," on the other hand, for whom every thought is already a tribe, "destroys images" and makes "thought a war machine."

Deleuze emphasizes that the nomad does not bring a rival image of thought that competes with the image inspired by the State apparatus, but "a force that destroys both the image *and* its copies."[35] In his work with Guattari, Deleuze does not use the concepts of depth, height, and surface in exactly the same way as he did in *Logic of Sense*. Nevertheless, we can see that the territorial machine has a special relation to bodies in their depth, the despotic machine appeals to a voice from on high, and the capitalist machine fills the surface with its extensive axiomatizations. Simulacra, icons, images. Mixing terminologies, we might say that the war machine produces the phantasm, releasing an absolute deterritorialization of thinking, acting, and feeling. At any rate, the war machine does not inscribe a clothed or striated "full body" upon which desiring-production "falls back" – everything keeps moving in the creation of smooth space.

This dynamic constitution of smooth space is always in tension with the striations of space by the other social-machines, especially despotism. Irreducible to the State, the war machine has a form of exteriority "such that it exists only in its own metamorphoses." This means it is operative *within* all sorts of innovations and inventions, even in *religious* creations (TP, 398). Here too Deleuze pays special attention to monotheistic religion, which in a certain sense is "a piece in the State apparatus." He points out that Christianity, although it became urban and imperial, also gave rise "to bands, deserts and war machines of its own" (TP, 481).

Deleuze also refers to the Crusades, which were a "properly Christian adventure," as an example of a case in which a religion takes over a war machine in order to project a universal or "spiritual" State that reterritorializes the entire world. "Despite all that," Deleuze insists, "when religion sets itself up as a war machine, it mobilizes a formidable charge of nomadism or absolute deterritorialization." The war machine cannot be entirely captured by the apparatus of the State or Religion. Something always secretes from its despotic overcoding. The nomad also has a sense of the absolute but – unlike that of the priest – it is "singularly *atheistic*."[36] Using the designation "religion" in the more precise sense I have been exploring throughout this book reveals another distinctive feature of the war machine. It may be captured by (or arise in flight from) the powerful theogonic forces of a monotheistic religious coalition, but in itself the war machine is inherently *theolytic*.

The most obvious example of the use of war imagery in the Christian doctrine of salvation is the *Christus victor* theory of atonement. Most versions of this soteriological motif also presuppose that the conditions for ideal axiological engagement were originally granted by a transcendent, moralistic Entity to the first human pair. After their "fall" from a paradisiac state, Adam and Eve were subordinated to the forces of sin and the Devil. All of their offspring are now powerless to resist worldly captivations and demonic captors. On this model, salvation can only be actualized if God defeats these forces and provides new conditions for the freedom of humanity.

The most popular version of this theory during the patristic and medieval periods, and a favorite of Martin Luther, depicted the Christ event as a cosmic victory over Satan (or Lucifer). Having tricked Adam and Eve into disobedience, this fallen angel became ruler of this world and now tempts human souls in life and imprisons them in hell after death. When Christ died on the cross, Satan thought he had won the greatest prize of battle, the Son of God. But death could not hold the latter, who defeated Satan and took the keys to death and Hades (Revelation 1:18). As the Apostle's creed puts it, Christ descended into hell and was then raised to heaven, sitting at the right hand of the Father almighty, "thence he shall come to judge the quick and the dead." Christ now has the power to release humanity from its captivity, not only from the Devil but from death itself.

Earthly religious coalitions could not hold together if this heavenly victory were taken as a fait accompli. There must be rituals that keep alive the fear of being deceived and captured again. During the Roman Catholic rite of confirmation, for example, the confirmand must publically reject Satan, his works and empty promises. In many Christian coalitions, especially among Pentecostals and charismatics, ambiguous experiences are commonly interpreted as demonic temptation (which calls for constant watchfulness) or even as demonic possession (which calls for an exorcism). Battling evil supernatural agents imaginatively detected by the in-group strengthens its cohesion. Besides the daily threat of deception, one must also worry about one's place in the eternal apparatus of capture, the ultimate segmentarity of heaven and hell. In the last century, many sacerdotal theologians attempted to develop atonement theories that downplayed this language of divine judgment, sometimes even rejecting the idea of a literal hell.

We can understand why such proposals are often met with hostility by in-group members: they undermine the sort of religious representations that help hold coalitions together. It is important to note, however, that new formulations of this doctrine, insofar as they appeal to a transcendent Agency that works for the flourishing of human coalitions, are still driven by and further activate anthropomorphic promiscuity and sociographic prudery. In contexts dominated by monotheism, these theogonic mechanisms all too easily lead to the sanctioning of "just" wars as well as "terrorist" reactions to such religiously inspired despotic overcodings. Research in the bio-cultural study of religion suggests that theogonic reproduction plays a significant role in the justification of war by Religions tied to despotic States, and in the justification of acts of terror by small-scale groups within those Religion-States who feel displaced and threatened by such wars.[37]

The distinctions I have been outlining in these chapters suggest that theology might be able to find its own revolutionary path, to escape from the religious warring of the sacerdotal apparatus of capture. Following its iconoclastic trajectory, theology can machine new hypotheses about the conditions for axiological engagement and produce new weapons for combating the judgment of God. Liberated from the sacerdotal machine, it can contribute to the constitution of smooth social space by drawing lines of flight that resist the repressing representations of theogonic reproduction. Like all machines, theology operates within the surface tension created by the various forms of social-production that fall back on desiring-production. In the following thought experiment, I briefly explore the ways in which theogonic and theolytic forces might play a role in the interplay between the four social-machines outlined by Deleuze in *Capitalism and Schizophrenia*. This experiment does not deal with all of the important variables that distinguish the four forms of the socius, but it does highlight one important set of differences that can help us clarify our options as we keep tinkering with our theological machines.[38]

Figure 5.1 plots the four social-machines onto the conceptual grid of cognitive and coalitional tendencies we have been utilizing throughout the book.

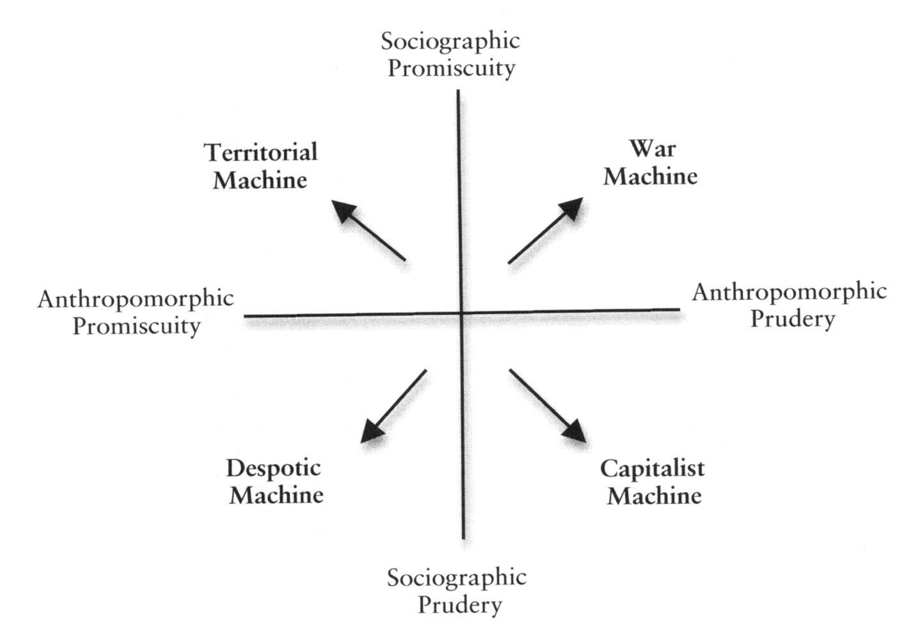

Figure 5.1

It is important to remember that these machines are abstract and are not intended to designate discrete social forms that have been historically realized in a particular order. They are effectuated or resisted to some degree in any human population. Moreover, the cognitive and coalitional tendencies marked out by the grid will vary in intensity and shift over time within and among persons and groups that make up any particular bio-cultural space. Finally, keep in mind that here we are conceptualizing theology as a machine for generating hypotheses about the conditions for axiological engagement. We might expect it to function quite differently as it tries to hook up with the various social-machines.

Let us begin with the despotic machine, whose special relation to the sacerdotal trajectory of theology we have already noted. Deleuze argues that "the primordial Urstaat" is not one concrete formation among others, but a "regulating idea or principle of reflection (terror)." In a sense, the despotic State is the origin, but "the origin as an *abstraction* that must include its differences with respect to the concrete beginning," namely, the territorial machine, upon which it forces an overcoding.[39] It makes sense to think that the small groups that began to outcompete all other hominid groups during the Late Pleistocene were those in which the territorial machine began to be overwritten by the despotic machine. Before the expansion of the hominid population and the depletion of ecological resources (or other factors) that led to the "god-bearing" traits, there would have been less need for sociographic prudery. Small-scale societies in relatively unconstrained geographical settings are bound up with their own gods and rituals, but tend to be characterized by less anxiety about whether their imaginative religious worlds are "right" or "best" and more openness to rearranging or adding supernatural objects in those worlds when faced with practical challenges.

Anthropomorphic promiscuity, already present as a set of cognitive tendencies that enhanced the chances for survival, would have been even more intensely activated as it was adapted to the complex social structures filled with more people and more gods of various ranks that emerged after the Neolithic. The installation of the abstract machine of despotism and the shift from shamans to priests were reciprocally related. Holding together the big groups that were assembled during the axial age required ever bigger gods. Eventually the sacerdotal machine of Christianity detected the biggest God imaginable (infinitely beyond representation yet mysteriously represented in Christ) and protected the cohesion of its Empire with threats of the most terrifying social segmentarity imaginable (the disjunction between eternal pleasure and eternal pain).

The decoding of flows that characterizes the capitalist machine has also always been present in human populations, even if only as that which was "warded off" by primitive and barbarian social inscriptions (and the nomads). The capitalist machine fosters anthropomorphic prudery; its operation does not require the detection of human-like supernatural agents. In its extreme forms, it is even blind to the qualities of natural human agents, which are reduced to their functions within the axiomatizations that cause the decoding of flows to fall back on the full body of Capital. It might seem that the capitalist machine is sociographically promiscuous because it allows and even encourages the multiplication of images, producing new idealized commodities that we lack and new modes of consuming them.

However, in the sense that it forces *all* surplus value to fall back into the same axiomatizing conjugation of decoded flows, converting all codes to abstract quantities (Money), it is at least as prudish as the despotic machine. Instead of promoting the demand that "everyone must follow the laws of our group's god," it spreads a different sort of universal anxiety: "everyone must accumulate surplus value for their own group." Like the territorial machine, the capitalist machine, in and for itself, has little use for theology. There is less need for hypotheses about the transcendental conditions of axiological engagement if values are automatically organized in relation to a constantly varying plurality of spirits or in relation to the constant uniformity of a capitalization of materials.[40]

The war machine is anthropomorphically prudish and sociographically promiscuous. It resists the facialization and landscapification of the despotic machine. It creates and populates smooth space with "probe-heads" that draw lines of flight, cutting edges of deterritorialization that become positive and absolute, "forming strange new becomings, new polyvocalities" (TP, 211). Just as the war machine combats the despotic machine, always escaping in order to create and produce new values, so the iconoclastic theological machine combats the sacerdotal machine, criticizing its appeals to an ideal human-like, coalition-favoring deity and constructing new pragmatic hypotheses for axiological engagement. Figure 5.1 illustrates how both the primitive and capitalist machines promote tendencies that partially challenge the despotic mode of theogonic reproduction.

In this sense, their inscriptions are problematic for the sacerdotal machine. The latter only survives by overcoding territories and resisting the axiomatizations of the immanent capitalist field that relativize its preferred Image of transcendence. The iconoclastic theological machine, on the other hand, fractures the repressive "representations" of all three modes of social-production. Nomadic "theology" has no time, and no place, for the segmentarity of Oedipus, much less the sedentary transcendence of the iconic Christ. In this sense, it is an atheist machine. Might its combat with the judgment of God diminish the need for cynical and pious declarations of war? Might it help to free desire from the numbing, an-aesthetizing effects of the Eidetic framework?

The Liberation of Feeling

The *Capitalism and Schizophrenia* project develops hypotheses about the conditions for this release of desiring-production, for the liberation of the ontological forces of affect or feeling (*aesthesis*, in the broadest sense).[41] Here we find a multiplicity of concepts assembling into what we might call Deleuze's theological aesthetics: creativity, art, diagrammatic lines of flight, pleasure, perception, the productivity of desire, etc. Consciousness is felt as a process of coming-to-be within a matrix of flows in which values are produced, registered, and consumed. How are we to account for this axiological engagement? For Deleuze, it is precisely the recording of *anti*-production on the surface of the Body without Organs that makes possible *both* the repression *and* the liberation of desiring-machines.

The "primal" repression of break-flows, the "breaks" in organ-machines that cause them to fall back on the BwO, frees them from a habitual or instinctual determinism. On the other hand, it also makes them liable to a "secondary" repression by the representations of social-production that fall back on the more or less striated full bodies of the earth, the despot or capital. The role of anti-production here is reminiscent of the affirmative disjunctive operation of the aleatory point or "non-sense" in *Logic of Sense*, and of the synthesizing differentiating function of (non)-being in *Difference and Repetition*. In each case, repression begins when a representation is mistaken as the genetic element of the real rather than a real effect.

The (revolutionary, schizoanalytic, pragmatic, nomadic) war machine works to emancipate desiring-production from the three main modes of social-production treated in *Anti-Oedipus*, freeing desire's continuous coupling of "flows and partial objects that are by nature *fragmentary and fragmented*."[42] This icono-clastic process is a real fragmentation, but one that liberates a creative or "artistic" force of fabulation. It seems clear enough that Deleuze is *not* proposing a value-free anarchy that blindly fights to overthrow the State, dismantle the global capitalist field and neutralize all territorial codes. In one way or another, all four of the "abstract" social-machines are likely to continue operating within human societies; the question is how we are going to respond to the repressive representations of the three modes of inscription that attempt to capture the creative force of the war machine. In contrast to the anxious attempt to fit in to the molar aggregate of everybody/everything, Deleuze describes a molecular *becoming*-everybody/everything, which is to make the world a becoming, to make a world, or to world (*faire monde*). To become everybody/everything is "to reduce oneself to an abstract line, a trait, in order to find one's zone of indiscernibility with other traits, and in this way enter the haecceity and impersonality of *the creator*."[43] Here "the creator" designates not a divine Person, or even human persons, but the creative process of the becoming-molecular of impersonal haecceities, intensities of difference that infinitely pass into one another and make all things new.

Deleuze links creativity with an atheism whose secretion, as we have seen, is already found within religion – and Christianity in particular. In his lectures on Spinoza, given in the same year that *A Thousand Plateaus* was published, he suggests that "atheism has never been external to religion: atheism is the artistic power at work on religion."[44] He illustrates this atheistic artistic power by referring to a variety of Christian paintings, some of which he had also alluded to in the *Capitalism and Schizophrenia* project. In *Anti-Oedipus*, for example, he suggests that something new emerged in painting as fifteenth-century Venetian capitalism begins to sense the signs of its own decline, "Christ's body is engineered on all sides and in all fashions, pulled in all directions, playing the role of a full body without organs, a locus of connection for all the machines of desire, a locus of sadomasochistic exercises where the artist's joy breaks free" (AO, 403). In *A Thousand Plateaus*, he emphasizes that it is not only the body, but also and especially the face of Christ that is "worked" by painters in order to "make it leak from the religious code in all directions" (TP, 332). He points to all sorts of deviations: the crucified Christ-turned-kite-machine sending stigmata to St. Francis, Christ-athlete-at-the-fair, Christ-Mannerist queer, etc.[45] Some of the paintings to which he referred obliquely in these volumes are treated more explicitly in his single-authored book on the painter *Francis*

Bacon: The Logic of Sensation, published the year after *A Thousand Plateaus*.

In that context, Deleuze wrote that Christianity contains "a germ of *tranquil atheism* that nurtured painting." He suggests that during the late middle ages and Renaissance some Christian painters began to "adhere literally to the idea that *God must not be represented*," which led to a "properly *pictorial atheism*." From the point of view of religious morality or aesthetics, it might seem that *without* God, everything would be permitted. Deleuze argues the opposite: "*with* God, everything is permitted." This is the case not only morally (e.g., even wars can be sanctioned as holy or just) but also *aesthetically*, and "in a much more important matter, because the divine Figures are wrought by a free creative work, by a fantasy in which everything is permitted." The idea of an infinite God beyond representation contributed to a sort of indifference among artists toward the religious subjects they were asked to represent; they felt free to decode divine Figures in creative ways. As the Figure began to lose its necessary connection to a transcendent essence, painters linked it to the accident, the changeable, the event. Christ is "besieged" in painting, replaced by all sorts of accidents, made to pass through diverse "areas of sensation" and through all "levels of different feelings." In other words, "Christ's body is fashioned by a truly *diabolical* inspiration."[46]

Diabolical? What does painting (or any other creative artistic expression) have to do with demonology? As in his earlier single-authored works, Deleuze continues to use a "demonic" vocabulary in the *Capitalism and Schizophrenia* project. In *Anti-Oedipus*, for example, he appeals again to Klossowski's contrasting of "God as the master of the exclusions and restrictions that derive from the disjunctive syllogism with an *Antichrist* who is the prince of modifications, determining instead the passage of a subject through all possible predicates."[47] He also describes the schizophrenic process as having a special relationship to the "demoniacal" in nature (AO, 26).

Some of the most interesting examples of "diabolical" language in *A Thousand Plateaus* appear in the tenth plateau ("1730: Becoming-Intense, Becoming-Animal, Becoming-Imperceptible . . ."). Throughout the three subsections on "Memories of a Sorcerer" Deleuze and Guattari use the first person plural in a rather intimate way. "*We* sorcerers have always known . . . that is *our* way, fellow sorcerers."[48] What do they know, and what is their way? Sorcerers have a special relation to multiplicities, to the becoming-animal that always involves a pack. Sorcerers know that transformations begin with an "initial relation of alliance with a demon" on the borderline of the pack. They sometimes require a "pact with the Devil." The way of the sorcerer is to find lines of flight, whose trajectories cannot be known ahead of time. The Devil is a "transporter" of "humors, affects, or even bodies." This is why the Church seeks to expose pacts with the Devil; "the church has always burned sorcerers."[49]

As in his earlier work, it is clear that Deleuze's use of diabolical vocabulary is not meant to "represent" actual (or virtual) supernatural agents, disembodied *intentional* entities that plague a particular coalition. Nor is he promoting magic, witchcraft, mysticism, alchemy or sorcery in the sense these were interpreted and practiced during the Inquisition. It seems to me most likely that he was utilizing such terms in much the same way as he did "schizophrenia" and "war." By using words that usually designate that which we most fear – powers that we cannot manage, powers that threaten to dissolve our grip on reality – Deleuze challenges our preconceptions. Perhaps the real problem is the way we are gripping reality, the way we try to manage our identities within in-groups. Perhaps it is our *representation* of these powers that is terrifying us, paralyzing us within repressive social assemblages and mobilizing us against defectors and out-groups.

Perhaps it is only by opening ourselves up to encounters with these (non-intentional) intensities that we can discover new modes of creativity that free us from anxiety. "There is in fact a *joy that is immanent to desire* as though desire were filled by itself and its contemplations, a joy that implies no lack or impossibility and is not measured by pleasure since it is what *distributes intensities of pleasure* and prevents them from being suffused by anxiety, shame, and guilt."[50]

Deleuze's theological aesthetics has no place for judgment, because it is packed with creative evaluations. Instead of judging other existing beings, Deleuze (following Spinoza and Nietzsche) encourages us to *sense* whether they bring creative forces to us or whether they return us to the miseries of war. "If it is so disgusting to judge, it is not because everything is of equal value, but on the contrary because *what has value can be made or distinguished only by defying judgment.*"[51] Judgment presupposes pre-existing criteria, whereas evaluation brings something new into existence by affirming the difference of being. "To affirm is still to evaluate, but to evaluate from the perspective of a will which enjoys its own difference in life instead of suffering the pains of the opposition to this life that it *has itself inspired*."[52] It is actually our judgments themselves, our representations of other beings (or ourselves) as valuable based on external, idealized criteria, that block creativity and restrict life, separating it from what it can do. Deleuze describes Nietzsche's transvaluation of values as a process in which life and thought (and we might add, action and desire) go in the same direction, carrying one another along "*smashing restrictions*, matching each other step for step, in a burst of *unparalleled creativity*."[53]

By disclosing the repressive power of social representations, Deleuze has helped clear the way for revolutionary experimentation. I have tried to show how *religious* machines, which integrate and intensify theogonic forces, and the *sacerdotal* theological machines coupled to them, complicate matters in a different way. The repressive representations they reproduce are reinforced by the naturally evolved mechanisms that all too easily lead to the detection of gods and the protection of in-groups. This may have helped (some of) our ancestors survive, but now theogonic reproduction is crushing the life out of us – while "representing" itself to us as our savior. The *iconoclastic* theological machine can help by clearing the field of religious icons, priestly erections of transcendence that make us anxious and distract us from creating new connections on the plane of immanence. As Nietzsche put it in *The Twilight of the Idols*, "there is nothing that can judge, measure, compare, or condemn our being." The concept of "God," he insists, has been the biggest objection to existence so far. For this reason, declares Nietzsche: "We reject God, we reject the responsibility in God: *this* is how we begin to redeem the world."[54]

What can a godless body do? Make a rhizome, move on the surface, liberate lines of flight, feel the movement of the pack, unleash the creative forces of affect. For all of the reasons we have been discussing, such movements threaten groups whose cohesion depends on shared imaginative engagement with supernatural agents. Religious societies, like the State apparatus, treat their secrets with gravity, but inevitably (it is the nature of secrets) something oozes out and something is perceived. The war machine treats secrets with celerity, molecularizing their content and linearizing their form (TP, 320). This is why the iconoclastic machine feels so dangerous to the sacerdotal machine, which uses its massive arsenal to crush or domesticate it. But we nomads have no reason to fear: we have weapons of mass secretion that work just by bringing them into the open.

6

Secreting Atheism

We have seen that Deleuze had several uses for a theological hammer. He broke icons of transcendence, pried apart the dogmatic shackles of thought, extended the crack that releases the eternal truth of events, and assembled nomadic war machines to combat the psycho-social repression of desiring-production. Deleuze had other ways of utilizing a hammer that we have not explored here; we might have added chapters, for example, on "forging theological intuitions" (*Bergsonism*) or "moving theological pictures" (*Cinema 1* and *Cinema 2*). All of his efforts contributed to the inversion of the Platonic Eidetic framework, to overturning the domain of representation in which philosophy has labored so long, by creating and connecting new concepts in the immanent field of univocal being.

Christian monotheistic coalitions live, breathe, and have their analogical being in that domain; they are held together, in part, by requiring their members to select one true Icon among rival images of idealized divine transcendence. This is why hammering theology of the Deleuzian sort inevitably increases the secretion of atheism. Throughout this book, I have explored how the *eidolon* of Christ (as one example of a Figure of transcendence) functions in the mental and social space of religious coalitions in a way that binds thinking, acting, and feeling. I have tinkered around with Deleuzian philosophy, attempting to amplify its liberating force by coupling it to a conceptual heuristic derived from the bio-cultural study of religion.

In this final chapter, I clarify the sense in which iconoclastic theology is *atheistic* and outline some of the ways in which its secretion is *productive*. For Deleuze, there is a sense in which neither atheism nor "the death of God" is a problem for philosophers. "Problems begin only afterward, when the atheism of the concept has been attained." He finds it amazing that so many philosophers still find the death of God tragic. "Atheism is not a drama but the philosopher's *serenity* and philosophy's *achievement*."[1] In *Anti-Oedipus*, he claimed that denying God is only a "secondary thing," especially if it is immediately followed by putting "man" in God's place. The person who realizes that "man" is no more central than "God" does not even entertain the question of "an alien being, a being placed above man and nature." Such a person, Deleuze observes, no longer needs "to go by way of this *mediation* – the negation of the existence of God – since he has attained those regions of an auto-production of the unconscious where the unconscious is no less *atheist* than orphan – *immediately atheist*, immediately orphan."[2] Once one recognizes the repressive power of social representations, Deleuze suggests that atheism is an unremarkable, somewhat obvious, place to begin.

As we have seen, however, unveiling this repression is not so easy – especially when it comes to *religious* representations. Deleuze was not aware of the cognitive mechanisms that reinforce (and are reinforced by) coalitional mechanisms. Developments in the bio-cultural sciences provide us with conceptual tools that can supplement the insights that arise in the debates among defenders and detractors of psychoanalysis. I have tried to show how powerfully and surreptitiously the evolved theogonic forces of anthropomorphic promiscuity and sociographic prudery work within religious minds and groups. It helps to point out the secrets of theism, especially the cognitive incoherence and coalitional irrelevance of representations of an infinite personal God. Such prodding exerts a pressure that intensifies the secretion of atheism. But this is not enough; the forces of theogonic reproduction have led to adaptive defenses that hold subjects within religious coalitions. For example, sacerdotal theologians can insist that these "mysteries" are part of what is adorable about the divine nature or part of what is hidden in the divine plan. Appealing to concealed secrets, secrets that are appealing in part because of their concealment, keeps the secretion in check.

Deleuze's overturning of the domain of representation reveals a different sort of secret. When Plato's hidden dualism is brought into the open, it challenges the whole enterprise of selecting among rival images to determine the true icon that resembles the ideal model of transcendence. This secretion is much more difficult to contain because the epistemological, moral, and metaphysical container itself has been destroyed. *Religious* representations, however, evolved long before the axial age and their reproduction does not depend on a Platonic or any other retroductive hypothesis about axiological engagement. They "naturally" repress analysis, activity, and affect regardless of what philosophers or theologians say. The inversion of Plato and the dissolution of Oedipus will have only a limited effect on Christ – or any other religious Figure of transcendence.

To move people to where Deleuze wants to *begin* will require unveiling the mechanisms that make it so easy to keep religious secrets in the first place. This process calls for therapeutic sensitivity to the real fear and anxiety that can arise when a person begins such a journey, and political sensitivity to the real agony and violence that can arise when a group feels threatened. Sledgehammers are rarely helpful in such contexts. On the other hand, a relentless pounding of the sacerdotal Icons whose representations "fall back on" and crush life, while arrogating to themselves the power to give life, may very well be a necessary first step; "only friends can set out a plane of immanence as a ground from which idols have been cleared" (WP, 43).

The Production of Atheism

It may indeed be the serenity of the philosopher, but achieving atheism (in the modern sense) was made possible, at least in part, by Christian theology.[3] We have noted several reasons for the exceptional atheistic secretion of the latter, all of which are related to its persistence in – and simultaneous resistance to – representing the infinite. It was precisely philosophy's "being so compromised with God," i.e., the absolutely unrepresentable monotheistic God, that enabled it to draw lines of flight that eventually fractured the whole domain of representation.[4] Although they are almost always pulled back by the bio-cultural gravitational field of the sacerdotal trajectory, some Christian theologians, especially logicians, egalitarians, and contemplatives, have also pursued intensifications of thinking, acting, and feeling that challenge the notion of an infinite supernatural Agent who cares for a particular human Group. The Christian idea of an infinite, transcendent moralistic Entity is simply unbearable – cognitively and coalitionally.

Human minds evolved in small-scale groups in an environment where the shared detection of finite, human-like, and coalition-favoring gods was naturally selected because it enhanced the chances of survival. In the west Asian axial age, the political emergency of increasingly large and pluralistic populations and the psychological emergency of increasingly complex reflection on "the self" in relation to the totality of "the world" were intertwined in a way that eventually led to the idea of an infinite God who fore-knows and fore-ordains the destinies of a finite set of souls in a closed cosmos. In early modern Europe, the escalation of philosophical deliberation on the theoretical implausibility and stultifying effects of such an idea and the slow deterioration of Christianity's monopolistic control of mental and social space were intertwined in a way that helped to produce contemporary atheism.

In what sense is atheism itself *productive*? This depends, of course, on what we mean by atheism – and how we evaluate productivity. Let me begin with the latter. In the broadest sense, Deleuze would argue that everything is productive; all that exists is desiring-production (and the socius, which is desiring-production under certain determinate conditions). The real question, then, is how and what does an atheist-machine produce? The actual products of self-professed "atheist" groups have been just as ambivalent as those of their "theist" counterparts. Moreover, just like theists, individual atheists may be tranquil or bellicose, lethargic or creative. How, then, can we use the designation *atheism* productively? One approach is to focus on the distinctive way in which hypotheses are produced when one intentionally follows out the theolytic forces of anthropomorphic prudery and sociographic promiscuity. This does not capture everything there is to say about atheism, any more than "shared engagement with axiologically relevant supernatural agents" captures everything there is to say about religion.

Both atheist and religious groups can provide a sense of belonging and give meaning to the lives of their members. Atheist and theist individuals alike can feel a sense of awe when contemplating the cosmos, work to heal suffering, support the arts, etc. They can clearly be distinguished, however, by the extent to which they rely on appeals to the revelation of (or ritual engagement with) gods in their production of hypotheses about what is happening in nature and what might happen in society. Religious hypotheses are fueled by the evolved forces of anthropomorphic promiscuity and sociographic prudery. They are driven by and reinforce theogonic reproduction. Ambiguous natural phenomena are explained by references to the supernatural agents imaginatively detected by members of the group. Prescriptions for organizing the social field are guided by references to the judgments of those same supernatural agents, shared ritual engagement with which helps to protect in-group cohesion. Atheists, on the other hand, resist such appeals in their hypothesis production.

In other words, they are *naturalists* and *secularists*. Here too we are dealing with terms that are highly contentious. Here too I am using these terms to designate tendencies that are related to the conceptual heuristic derived from the bio-cultural study of religion. Definitions of naturalism vary widely, but it seems to me that most have a common feature: resistance to appeals to supernatural agency in theoretical explanations of the natural world. In the academic sphere, this is often called *methodological* naturalism. Individual scholars might feel very differently about the actual existence of gods, but the excision of such agents from scientific hypotheses has led to enormous productivity across the disciplines.

Proposals for defining secularism are also quite diverse, but most could incorporate the following feature: resistance to appeals to supernatural authority in practical inscriptions of social worlds. We might refer to this tendency in the public sphere as *methodological* secularism. Individual civil leaders or politicians might belong to various religious groups, but opposition to appeals to the revelation or ritual of a particular coalition in pluralistic contexts has contributed to the production of new forms of shared social space. Now, there is no doubt that the valence of such productivity is open to debate. The effects of scientific technologies and the results of political experiments are impossible to predict.

We do not know what naturalist-secularist bodies can do. Whatever they *can* do, hypothesizes the atheist, their axiological engagement is not conditioned by human-like, coalition-favoring gods. Atheism follows out the logic of the theolytic forces, pressing beyond methodological versions of anthropomorphic prudery and sociographic promiscuity and insisting on *metaphysical* naturalism and secularism. If gods play no role in the inter-subjective and trans-communal academic hypotheses that have the most explanatory power, why postulate their existence? If the revelatory rituals of particular religious coalitions are not necessary for inscribing the shared space of complex, pluralistic societies, why participate within them? In response to such questions, religious people often appeal to their own experiences of imaginative engagement with supernatural agents, making inductions and deductions that flow naturally from the abductive hypotheses shared within their coalitions. Debate at this level is rarely fruitful. This is why it is necessary to engage in the critique and construction of *retroductive* hypotheses about the conditions for creating new values.[5] Theology is simply too important to leave to theists.

If it were just a question of otiose relics of bygone days, atheists might leave well enough alone. But shared imaginative engagement with supernatural agents has a powerful function indeed, producing intensified anxiety about in-group identity within the psyche and intensified antagonism toward out-groups within the polis. Of course religion has *other* uses as well; for example, imagining a caring divine attachment figure can provide a sense of elation and imagining an eschatological reward can motivate impressive displays of altruism. The question is whether joy and kindness can be promoted without appealing to gods. And the answer is yes. In their combat with the "judgment of God," there is always the danger that atheists will form their own in-groups in ways that simply antagonize theists, reinforcing their hyper-sensitive detective and protective tendencies, which only makes things worse.

Atheists are human too, and will naturally be interested in finding relevant agents and forming enjoyable groups – but they will resist the evolved predisposition to organize their axiological engagement around appeals to divine revelations and rituals. I have been writing about theists and atheists as though we are dealing with distinct identities or groups, which is not very Deleuzian. Nor is it consistent with the conceptual framework of cognitive and coalitional forces we have been discussing. Better to say that we are all shaped by theogonic and theolytic forces, to which we respond in various ways as we continuously adapt to the complex and changing natural and social environments within which we produce, register, and consume valuables.

The productivity of naturalism and secularism (in the senses described above) challenges the plausibility of belief in gods and the feasibility of adaptive strategies that rely on them to save us. Iconoclastic theology can be emboldened by the discoveries in the bio-cultural study of religion that support the hypothesis that shared imaginative engagement with gods emerged over time as naturally evolved hyper-sensitive cognitive tendencies led to mistaken perceptions that slowly became entangled within erroneous collective guesses about the number of relevant actors in the social field. Even if only "secondarily," the iconoclastic production of new retroductive hypotheses about the conditions for axiological engagement are clearly *atheistic* (in the sense described above). Secreting this sort of productive atheism will not solve all our problems and will surely create some new ones. However, insofar as it clears the ground of icons of transcendence that distract us with mythical interpretations of nature and divide us through supernatural inscriptions of society, at least it gets us moving. In this sense, the production of atheism is good news.

The Gospel According to Deleuze

Deleuze's Anti-Christ theology is clearly not a "Gospel" in the traditional sense; he has no interest in the salvation of the world, whether by divine or any other means. "The world" does not need to be "saved." It lacks nothing, and there is no transcendent, regulative ideal against which to judge it as more or less salvageable. However, the iconoclastic force of Deleuzian theology is "gospel" in the literal sense of the term; that is, it is a message of "good news." Deleuze calls us to *believe* in *this* world, to counter-effectuate the events of this life, to affirm the unlimited creativity of pure becoming as we cast planes of immanence across the chaos.[6]

As we saw in Chapter 2, already in his early writings, and especially when dealing with Nietzsche, Deleuze argued that philosophy is pure affirmation – a creative rejoicing in life and being in all its multiplicity. In both its speculative and practical moments, philosophy is a joyful "yes" that overcomes the "no" of ideologies of *ressentiment* that are bound up in religious representations. It is the affirmation of the good news that being itself is the affirmation of difference. For Deleuze, following Nietzsche, the "practical joy of the diverse" lies in the "affirmation of the multiple." From this perspective, "joy emerges as the sole motive for philosophizing" (PI, 84). Joy and philosophy are still connected in Deleuze's last published essay, "Immanence: A Life." Pure immanence is "a life," and nothing else. "A life is the immanence of immanence, absolute immanence: it is complete power, complete *bliss*."[7] This may not be the sort of gospel we evolved to appreciate naturally, but it is good news for those with "ears to hear" (cf. Mark 4:9, Luke 8:8).

As we saw in Chapters 3 through 5, Deleuze's philosophy brings glad tidings to those who seek to liberate thinking, acting, and feeling from the stultifying icons of transcendence that bind them within the Platonic domain of representation. Affirming the complex repetition of pure difference (the eternal return) breaks the fetters of the dogmatic image of thought that bind thinking to the analogous, the same, the opposed, and the similar. Counter-effectuating events releases their eternal truth so that the actor can be reborn, break with her carnal birth, and become the offspring of her events rather than her actions and passions. Assembling creative, revolutionary war machines smoothes out the striated space of fascist modes of social-production, freeing desiring-production to distribute intensities of pleasure that are not suffused with anxiety, shame, and guilt. None of this happens easily, and there are dangers all along the way; too much of the wrong kind of hammering can be disastrous. Given the cognitive and coalitional forces that lead us to scan for judgmental supernatural agents who will enforce transcendent ideals in a way that protects our coalitions, it is no surprise that a Deleuzian voice calling out from the nomadic wilderness can sound like craziness. But it is just the sort of gospel that can wake us from our theogonic slumbers.

Deleuze's "theology" is good news for atheists looking for resources for the construction of plausible *naturalist* retroductive hypotheses about the conditions for axiological engagement, and for inspiration for the development of feasible *secularist* strategies for habilitating pluralistic, social space in ways that are hospitable to and for difference. In the preceding chapters, I pointed to several places in Deleuze's work where one can find resources for such "atheist" production. There is no doubt that Deleuze is a metaphysical naturalist. He defines naturalism as the celebration of the positivity of Nature, as the philosophy of affirmation: "pluralism linked with multiple affirmation; sensualism connected with the joy of the diverse; and the practical critique of all mystifications."[8]

Deleuze is also a metaphysical secularist, insofar as he insists that the transcendental conditions for real experience are worldly (*saecularis*). The difficult task facing us today, he argues, is "believing in *this world*."[9] Deleuze's language about a "new earth" and his anticipation of a "people to come" can sound naively utopian, but such interpretations miss the point. There is no external, ideal "goal" toward which our social inscriptions are oriented. The point is the value of being itself, the value-creating process of desiring-production "that is always and already complete as it proceeds, and as long as it proceeds" (AO, 417). The abstract social-machines that try to capture the nomads are not likely to be disassembled any time soon (probably not until there are no more people). The key question today is how (and whether) we can go on peopling the earth in creative and life-affirming ways.

It is important to emphasize that it is not the Deleuzian corpus itself that is gospel. However enthusiastic we may be about his material hypotheses, they are not the good news. It would be ironic (even tragic) to set up Deleuze as a "model." He worked hard at constantly constructing new concepts, creating them anew and keeping them moving precisely so that his work would not be idealized or idolized, so that he would not become a new Icon around which thinking, acting, and feeling were colonized once again. In *Dialogues*, Deleuze described his early experience of Sartre, not as "a model, a method or an example, but a little fresh air . . . an intellectual who singularly changed the situation of the intellectual" (D1, 12). This is what Deleuze can be for iconoclastic theology – not a model, but a gust of air, an inspiration to get us moving. Like the perverse "breaths/spirits" in Klossowski's *The Baphomet*, the intensities of difference in Deleuze's writing can "sufflate" bodies – bodies of theological literature, as well as other sorts of literature and other sorts of bodies. "Insufflation" sounds scary; how will we hold together? Deleuze invites us to consider the inverse; perhaps it is precisely our fear of falling apart that leads us to resist the creative "diabolical" processes of schizogenesis, that makes us desire our own religious repression.

In this sense, Deleuze can also be an "inspiration" for theologians trained in the major religious traditions that trace their roots to the west Asian axial age. As we have seen, the iconoclastic trajectory has always been operative within Christian theology, although its secretion has usually been blocked and reterritorialized by the sacerdotal trajectory. For theologians who are already tempted by the logical, egalitarian, and contemplative lines of flight within the Christian religion, Deleuze can provide a stimulus to escape the pull of the integrated theogonic forces and to create new values with "the nobility and the courage" (TR, 364) of the atheism it inspires. Their scholarly expertise will be an invaluable asset in finding the cracks within monotheistic coalitions from which this revolutionary force secretes, and they will not need to leave behind their passion for intensity, infinity, and intentionality.

What conditions the intense experience of finite intentionality? Sacerdotal hypotheses have typically appealed to a transcendent moralistic Entity who resembles what he conditions (intentionality), and conditions it by ordering intensities with his infinite knowledge and power. Deleuze hypothesizes that the condition for the real experience of intentionality is the immanent causality of infinite intensities of difference (simulacra, schizzes, etc.), which bear no resemblance to that which they condition. Iconoclastic theology is no less intense, and no less concerned about infinity and intentionality – but its hypothesis production is animated by the explanatory and pragmatic power of the integrated theolytic forces.

In this context I have consistently focused on the atheism secreted by Christianity, but of course there are revolutionary resources to be extracted from other religions as well. Coalitions within Judaism and

Islam have produced their own creative, nomadic war machines and, in a variety of different ways and with varying degrees of success, have worked hard to capture them again with the auxiliary apparatuses of monotheism. The secretion of atheism looks quite different in the major religious traditions that originated in east and south Asia because most of their theologians did not attempt to represent the *infinite* as a Person in the same way as the Abrahamic traditions. Despite popular portrayals of Daoism and Buddhism (for example) in the west, most members of these coalitions regularly participate in imaginative ritual engagement with all sorts of *finite* supernatural agents, both nasty and nice.[10] What secular westerners tend to find most attractive in these (and other) traditions are the philosophical and "spiritual" texts that draw lines of flight that promote anthropomorphic prudery and sociographic promiscuity.

It seems to take an enormous investment of energy to unveil the forces of theogonic reproduction, and even more to overcome them. In another sense, however, it just takes letting go. This is an insight shared by many Daoist and Buddhist sages. Let go. Release. Flow. Trying to control the world in order to manage our anxiety only makes it worse. This is also what the Stoics (and in a different sense, the Epicureans) were trying to tell us. A gospel they shared with Deleuze.

The Forces of Theology

The evolved cognitive and coalitional forces at work in our lives are exceptionally powerful, especially when we are unaware of their functioning. Like all hammers, theology operates as a force amplifier, converting basic mechanical work into kinetic energy (and back). Physically speaking, a hammer-blow delivers an amount of energy to its target equivalent to one half the mass of the head times the square of the speed of the head at the time of contact. This means that energy increases linearly with mass, but quadratically with speed. Metaphysically speaking, the hammer-blows of theology (regardless of the trajectory it follows) are also force amplifiers, converting mental and social forces into a kinetic energy that amplifies their effect exponentially. Sacerdotal hammering is reinforced by the gravity and molar mass of cognitive and cultural evolution. "You will be a subject, nailed down as one" (TP, 177). The energy of iconoclastic hammering comes from its velocity, but the issue is not simply relative speed or slowness. Its force derives from the celerity of pure becoming, from pure affects that are below and above the threshold of perception, from the "becoming-molecular" and "becoming-imperceptible" that have an essential relation to movement itself (TP, 309).

Deleuze argued that only Friends can set out a plane of immanence as a ground from which transcendent religious Figures have been cleared. Such planes are cast over the chaos and constructed of concepts that are always created anew.[11] This is why Deleuze was always going beyond himself, prying his own concepts out of earlier planar presentations, fragmenting them and moving on to new fabulations. This is also why iconoclastic theology must go (and keep on going) beyond Deleuze. As it keeps going, of course, it can also keep extracting fragments from his (and other) literary products, mobilizing and connecting them in novel ways as it casts new speculative and practical planes over the chaos – that's what Friends are for.

Interest in the potential impact of Deleuzian concepts on theology has been increasing rapidly in recent years. This is true both among Christian theologians and among Deleuze scholars who have little or no interest in Christianity or other religions. One of the features common to most proposals in this expanding body of literature is an evident passion for hypotheses about the conditions for axiological engagement. One way of distinguishing between them is by exploring the extent to which their (more or less Friendly) appropriation of Deleuze is shaped by the sacerdotal and iconoclastic trajectories. For some Christian theologians, engaging Deleuze is primarily a defensive maneuver. Writing from an ardently confessional (i.e., sacerdotal) perspective, their main concern seems to be protecting the doctrinal formulations of their coalition from attack or showing that what they find most fascinating in Deleuze can be (or already has been) incorporated into the Christian tradition.[12]

However, as we might expect, most Christian theologians who are attracted to Deleuze are also strongly attracted to the iconoclastic lines of flight already present within Christianity. That is, they are more willing to allow logical reflection, egalitarian concern, or intense contemplative experience to challenge traditional formulations and ecclesial practices. They tend to be on the cutting edges of the deterritorialization of their religious coalitions.[13] Nevertheless, insofar as such efforts at liberation also include appeals to divine revelation and ritual engagement with Christ as the ideal representative of God, whose moral judgments and promises are the basis for holding together religious Groups, they are held back by the forces of the sacerdotal trajectory. This weakens the plausibility of their hypotheses by (partially) immunizing them from the critique of those who do not share their imaginative engagement with this supernatural Agent. This strategy functioned relatively well from the axial age to the early modern period, but it is rapidly losing its viability (and proving itself detrimental) in our current globally interconnected, ecologically stressed environment.

On the other hand, one also finds a growing number of scholars who are passionate about "theology," and even enthusiastic about extracting resources from the Christian religion, but who resist appeals to a transcendent moralistic Entity and have little or no interest in protecting the boundaries of "the Church." Their appropriations of Deleuze are characterized by a far more robust anthropomorphic prudery and sociographic promiscuity.[14] For all of the reasons outlined in this book, I believe this is a more productive path. I have argued that it will be easier to liberate the iconoclastic trajectory of theology from the sacerdotal if we attend to the distinct qualities of "religion" drawn out by empirical research in the bio-cultural sciences: shared imaginative engagement with axiologically relevant supernatural agents.

In my view, iconoclastic proposals can be strengthened by avoiding vague definitions of religion (orientation toward ultimate meaning, potency of awareness, etc.), definitions so *broad* that they apply to virtually all human beings, including atheists. They can also be strengthened by avoiding definitions that begin (and end) by asserting that the term "religion" was a Christian invention used as a tool for colonizing other cultures (and academic disciplines). The term may very well have been so invented and so used, but such *narrow* definitions, which are popular among some humanist scholars of religion, ignore the inventive ways the term has been used in a variety of other fields. There is no "right" use of a term, but I hope the concepts I have derived from the bio-cultural sciences may encourage iconoclastic theological Friends to make connections with other empirically oriented disciplines.

Finally, there are an increasing number of Deleuze scholars who are focusing on his "theology" (or "anti-theology," which, in light of his Klossowskian definition, is the same thing), but who have little or no interest in Christianity or other religions. Coming from a wide variety of fields such as philosophy, literature, and social theory, these tend to be experts on Deleuze who are already somewhat enthusiastic about his approach to the science of non-existent entities and the way in which they animate language and make for it a body divided into disjunctions. They may not designate his – or their own – work as *theological*, but these scholars are certainly in the business of critiquing and constructing hypotheses about the conditions for real axiological engagement.[15]

As they bring the resources of their own disciplines to bear on this field of inquiry, which was once the protected domain of (Christian) theology, they more or less explicitly reject hypotheses that appeal to the sort of transcendent, moralistic Entity imaginatively engaged in monotheistic coalitions. In my view this sort of constructive critique can provide an impetus for innovation in the academic field of theology, opening up new possibilities for serious, productive dialogue with other disciplines. Why should it be the only academic field whose members get away with appealing to the revelations of supernatural agents detected in the rituals and behind the texts of their own religious in-groups? Not all theologians do this and, as we have seen, this is not all that theologians can do. The ongoing transgression of the boundaries of this field, which have for too long been marked off and policed by sacerdotal forces that immunize the abductions of religious coalitions from retroductive critique, can help to liberate the creative forces of the iconoclastic trajectory that are always and already secreting from it.

I have tried to contribute to the evolving dialogue among my transgressing Deleuzian Friends in three ways. First, I have attempted to demonstrate the centrality and pervasiveness of theological hypotheses in Deleuze's work. Reading him from this perspective draws attention to connections and discloses patterns across his writings that might otherwise be missed. It also helps to make sense of his consistent affirmation of the "diabolical" throughout his career; as a conceptual motif, Anti-Christ is at least as generative as Anti-Oedipus. Second, I have shown how several of his key concepts can be mapped onto a conceptual heuristic derived from the bio-cultural study of religion. Reading him from this perspective renders more explicit the theolytic force of his hypothesis-production, highlighting the role of anthropomorphic prudery and sociographic promiscuity in his creative process. It also introduces a definition of religion that helps us identify where we can creatively fragment his hypotheses and make new rhizomic connections. Third, I hope to have demonstrated how fruitful it can be to release the flows of the iconoclastic trajectory of theology by cracking open the arboreal edifices of monotheistic religion with a precision hammering that is even more intense than Deleuze's, thereby increasing the secretion of a productive atheism that liberates thinking, acting, and feeling. Whether or not we call this "theology," it is, as Deleuze would say, interesting and important work to do.

Can't we all be Friends? Probably not. The findings of the biocultural sciences suggest that human cognition has evolved in such a way that coalitional binding depends upon widespread anxiety about in-group identity and hostility toward defectors and out-groups. These evolved defaults are deeply embedded in the matrix of psychological and political networks that organize our lives. They have been reinforced by thousands of years of religious entrainment involving shared imaginative engagement with axiologically relevant supernatural agents. It takes an enormous amount of energy to reverse the tendency to guess "disembodied intentional force" when confronted with ambiguous phenomena. It takes even more energy to overturn the tendency to hold groups together by relying on collective guesses that those forces are watching and waiting (to help or to harm). On the other hand, unveiling the forces of theogonic reproduction automatically weakens them because they only work well when they are adequately hidden. As the theolytic forces are integrated, they grow in intensity and reinforce one another. Iconoclastic trajectories of the sort traceable from the Stoics through Deleuze are gaining momentum. Creative naturalist and secularist hypotheses are resonating ever more productively across a wide variety of academic disciplines and public fields of discourse. Who knows what Friendly atheist bodies can do?

Notes

Chapter 2

1. WP, 43, emphasis added. Throughout this book, I will synecdochally refer to "Deleuze" when discussing works co-authored with Guattari – a common practice in the secondary literature on Deleuze, especially when dealing with concepts that the latter treated separately in single-authored texts. I extract resources from across Deleuze's writings, but my main task is to draw out a motif that I will refer to as his "iconoclastic theology." For a general introduction to Deleuze's work from a broader perspective, see Buchanan, *Deleuzism*; Colebrook, *Gilles Deleuze*; Hughes, *Philosophy After Deleuze*; Crockett, *Deleuze Beyond Badiou*; Due, *Deleuze*; Patton, ed., *Deleuze: A Critical Reader*; Ansell Pearson, ed., *Deleuze and Philosophy*; Stivale, ed., *Gilles Deleuze: Key Concepts*; and Smith, *Essays on Deleuze*.
2. In "A Letter to a Harsh Critic," Deleuze described his view of the history of philosophy as "a sort of buggery or (it comes to the same thing) immaculate conception. I saw myself as taking an author from behind and giving him a child that would be his own offspring, yet monstrous. It was really important for it to be his own child, because the author had to actually say all I had him saying. But the child was bound to be monstrous too, because it resulted from all sorts of shifting, slipping, dislocations and hidden emissions that I really enjoyed" (N, 6).
3. TR, 364, emphasis added.
4. WP, 92, emphasis added. Deleuze commonly singles out "Christian transcendence" for its role in misleading western thought (e.g., WP, 101).
5. NP, 93, 118, 162.
6. For example, DR, 262; SPP, 24; AO, 294; TP, 278; TF, 76.
7. LS, 253–4, emphasis added.
8. The "axial age" refers to the transitional period between about 800–200 BCE, during which new kinds of complex, literate states emerged in the most populated areas across west, south and east Asia. For an introduction to the way in which religion evolved during this period, see Bellah, *Religion in Human Evolution* and Armstrong, *The Great Transformation*.

9. For example, even in the same essay on Klossowski in *Logic of Sense* from which I have taken the definition of theology that will serve as a starting point for my rhizomic extension of his project, Deleuze refers to the importance of distinguishing between theology and anti-theology (LS, 323). Without making any claims that Deleuze is consistent in his use of the term "theology," I am extracting one particular usage and exploring its revolutionary force. In the sense in which I am using the terms, I hope to show that Deleuze can indeed be appropriately designated an *iconoclastic theologian*.
10. For Aristotle theology was the highest theoretical science, the study of being *qua* being (*Metaphysics*, 1025a19, 1064b3). Slavoj Žižek proposes a "materialist theology" in Chapter 2 of *The Parallax View*. Unfortunately, Žižek's reading of Deleuze in *Organs Without Bodies* seems, in my view, to be less about reading Deleuze and more about supporting his own interpretation of Lacan. See Smith, *Essays on Deleuze*, Chapter 18.
11. For a discussion of hermetic themes in Deleuze's early writings, and their impact on his later work, see Ramey, *The Hermetic Deleuze*.
12. Cf., e.g., DR, 84; TP, 189, 551.
13. NP, 17, emphasis added.
14. For a more thorough reconstruction, see Shults, "Science and Religious Supremacy," "The Problem of Good," and especially *Theology After the Birth of God: Atheist Conceptions in Cognition and Culture* (Palgrave Macmillan, forthcoming). For extensive bibliographies and reviews of the literature within this trans-disciplinary "field," see the website for the *Institute for the Bio-Cultural Study of Religion*: http://www.ibcsr.org. Given the limitations of space and the specific goal of the current project, my strategy here is to refer the interested reader to some of the most relevant scientific theories and empirical findings in the endnotes, but to remain focused in the main text on the broader engagement with Deleuze's "theology."
15. For an introduction to some of the empirical evidence and theoretical developments relevant to what I am calling anthropomorphic promiscuity, see Guthrie, *Faces in the Clouds*; Atran, *In Gods We Trust*; Boyer, *The Naturalness of Religious Ideas*; Barrett, *Why Would Anyone Believe in God?*; Pyssiäinen, *Supernatural Agents*; Schaller et al., *Evolution, Culture and the Human Mind*; Tremlin, *Mind and Gods*; Lewis-Williams, *Conceiving God*; Kirkpatrick, *Attachment, Evolution, and the Psychology of Religion*.
16. For an introduction to some of the empirical evidence and theoretical developments relevant to what I am calling sociographic prudery, see Sosis, "Religious Behaviors, Badges, and Bans: Signaling Theory and the Evolution of Religion"; Bulbulia et al., *The Evolution of Religion*; Boyer, *Religion Explained*; Rossano, *Supernatural Selection*;

Whitehouse, *Modes of Religiosity*; McCauley, *Why Religion is Natural and Science is Not*; Wildman, *Science and Religious Anthropology*; Pyysiäinen, *How Religion Works*.

17. AO, 318 (French, 348: "*bioculturelle*").
18. Several authors have examined the role of evolution in Deleuze's work. For example, Ian Buchanan argues that Deleuze and Guattari's discussion of the problem of the evolution of the thought-brain (in *What is Philosophy?*) broaches a new sort of question "that effectively turns the history of philosophy into a kind of evolutionary psychobiology," in which the "biological" is understood as already "philosophical." For Deleuze, Buchanan explains, all creatures engage in "contemplation," that is, converting the chaos of undirected stimulus into directed stimulus (or excitation into sensation), and transforming sensation into "thought" (*Deleuzism*, 41, 63). For additional explorations of the relationship between Deleuze and evolutionary sciences, see Bell, *Philosophy at the Edge of Chaos*; Ansell Pearson, *Germinal Life*; Protevi, *Life, War, Earth*; Jensen and Rodje, eds., *Deleuzian Intersections*.
19. See, for example, Tremlin, *Minds and Gods*, and Whitehouse, *Modes of Religiosity*.
20. See references in endnote 14.
21. For a discussion of minimally counter-intuitive concepts within religions across cultures, see Boyer, *Religion Explained*.
22. Cf. Shults, "The Problem of Good" and *Theology After the Birth of God*.
23. FB, 100, emphasis added.
24. Gilles Deleuze, "Seminar on Spinoza/Course Vincennes 25/11/1980," available at www.webdeleuze.com (accessed 10 September 2013). Cf. DR, 276.
25. N, 10–11. For a discussion of the concept of secret in Deleuze's work, see Colebrook, "The Secret of Theory."
26. For an overview of some of the relevant empirical research in cognitive science that bears on this issue, see Slone, *Theological Incorrectness*, and Barrett, "Dumb Gods." Several psychological studies have shown that even religious people who are able to understand and articulate the "orthodox" doctrines of divine omnipotence and omniscience automatically default to "theologically incorrect" answers involving "dumb gods" when asked to respond under time constraints to (for example) existentially relevant narratives involving petitionary prayer.
27. For an introduction to some of the empirical research on the relation between rituals and cognitive evolution, see McCauley and Lawson, *Bringing Ritual to Mind*, Whitehouse and Laidlaw, eds., *Ritual and Memory*, and Schaller et al., *Evolution, Culture, and the Human Mind*.

28. NP, 3, emphasis added.
29. E.g., NP, 55, 84, 87, 174, 179.

Chapter 2

1. LS, 303, emphasis added.
2. Deleuze scholars with different tasks may well choose to highlight other examples of his early works of philosophical portraiture. Along with Nietzsche and Spinoza one commonly finds Bergson high on the list of inspirational influences. This "trinity" of influential thinkers is emphasized, for example, by May, *Gilles Deleuze: An Introduction*, and Hardt, *Gilles Deleuze: An Apprenticeship in Philosophy*. I will treat Bergson as well, but for reasons that will soon become clear, I have highlighted Kant instead. My main concern in the expository sections of this chapter is not primarily whether Deleuze got them "right" (a question that would be more important in other contexts), but on the "monstrous" creations that resulted from his penetration of their literary bodies.
3. E.g., C1, 61; C2, 127. Cf. N, 42. For a fuller discussion of this theme, see Colebrook, *Gilles Deleuze*, especially Chapters 2 and 5. For two quite different treatments of the creative role of the concept of image in Deleuze's thought, compare Lambert, *In Search of a New Image of Thought: Gilles Deleuze and Philosophical Expressionism*, and Flaxman, *Gilles Deleuze and the Fabulation of Philosophy*.
4. LS, 197. Cf. Deleuze's more exhaustive treatment of Leibniz in *The Fold*.
5. Leibniz, "Conformity of Faith with Reason," in *Theodicy*, 99, 103.
6. Leibniz, *Philosophical Texts*, 280, emphasis added.
7. Hegel, *Lectures on the Philosophy of Religion*, volume III, "The Consummate Religion," 290–328.
8. LS, 121, emphasis added.
9. LS, 314, emphasis added.
10. For examples of the way these tendencies work together see, for example, Atran, *Cognitive Foundations of Natural History*, Boyer, *Religion Explained*, and Teehan, *In the Name of God*.
11. "Qu'est-ce que fonder?" Lectures given at Lycee Louis le Grand, 1956–1957, available at www.webdeleuze.com (accessed 10 September 2013).
12. For treatments of Deleuze's search for the conditions of *real* experience and his critical engagement with Kant, see Smith, *Essays on Deleuze*, Chapter 14; Hughes, *Deleuze's Difference and Repetition*; and Voss, *Conditions of Thought*. For an analysis of the way these concerns, which lead Deleuze to propose a "transcendental empiricism," can be traced back to his earlier engagement with Hume, see Bell, *Deleuze's Hume*.

13. DR, 87, emphasis added.
14. AO, 27, emphasis added.
15. For a discussion of Deleuze's treatment of the three Critiques, see Hughes, *Deleuze's Difference and Repetition*, Chapter 1, and Smith, *Essays on Deleuze*, Chapter 7.
16. LS, 336, emphasis added.
17. *Critique of Pure Reason*, 135, emphasis added.
18. *Critique of Pure Reason*, 29, emphasis in original.
19. *Religion Within the Limits of Reason Alone*, 54. Cf. his later discussion of the archetype on page 109.
20. SPP, 11, emphasis added.
21. For analyses of the role of the concept of immanence throughout Deleuze's work, see de Beistegui, *Immanence: Deleuze and Philosophy*, and Kerslake, *Immanence and the Vertigo of Philosophy*.
22. Published as Chapter 1 in *Pure Immanence*. For a more detailed discussion of the concept of immanent causality in Deleuze's reading of Spinoza, see Nail, "Expression, Immanence and Constructivism."
23. See Deleuze's lectures on "Les aspects du temps, la lumière, Bergson, Le mouvement, Kant, Le sublime dynamique," 22/03/1983, available at www.webdeleuze.com (accessed 10 September 2013).
24. EP, 165; cf. 48.
25. Seminar on Spinoza, 25/11/1980, available at www.webdeleuze.com (accessed 10 September 2013).
26. Cf. EP, 172–3.
27. DR, 40. Cf. his discussion of Spinoza and Scotus in EP, Chapter 3.
28. SPP, 24, emphasis added.
29. *A Theologico-Political Treatise*, 64, 195.
30. EP, 123. Cf., e.g., 185, 225, 301, and 307.
31. Deleuze's reading relies heavily on Klossowski's *Nietzsche and the Vicious Circle*.
32. LS, 299, emphasis added.
33. LS, 300, emphasis added. In this context Deleuze also refers to Nietzsche's apparent allusion to Plato's allegory of the cave in *Beyond Good and Evil* (§289): "behind each cave another that opens still more deeply, and beyond each surface a subterranean world yet more vast, more strange. Richer still and under all foundations, under every ground, a subsoil still more profound."
34. NP, 84, translation emended, emphasis added.
35. *Thus Spake Zarathustra*, 66 (Part II, On the blessed isles), emphasis added.
36. For example, *The Will to Power*, 379 (§712).
37. NP, 16, emphasis added.
38. DR, Preface, xx, emphasis added.
39. See, for example, Grant, "At the Mountains of Madness."

40. For an introduction to some of the relevant empirical research and theoretical formulations on this theme see, for example, Atran, *In Gods We Trust*, and Pyysiäinen, *Supernatural Agents*.

Chapter 3

1. For overviews and analyses of the arguments of this book, see Williams, *Gilles Deleuze's Difference and Repetition*; Hughes, *Deleuze's Difference and Repetition*; Voss, *Conditions of Thought*; and Bryant, *Difference and Givenness*. For a discussion of its role in the broader development of the philosophy of difference, see Widder, *Genealogies of Difference*.
2. DR, English introduction, xvii.
3. DR, 156, emphasis added.
4. DR, 132. Although in this context Deleuze insists on a "thought without image," elsewhere he sometimes refers to the need for a "new image" of thought. For example: "The plane of immanence is not a concept that is or can be thought but rather the image of thought, the image thought gives itself of what it means to think, to make use of thought, to find one's bearings in thought . . . The image of thought demands 'only' movement that can be carried to infinity. What thought claims by right, what it selects, is infinite movement or the movement of the infinite. It is this that constitutes the image of thought" (WP, 37).
5. DR, 50, 262. "Difference is 'mediated' to the extent that it is subjected to the fourfold root of identity, opposition, analogy and resemblance." In relation to concepts, it has four aspects: "identity in the form of the *undetermined* concept; analogy, in the relation between ultimate *determinable* concepts; opposition, in the relation between *determinations* within concepts; resemblance, in the *determined* object of the concept itself" (DR, 29).
6. Cf. DR, 270–1.
7. DR, 167, emphasis added.
8. DR, 167. All of the postulates, says Deleuze, involve the same confusion: "elevating a simple empirical figure to the status of a transcendental, at the risk of allowing the real structures of the transcendental to fall into the empirical" (DR, 154). Deleuze's solution is a transcendental empiricism that overturns the dogmatic image of thought.
9. For the full text of Chalcedon, including the Tome of Leo and all of the condemnations, see Schaff and Wace, eds., *Nicene and Post-Nicene Fathers*, second series, volume XIV, *The Seven Ecumenical Councils*.
10. For a discussion of Deleuze's engagement with this tradition, see Ramey, *The Hermetic Deleuze*. Deleuze also reworks the language of complication, implication, and explication in EP, PS and TF.
11. DR, 265, emphasis added.

12. For a concise summary of Deleuze's treatment of the differential calculus, see Smith, *Essays*, 245–6. For a discussion of his treatment of mathematics in general, see DeLanda, "Deleuze, Mathematics, and Realist Ontology."
13. Deleuze proposes the concept of different/ciation "to indicate at once both the state of differential relations in the Idea or virtual multiplicity, and the state of the qualitative and extensive series in which theses are actualized by being differenciated" (DR, 245).
14. DR, 211, emphasis added.
15. DR, 222, emphasis added.
16. DR, 211, emphasis added.
17. In his book on *Bergsonism*, published two years before *Difference and Repetition*, Deleuze suggested that the critical aspects of Bergson's philosophy all form part of a single theme: "a critique of the negative of limitation, of the negative of opposition, of general ideas" (B, 47). In his later work with Guattari as well, Deleuze challenges traditional predication theories: "Spatiotemporal relations, determinations, are not predicates of the thing but dimensions of multiplicities . . . the plane of consistency contains only haecceities, along intersecting lines. Forms and subjects are not of that world" (TP, 290).
18. This also helps to explain the difference between Deleuze and Badiou, who relies more heavily on set theory in the development of his ontology. In Badiou's *Deleuze: The Clamor of Being* he insists that the "fundamental problem" that allegedly drives Deleuze is "to submit thinking to a renewed concept of the One" (11). This seems to be a projection of his own assumption that mathematics is ontology, and that mathematics involves the strategy of "forcing" an *indiscernible* to the point that "the extension in which it appears is such that an *undecidable* statement of ontology is veridical therein, thus decided" (*Being and Event*, 428). This may very well be consistent with the formalism of the language of set theory in which one learns to "count-as-one," but it is not consistent with anything that Deleuze does anywhere in his work.
19. DR, 202, emphasis added.
20. DR, 191, 209, emphases added.
21. DR, 64, emphasis added.
22. DR, 1, emphasis added.
23. DR, 212, emphasis added.
24. DR, 13, 246, emphasis added
25. DR, 91, emphasis added.
26. For example, he observes that Nietzsche himself explicitly opposed his view to the simple "cyclical hypothesis" of ancient philosophy (DR, 242–3).
27. DR, 126, 128, emphasis added.
28. DR, 125, emphasis added in first quotation.

29. DR, 243, emphasis added
30. DR, 145, emphasis added.
31. WP, 129, emphasis added.
32. DR, 222, emphasis added.
33. DR, 95–6, emphasis added.

Chapter 4

1. It may be that the relative lack of attention to this book in the secondary literature (in comparison with *Difference and Repetition*) is related to the odd way in which it is structured. As we will see in Chapter 5, *A Thousand Plateaus* also broke the traditional rules by which books are organized. It takes more effort to engage these texts, but it helps to know that working through Deleuze's unfolding (and folding back in) of new concepts in and across series (or plateaus) itself provides an experience of how these concepts "work." Concepts like "series" (as well as "expression") continue to play a significant role in Deleuze's later collaboration with Guattari; see, for example, their analysis of literary machines in *Kafka: Toward a Minor Literature*.
2. LS, 113, emphasis added.
3. For an overview and analysis of the whole argument, see Williams, *Gilles Deleuze's Logic of Sense*, and Bowden, *The Priority of Events: Deleuze's Logic of Sense*. Although the English translation of this book renders the French title *Logique du sens* as *The Logic of Sense,* I agree with Williams and Bowden (among others) who prefer the translation *Logic of Sense*. For concise treatments of the concept of event and its relation to ethics, see Colebrook, "Deleuze and the Meaning of Life," and Boundas, "What Difference Does Deleuze's Difference Make?" For a concise treatment of the concept of sense, see Voss, "Deleuze's Rethinking of the Notion of Sense." For a fuller treatment of the theme of "the event" in Deleuze's work as a whole, see Zourabichvili, *Deleuze: A Philosophy of the Event*. For fuller treatments of Deleuze's ethics throughout his work, see the essays in Jun and Smith, eds., *Deleuze and Ethics*.
4. LS, 38, 7, emphasis added in both citations.
5. LS, 254, emphasis added.
6. LS, 109, 92, 83, emphasis added.
7. Deleuze uses a variety of terms to indicate this creative force of "paradox," including "nonsense" and the two-sided "aleatory point." In addition to the phrase *l'instance paradoxale* (the paradoxical "instance" or "agency"), he also sometimes uses *l'élément paradoxal* (the paradoxical element). The former is occasionally translated in the English version as "paradoxical entity." Although Deleuze sometimes uses these terms in distinctive ways, they often appear virtually

interchangeable (see especially the ninth series on the Problematic and the eleventh series on Nonsense).

8. See, for example, Bloom, *Descartes' Baby*, and Tremlin, *Minds and Gods*.
9. LS, 9, emphasis added. Cf. LS, 206: "Being pure saying and pure event, univocity brings in contact the inner surface of language (insistence) with the outer surface of Being (*extra-Being*)" (emphasis added).
10. LS, 108, emphasis added.
11. LS, 49. Deleuze illustrates this with Alice's discovery in the Sheep Shop of the complementarity of the "empty shelf" and the "bright thing always in the shelf next above." In *Logic of Sense* the work of Lewis Carroll is as prominent as that of the Stoics, but given our interest in theological questions, it makes more sense to focus here on the latter.
12. LS, 133, emphasis added.
13. LS, 339–40, emphasis added.
14. LS, 334. In this essay, Deleuze also reflects on the philosophical import of two of Klossowski's novels: *Roberte Ce Soir*, in which one of the main characters, Octave, is a theologian, and *The Baphomet*, in which "the spirits" rebel against the order (and judgment) of God and insufflate bodies in all sorts of devious ways.
15. TF, 61.
16. LS, 196, emphasis added.
17. LS, 323. Here "pornology" should not be confused with uncreative "pornography" that merely repeats the same.
18. LS, 118, emphasis added.
19. LS, 30, emphasis added.
20. LS, 64, 120, emphasis added.
21. LS, 139, emphasis added.
22. LS, 92, emphasis added.
23. LS, 210, emphasis added.
24. See, especially, McCauley and Lawson, *Bringing Ritual to Mind*.
25. LS, 204, emphasis added.
26. LS, 75, translation emended.
27. LS, 187, emphasis added.
28. LS, 73, emphasis added.
29. LS, 192, emphasis added.
30. The possibility of a link between *sacramentum tantum* and *eventum tantum* was suggested by Williams, *Gilles Deleuze's Logic of Sense*, 158.
31. LS, 166, emphasis added.
32. LS, 141–2, emphases in original.
33. LS, 164, emphasis added.
34. LS, 11, emphasis added.
35. For more detailed analyses of Deleuze's treatment of psychoanalysis

within this part of *Logic of Sense*, see Bowden, *The Priority of Events*, Chapter 5, and Widder, "From Negation to Disjunction."

36. LS, 261, first emphasis added.
37. LS, 250, emphasis added.
38. LS, 247, emphasis added.
39. LS, 252–4, emphases added.
40. LS, 171, translation emended (French, 176: "comédiene").
41. LS, 170, emphasis added.
42. WP, 159, first two emphases added. "From everything that a subject may live ... the event releases a vapor that does not resemble them ... the event is actualized or effectuated whenever it is inserted, willy-nilly, into a state of affairs; but it is counter-effectuated whenever it is abstracted from states of affairs so as to isolate its concept" (WP, 159).
43. See, e.g., Hallward, *Out of this World*. For reasons that should be clear from my analysis of the text, I disagree with this reading of Deleuze – and of the Stoics.
44. LS, 243, emphasis added, translation emended. Here and throughout the chapter, I have translated the French terms *effectuation* and *contre-effectuation* as "effectuation" and "counter-effectuation" rather than as actualization and counter-actualization as in the English translation *The Logic of Sense*. Deleuze could have used the French term *actualisation*, as he did throughout *Difference and Repetition*. In my view, it seems reasonable that he intentionally used the terms *effectuation* and *contre-effectuation* instead in order to link his discussion of ethics more explicitly to his reading of the Stoic cleavage of cause and *effect* (*effet*).
45. LS, 254, first emphasis added, translation emended.
46. LS, 204, translation emended.
47. LS, 179, emphasis added.
48. LS, 182, emphasis added, translation emended.

Chapter 5

1. For more detailed analyses of the *Capitalism and Schizophrenia* project, see Buchanan, *Deleuze and Guattari's Anti-Oedipus: A Reader's Guide*; Holland, *Deleuze and Guattari's Anti-Oedipus: Introduction to Schizoanalysis*; Massumi, *A User's Guide to Capitalism and Schizophrenia: Deviations from Deleuze and Guattari*; Kerslake, *Deleuze and the Unconscious*; and Patton, *Deleuze and the Political.* For a discussion of the shift in vocabularies from Deleuze's earlier work to his collaboration with Guattari, see Smith, "From the Surface to the Depths."
2. Deleuze emphasizes that even "arboreal" and "rhizomic" are not rival images to be judged according to their likeness to an ideal model;

rather, the first is that which "operates as" a transcendent model while the latter "overturns the model and outlines a map" (TP, 22).

3. AO, 342, emphasis added.
4. AO, 85, emphasis added.
5. TP, 168, 169, emphasis added.
6. AO, 9, 17.
7. AO, 309. Cf. AO, 271, for a discussion of the sense in which the capitalist full body is also "naked."
8. TP, 183, emphasis added.
9. TP, 157, emphasis added.
10. TP, 562, 563, emphases added.
11. ECC, 129, second emphasis added.
12. ECC, 127, first emphasis added.
13. Nietzsche, *The Anti-Christ*, 39 (§42).
14. ECC, 46, emphasis added.
15. AO, 121, emphasis added.
16. As Eduardo Viveiros de Castro puts it, Deleuze and Guattari's use of such terms can appear "quaintly archaic," and is sure to make the anthropological reader wince ("Intensive Filiation and Demonic Alliance," 222). However, even a cursory reading of *Anti-Oedipus* reveals a revolutionary usage of these terms, a provocative appropriation of old designations that is designed to challenge prejudices rather than reinforce them.
17. AO, 353–4, 417.
18. AO, 13. Cf. the translator's note on the French phrase "se rebattre sur" at AO, 11.
19. AO, 202, emphasis added.
20. AO, 217, emphasis added.
21. "When the Christians took possession of the Empire, a complementary duality reappeared between those who wanted to do everything possible to reconstruct the Urstaat from the elements they found in the immanence of the objective Roman world, and the purists, who wanted a fresh start in the wilderness, a new beginning for a new alliance, a rediscovery of the Egyptian and Syriac inspiration that would provide the impetus for a transcendent Urstaat. What strange machines those were that cropped up on columns and in tree trunks! In this sense, Christianity was able to develop a whole set of paranoiac and celibate machines, a whole string of paranoiacs and perverts who also form part of our history's horizon and people our calendar" (AO, 241–2).
22. TP, 196–7, emphasis added.
23. TP, 126–8. For a discussion of faciality and politics, see Bignall, "Dismantling the Face."
24. AO, 219, emphasis added.
25. CC, 97. In Chapter VIII, Deleuze discusses Masoch's portrayal of both

Cain and Christ who, with the help of Eve and Mary, abolish the likeness to the father and expel the father from the symbolic realm; this involves a desexualization and resexualization, a painful second birth mediated only by, or totally invested upon, the mother. In Chapter X, he notes Nietzsche's treatment of the "essentially religious" problem of the meaning of pain. For Nietzsche if pain and suffering are meaningful, it must be because someone enjoys them. Three possibilities arise. The "normal" answer is that the gods are pleased by human pain; the "perverse" answers are that the one who inflicts or the one who suffers must enjoy it. Deleuze observes: "It should be clear that the normal answer is the most fantastic, the most psychotic of the three" (CC, 188).

26. Cf. AO, 244, 284.
27. AO, 249, emphasis added.
28. AO, 248. For discussions of the capitalist "axiomatic," see Holland, *Deleuze and Guattari's Anti-Oedipus*, Chapter 3; Patton, *Deleuze and the Political*, Chapter 5; Buchanan, "Power, Theory and Praxis."
29. AO, 245, translation emended, emphasis added.
30. AO, 289; cf. 236.
31. AO, 91, emphasis added.
32. TP, 460, emphasis added.
33. AO, 354, 374. Although *Anti-Oedipus* does not use the designation "war machine," the summary task of schizoanalysis sounds very much like the nomadic creation of smooth space: "the task of schizoanalysis is that of tirelessly taking apart egos and their presuppositions; liberating the prepersonal singularities they enclose and repress; mobilizing the flows they would be capable of transmitting, receiving or intercepting; establishing always further and more sharply the schizzes and the breaks well below conditions of identity; and assembling the desiring-machines that countersect everyone and group everyone with others" (AO, 396).
34. TP, 402, emphasis added.
35. TP, 415–16.
36. TP, 422–3, emphasis added.
37. For accessible introductions to some of the relevant research on these themes within the bio-cultural study of religion, see Atran, *Talking to the Enemy*; Teehan, *In the Name of God*; Strozier et al., *The Fundamentalist Mindset*; and Stern, *Terror in the Name of God*.
38. For a different sort of typology, based on a logical combinatoire formed by the categories of power and economics, see Holland, *Deleuze and Guattari's Anti-Oedipus*, 59.
39. AO, 238–9, emphasis added.
40. Elsewhere I have explored the relative infeasibility of the (doubly promiscuous) upper left and the (doubly prudish) lower right quadrants,

which we might call the "prodigal" and "penurious" trajectories, respectively. See Shults, "Theology After Pandora."

41. In some places, Deleuze makes a strong distinction between "affect" and "feeling" (French, *sentiment*) preferring the former designation over the latter (e.g., TP, 441). On the other hand, as we saw in Chapter 2, he also approvingly describes Nietzsche's overman as "a new way of feeling" (NP, 163). Even within TP, he describes the apprehension of a rhizomic multiplicity as an "*I feel*" (TP, 35; French, *je sens*). Indeed, he wrote an entire book on *Logique de Sens*. Like Deleuze, I am less interested in the designation "feeling" than the use to which it is put.
42. AO, 6, emphasis added.
43. TP, 309, emphasis added.
44. Deleuze, "Seminar on Spinoza/Course Vincennes," 25/11/1980, available at www.webdeleuze.com (accessed 10 September 2013). Cf. DR, 276.
45. TP, 198. Cf. AO, 404. For an analysis of Deleuze's approach to these paintings from the perspective of art history, see Watson, "The Face of Christ."
46. FB, 11, 101, emphasis added.
47. AO, 85–6, emphasis added.
48. TP, 264, 266, emphasis added.
49. TP, 268–77.
50. TP, 172, emphasis added.
51. ECC, 135, emphasis added
52. NP, 185, emphasis added.
53. NP, 101, emphasis added.
54. Nietzsche, *Twilight of the Idols*, 182.

Chapter 6

1. WP, 92, emphasis added.
2. AO, 65–6, emphasis added. Cf. AO, 342.
3. For additional arguments, based on other warrants, that support the claim that Christianity played a special role in the production of contemporary atheism, see Bloch, *Atheism in Christianity*; Buckley, *At the Origins of Modern Atheism*; and Berger, *The Social Reality of Religion*.
4. See Deleuze's lectures on Spinoza, available at www.webdeleuze.com (accessed 10 September 2013).
5. Here I mean "retroductive" in the sense explained in Chapter 1 above. Cf. Shults, "The Problem of Good," and *Theology After the Birth of God*.
6. See C2, 166, 181; WP, 202, and the discussion below.
7. PI, 27, emphases added.
8. LS, 316. See also his discussion of the "pleats of matter," and the

folding, unfolding, and refolding forces of nature in *The Fold*. Published in French in 1988, after his initial collaborations with Guattari, this book offers another analysis of Leibniz that goes beyond his earlier treatments in *Difference and Repetition* and *Logic of Sense* but still appropriates resources he finds in the Stoics (e.g., 120).

9. WP, 75, emphasis added. Reading through interviews of Deleuze, especially those in *Two Regimes of Madness*, it quickly becomes clear that he is a "secularist" in the sense I am using the term. This also comes through in his treatments of or discussions with Foucault; see, for example, Deleuze, *Foucault*, and "Intellectuals and Power."
10. For examples, see Kohn and Roth, eds., *Daoist Identity*, and Pyysiäinen, *Supernatural Agents*.
11. Cf. WP, 5, 43, 202.
12. See, for example Simpson, *Deleuze and Theology*; Sherman, "No Werewolves in Theology?"; and Davies, "Thinking Difference." Simpson defends a position called "Radical Orthodoxy" and the availability of salvation in the ecclesial assemblage; Sherman the transcendent becomings of the Eucharist and *theosis*; and Davies the *analogia entis* of the "apophatic" tradition in Christianity. The positions of all three explicitly rely on appeals to divine revelation in Christ and the ritual mediation of the Church.
13. See for example Justaert, *Theology After Deleuze*; Adkins and Hinlicky, *Rethinking Philosophy and Theology with Deleuze*; and Goodchild, "A Theological Passion for Deleuze." Justaert appropriates Deleuze at the cutting edge of a Roman Catholic assemblage. Inspired by Deleuze, she argues that liberation theologies can envision churches that are radically different – churches that resist the captivation of desire and the exploitation endemic to capitalist society (130). This is a clear example of what I have called an "egalitarian" line of flight within Christianity, and it offers resources for battling the sociographic prudery of the Church and male-dominated expressions of its anthropomorphic promiscuity. However, one can still see evidence of sacerdotal forces. For example, she refigures the Catholic Eucharist as an experience of the power of the life of Christ, a repetition of the Christ-event as that moment at which God's power was "at its summit" (99).

    Adkins and Hinlicky are at the cutting edge of a deterritorialization of Lutheran theology. They appropriate a variety of Deleuzian concepts in their critique of the "apophatic" escape route they find so prevalent in Christian theology, and call for a robustly "kataphatic" or affirmative approach in theology. In their attempt to develop a cartography of the assemblages of philosophy, religion, and theology, they reject any appeal to transcendence that relies on the "analogy of being." Nevertheless, insofar as Adkins and Hinlicky finally end up preserving the "genuine" divine transcendence of the Triune God through a refigured version of Luther's distinction between *deus absconditus* and *deus revelatus*, and explicitly affirm the eschatological presence of the crucified Messiah in the Eucharistic community, they are pulled back by the forces of the sacerdotal trajectory.

Goodchild was one of the earliest scholars to engage Deleuzian "theology" in detail. Inspired by Deleuze, he calls for the reconstitution of theology as the "discipline which creates, relates and assesses possible modes of existence." Unlike Justaert, Adkins and Hinlicky, Goodchild explicitly rejects the idea of God as "a subject with specific intentions" or a "manifestation in the form of a specific society or Church." Nevertheless, his early work emphasized the role of divine revelation in Christ and the need for Transcendence (e.g., "Theological Passion," 363; *Gilles Deleuze and the Question of Philosophy*, 159). In my reading of the development of his thought, it seems like these emphases wane when he shifts his focus to a critique of capitalism (e.g., *Capitalism and Religion*, more so in *Theology of Money*, and even more so in "Philosophy as a Way of Life"). In these later works, as well as in his contributions to *Rethinking Philosophy of Religion*, Goodchild is part of the group I identify in the next endnote. For his definition of "religion," see *Capitalism*, 227.

14. See, for example Crockett, *Radical Political Theology*; Barber, "Immanence and the Re-expression of the World"; Anthony Paul Smith, "The Judgment of God and the Immeasurable"; and Goodchild (see endnote 13 above). Crockett engages not only Deleuze, but also Derrida, Badiou, Nancy, Agamben, Žižek, and others, in his proposal for a radical postmodern theology that benefits from the momentum of the "death of God" movement in the 1960s, but takes political and ecological concerns more seriously. Instead of emphasizing the "messianic," he opts for what he calls (following Malabou) a "plastic" deconstruction of Christianity. Inspired by Deleuze, he argues that the task of theology is "to think the event" (144). As he puts it elsewhere, "we need to learn how to think and how to live, and this is what theology is truly about" (*Religion, Politics and the Earth*, 145). This fits with my description of theology as the critique and construction of hypotheses about the conditions for axiological engagement. For the reasons explained in the main text, however, I believe that his definition of religion as dealing with "orientations in the ultimate sense" is problematic, at least in the context of dialogue with the wider empirical study of religion in the bio-cultural sciences, which he dismisses, in my view, all too quickly (*Radical Political Theology*, 15, 154).

    In his analysis of Deleuze's "theology," Barber wants to make a strong distinction between religion and transcendence. Deleuze rejects transcendence but that does not mean, insists Barber, he is not "already religious" (38). Deleuze shares with religion a "desire to heal suffering"

(46). This use of the term religion, in my view, is not helpful. Many atheists want to heal suffering too. Why call this "religion?" Elsewhere, Barber describes the secular as "reinstituting a new transcendence of natural signification" ("Secularism," 169), which is just as ignorant of its fictive production as religion. I share Barber's enthusiasm for being intentional about naming the differences between immanence and its fictive productions, but prefer other ways of designating secularity. In his recent book *Deleuze and the Naming of God*, Barber consistently fights against the equation of religion with Christianity, a presumption he finds too common in the philosophy of religion. Such a presumption is indeed too common in that field, but the empirically based sciences in the bio-cultural study of religion moved beyond such naive and colonizing equations long ago. This is another reason I propose bringing the latter into critical dialogue with the former. Barber's own proposal, building on Deleuze's concept of differential immanence, calls for the "fabulation of icons" in the naming of "God." Given Deleuze's consistent hammering on *icons*, it seems to me that the "fabulation of simulacra" would be more appropriate. Nevertheless, I appreciate his Friendly recognition that Deleuze is indeed a "theologian."

Following Laruelle's concept of "non-philosophy," Anthony Paul Smith proposes a "non-theology," which would be a "science of theology" that is not itself "theological" and would "think past political theology in a way that would allow us to select the best political theology" (85). This proposal is explicitly offered as an alternative to what Smith calls Deleuze and Guattari's "political anti-theology," which in his approach would be used as "simple material" for the constructions of "non-theology." I include Smith in this group because of his consistent rejection of transcendence and his interest in finding resources within Christianity for developing new hypotheses about the conditions for axiological engagement, despite the fact that he calls this "non-theology." As we have seen, Deleuze has his own versions of "anti-theology" that are "theological" in this sense. Laruelle himself provides an example of an "atheist practice" that tries to make "God and Christ intelligible without simply renouncing them or believing in them" (*Future Christ*, 25). One of his main projects in that context is the extraction of the notion of "heresy" from Christianity, which he uses to alter the practice of philosophy. The danger with Laruelle's continuing use of the messianic language of the "coming" of Christ and the ecclesial language of "Future Christianity," in my view, is that it inadvertently activates theogonic forces and is far more confusing than Deleuze's straightforward use of the concept *Anti-Christ*.

15. Three of the chapters in *Deleuze and Religion*, edited by Mary Bryden, illustrate this Friendly Deleuzian business. In "The Organism as the Judgment of God," Protevi explicitly deals with the relation between

Deleuze's theology and his treatment of biological and social organization. In fact, his chapter is subtitled "on biology, theology and politics." When Deleuze says "God is a Lobster," he is referring to the process of stratification, to one aspect of the abstract machine of nature. When this process is overcoded by the despotic machine, the illusion of a transcendent God is produced. In this sense, argues Protevi, the crustacean God produces, but does not resemble, the "illusion of the organism as the judgment of God" (40). In "Embodied Anti-theology," Poxon also deals with Deleuze's battle with the judgment of God and exposits his treatment of the Antichrist "as a vital anti-theological trope, challenging the divine order and expressing the creative power of pure affirmation." This Deleuzian "anti-theology," she suggests, may in fact be "a 'true' *liberation* theology" (42, 50). In "The Doctrine of Univocity," Daniel Smith notes Deleuze's fascination with theological concepts, especially those developed in medieval theology, and explains the significance of his appropriation of the concept of univocity in his reading of Spinoza's reaction to it. This chapter was reprinted in Smith's *Essays*, which contains several other analyses of Deleuze's hypotheses about the conditions for real experience.

Many other Deleuze scholars have pointed to the centrality of his "theology" – and developed their own "theological" hypotheses about the conditions for axiological engagement – even when they do not use those designations (and there is no reason they should). I offer just a few examples, in alphabetical order. In his analysis of Deleuze's philosophy of difference, Bell notes that philosophy itself seems to have affected the development of the relationship between human beings and their tools. He argues that the task of philosophy is "to engender the *conditions* that allow for something to be thought," and that to accomplish this it is necessary for the thinking that is engendered in thought to "maintain itself as a dynamic system at the edge of chaos" (*Philosophy at the Edge of Chaos*, 207–9, emphasis added). In discussing Deleuze's "transcendental empiricism," Buchanan points to the importance of the theory of relations as external to their terms. This determination, according to Deleuze, "is the condition of possibility for a solution to the empiricist problem: *how can a subject transcending the given be constituted in the given*? It is this 'solution', as it were, that gives rise to transcendental empiricism, for what it does is flatten the ascension of the transcendental term so that the synthetic process is rendered as movement across a surface instead of a rising-up" (*Deleuzism*, 85). The conditions *for* axiological engagement are "flat" and "at the edge of chaos."

In several places, some of which I have already identified in earlier notes, Hughes argues that Deleuze's project as a whole can be clarified by careful attention to his relation to Kant and Husserl, both of whom were "theologians" in my sense. In discussing his relation to the latter in *Deleuze and the Genesis of Representation*, Hughes suggests that Deleuze's thought takes place "entirely under the sign of the reduction, and that it is concerned almost exclusively with the problem of genesis" (19). Although Deleuze goes beyond Husserlian "phenomenology," just as he went beyond Kant, to understand his texts requires reading them as a "theorization of genesis" (16). Hughes helpfully identifies a stable structure that underlies several of his major works, a structure that is systematically developed despite the use of vocabularies that do not cohere. This structure is meant to account for the way in which representation is produced out of the field of materiality (for a summary, see 156). Ansell Pearson summarizes Deleuze's contribution to philosophical discourse and "our practices of becoming who we are" in the following way: it is a fundamental reconfiguration that opens up "history and politics to a 'creative evolution' by showing the vital possibilities of what one might call a rhizomatics of historical time, in which the diagram moves beyond the limits of a filiative history and politics and weaves a supple and transversal network of novel alliances that is always perpendicular to the vertical structure of established and official history" (*Germinal Life*, 223). In other words, Deleuze analyzed *and* altered the conditions for axiological engagement.

More than most Deleuze scholars, Widder draws special attention to the way in which Deleuze's rejection of transcendence and hypotheses about an "originary web" of differences "demolishes the Christian God." Widder offers his own analysis of Ockham, who goes beyond Scotus, arguing that the former's dissolution of universals contributed even more powerfully to the liberation of individual difference. "It is only appropriate, even if ironic, that this conclusion – which dissolves the Christian God as well – should follow from Christian philosophy itself" (*Genealogies of Difference*, 148). In other words, Christianity secretes atheism, once it is appropriately hammered. For Widder's analysis of the way in which Deleuze's hypotheses pragmatically alter the conditions for axiological engagement, see his *Political Theory After Deleuze*. Williams has explored and expanded Deleuze's speculative and practical hypotheses in a variety of places, some of which we have noted in previous chapters. Here I draw attention to Chapter 4 of his *Gilles Deleuze's Logic of Sense*, which provides a detailed analysis of Deleuze's ethics. At its heart, argues Williams, is the claim that "only by affirming our singular place along series that also consume it can we live well with the ever present danger of resentment and discouragement. *Only acts that redouble the event can express all its most intense potentials while avoiding the fatal beliefs in eternal beings or values, for these can never outlive the certainty of future waste and collapse that stand as a condition for any action*" (174, emphasis in original).

Bibliography

Adkins, Brent and Paul R. Hinlicky, *Rethinking Philosophy and Theology with Deleuze: A New Cartography* (Edinburgh: Edinburgh University Press, 2013).
Ansell Pearson, Keith, ed., *Deleuze and Philosophy: The Difference Engineer* (London: Routledge, 1997).
Ansell Pearson, Keith, *Germinal Life: The Difference and Repetition of Deleuze* (London: Routledge, 1999).
Armstrong, Karen, *The Great Transformation: The Beginning of our Religious Traditions* (New York: Knopf, 2006).
Atran, Scott, *Cognitive Foundations of Natural History: Towards an Anthropology of Science* (Cambridge: Cambridge University Press, 1990).
Atran, Scott, *In Gods We Trust: The Evolutionary Landscape of Religion* (Oxford: Oxford University Press, 2002).
Atran, Scott, *Talking to the Enemy: Faith, Brotherhood, and the (Un) Making of Terrorists* (New York: HarperCollins, 2010).
Badiou, Alain, *Being and Event*, trans. Oliver Feltham (New York: Continuum, [1988] 2005).
Badiou, Alain, *Deleuze: The Clamor of Being*, trans. Louise Burchill (Minneapolis: University of Minnesota Press, [1997] 2008).
Barber, Daniel Colucciello, "Secularism, Immanence, and the Philosophy of Religion," in Anthony Paul Smith and Daniel Whistler, eds., *After the Postsecular and the Postmodern: New Essays in Continental Philosophy of Religion* (Newcastle upon Tyne: Cambridge Scholars Publishing, 2010), 152–71.
Barber, Daniel Colucciello, "Immanence and the Re-expression of the World," *SubStance* 39.1 (2010): 38–48.
Barber, Daniel Colucciello, *Deleuze and the Naming of God: Post-Secularism and the Future of Immanence* (Edinburgh: Edinburgh University Press, 2013).
Barrett, Justin, "Dumb Gods, Petitionary Prayer and the Cognitive Science of Religion," in Illka Pyysiäinen and Veikko Anttonen, eds., *Current Approaches in the Cognitive Science of Religion* (London: Continuum, 2002), 93–109.
Barrett, Justin, *Why Would Anyone Believe in God?* (Lanham, MD: AltaMira Press, 2004).

Bell, Jeffrey A., *Philosophy at the Edge of Chaos: Gilles Deleuze and the Philosophy of Difference* (Toronto: University of Toronto Press, 2006).
Bell, Jeffrey A., *Deleuze's Hume: Philosophy, Culture and the Scottish Enlightenment* (Edinburgh: Edinburgh University Press, 2009).
Bellah, Robert, *Religion in Human Evolution: From the Paleolithic to the Axial Age* (Cambridge, MA: Harvard University Press, 2011).
Berger, Peter, *The Social Reality of Religion* (London: Faber & Faber, 1969).
Bignall, Simone, "Dismantling the Face: Pluralism and the Politics of Recognition," *Deleuze Studies* 6.3 (2012): 389–410.
Bloch, Ernst, *Atheism in Christianity* (New York: Herder & Herder, 1972).
Bloom, Paul, *Descartes' Baby: How the Science of Child Development Explains What Makes Us Human* (New York: Basic Books, 2004).
Boundas, Constantin, "What Difference Does Deleuze's Difference Make?," in Constantin Boundas, ed., *Deleuze and Philosophy* (Edinburgh: Edinburgh University Press, 2006), 3–30.
Bowden, Sean, *The Priority of Events: Deleuze's Logic of Sense* (Edinburgh: Edinburgh University Press, 2011).
Boyer, Pascal, *The Naturalness of Religious Ideas: A Cognitive Theory of Religion* (Berkeley: University of California Press, 1994).
Boyer, Pascal, *Religion Explained: The Human Instincts that Fashion Gods, Spirits and Ancestors* (London: Random House, 2001).
Bryant, Levi, *Difference and Givenness: Deleuze's Transcendental Empiricism and the Ontology of Immanence* (Evanston: Northwestern University Press, 2008).
Bryden, Mary, ed., *Deleuze and Religion* (London: Routledge, 2001).
Buchanan, Ian, *Deleuzism: A Metacommentary* (Durham, NC: Duke University Press, 2000).
Buchanan, Ian, *Deleuze and Guattari's Anti-Oedipus: A Reader's Guide* (London: Continuum, 2008).
Buchanan, Ian, "Power, Theory and Praxis," in Ian Buchanan and Nicholas Thoburn, eds., *Deleuze and Politics* (Edinburgh: Edinburgh University Press, 2008), 13–34.
Buckley, Michael J., *At the Origins of Modern Atheism* (New Haven: Yale University Press, 1987).
Bulbulia, Joseph et al., eds., *The Evolution of Religion: Studies, Theories and Critiques* (Santa Margarita, CA: Collins, 2008).
Colebrook, Claire, *Gilles Deleuze* (London: Routledge, 2002).
Colebrook, Claire, "Deleuze and the Meaning of Life," in Constantin Boundas, ed., *Deleuze and Philosophy* (Edinburgh: Edinburgh University Press, 2006), 121–32.
Colebrook, Claire, "The Secret of Theory," *Deleuze Studies* 4.3 (2010): 287–300.

Crockett, Clayton, *Radical Political Theology: Religion and Politics after Liberalism* (New York: Columbia University Press, 2011).
Crockett, Clayton, *Deleuze After Badiou: Ontology, Multiplicity and Event* (New York: Columbia University Press, 2013).
Crockett, Clayton and Jeffrey W. Robbins, *Religion, Politics and the Earth: The New Materialism* (New York: Palgrave Macmillan, 2012).
Davies, Oliver, "Thinking Difference: A Comparative Study of Gilles Deleuze, Plotinus and Meister Eckhart," in Mary Bryden, ed., *Deleuze and Religion* (London: Routledge, 2001), 76–86.
De Beistegui, Miguel, *Immanence: Deleuze and Philosophy* (Edinburgh: Edinburgh University Press, 2010).
De Castro, Eduardo Viveiros, "Intensive Filiation and Demonic Alliance," in Casper Bruun Jensen and Kjetil Rodje, eds., *Deleuzian Intersections: Science, Technology, Anthropology* (New York: Berghahn Books, 2010), 219–53.
De Gaynesford, Maximilian, "Bodily Organs and Organisation," in Mary Bryden, ed., *Deleuze and Religion* (London: Routledge, 2001), 87–98.
DeLanda, Manuel, "Deleuze, Mathematics, and Realist Ontology," in Daniel Smith and Henry Somers-Hall, eds., *The Cambridge Companion to Deleuze* (Cambridge University Press, 2012), 220–38.
Deleuze, Gilles, *Empiricism and Subjectivity: An Essay on Hume's Theory of Human Nature*, trans. Constantin V. Boundas (New York: Columbia University Press, [1953] 1991).
Deleuze, Gilles, *Nietzsche and Philosophy*, trans. Hugh Tomlinson (New York: Columbia University Press, [1962] 1983).
Deleuze, Gilles, *Kant's Critical Philosophy: The Doctrine of the Faculties*, trans. Hugh Tomlinson and Barbara Habberjam (Minneapolis: University of Minnesota Press, [1963] 1984).
Deleuze, Gilles, *Proust and Signs: The Complete Text*, trans. Richard Howard (New York: George Braziller, [1964, revised 1970 and 1976] 1972).
Deleuze, Gilles, *Bergsonism*, trans. Hugh Tomlinson and Barbara Habberjam (New York: Zone Books, [1966] 1988).
Deleuze, Gilles, *Coldness and Cruelty*, trans. Jean McNeil (New York: Zone Books, [1967] 1989).
Deleuze, Gilles, *Difference and Repetition*, trans. Paul Patton (New York: Columbia University Press, [1968] 1994).
Deleuze, Gilles, *Expressionism in Philosophy: Spinoza*, trans. Martin Joughin (New York: Zone Books, [1968] 1990).
Deleuze, Gilles, *The Logic of Sense*, trans. Mark Lester with Charles Stivale (New York: Continuum, [1969] 2004).
Deleuze, Gilles, *Spinoza: Practical Philosophy*, trans. Robert Hurley (San Francisco: City Lights, [1970] 1988).

Deleuze, Gilles, *Cinema 1: The Movement-Image*, trans. Hugh Tomlinson and Barbara Habberjam (London: Continuum, [1983] 2005).
Deleuze, Gilles, *Cinema 2: The Time-Image*, trans. Hugh Tomlinson and Robert Galeta (London: Continuum, [1985] 2005).
Deleuze, Gilles, *Foucault*, trans. Seán Hand (London: Continuum, [1986] 1999).
Deleuze, Gilles, *The Fold: Leibniz and the Baroque*, trans. Tom Conley (London: Continuum, [1988] 2006).
Deleuze, Gilles, *Negotiations*, trans. Martin Joughin (New York: Columbia University Press, [1990] 1995).
Deleuze, Gilles, *Essays Critical and Clinical*, trans. Daniel W. Smith and Michael A. Greco (Minneapolis: University of Minnesota, [1993] 1997).
Deleuze, Gilles, *Two Regimes of Madness: Texts and Interviews 1975–1995*, trans. Ames Hodges and Mike Taormina (Los Angeles: Semiotext(e), [2001] 2007).
Deleuze, Gilles, *Desert Islands and Other Texts*, trans. Michael Taormina (Los Angeles: Semiotext(e), [2002] 2004).
Deleuze, Gilles, *Pure Immanence: Essays on A Life*, trans. Anne Boyman (New York: Zone Books, 2005).
Deleuze, Gilles and Claire Parnet, *Dialogues*, trans. Hugh Tomlinson and Barbara Habberjam (London: The Athlone Press, [1977] 1987).
Deleuze, Gilles and Claire Parnet: *Dialogues II*, trans. Hugh Tomlinson and Barbara Habberjam (London: Continuum, [1977] 2006).
Deleuze, Gilles and Félix Guattari, *Anti-Oedipus: Capitalism and Schizophrenia*, trans. Robert Hurley, Mark Seem, and Helen R. Lane (London: Continuum, [1972] 2004).
Deleuze, Gilles and Félix Guattari, *Kafka: Toward a Minor Literature*, trans. Dana Polan (Minneapolis: University of Minnesota Press, [1975] 1986).
Deleuze, Gilles and Félix Guattari, *A Thousand Plateaus*, trans. Brian Massumi (London: Continuum, [1980] 2004).
Deleuze, Gilles and Félix Guattari, *What is Philosophy?*, trans. Hugh Tomlinson and Graham Burchell (London: Verso, [1991] 1994).
Deleuze, Gilles with Michel Foucault, "Intellectuals and Power," in Foucault, *Language, Counter-Memory, Practice*, ed. Donald F. Bouchard and Sherry Simon (Ithaca: Cornell University Press, 1977), 205–17.
Due, Reidar, *Deleuze* (Cambridge: Polity, 2007).
Flaxman, Gregory, *Gilles Deleuze and the Fabulation of Philosophy* (Minneapolis: University of Minnesota Press, 2012).
Goodchild, Philip, *Gilles Deleuze and the Question of Philosophy* (London: Associated University Press, 1996).
Goodchild, Philip, *Deleuze and Guattari: An Introduction to the Politics of Desire* (London: Sage Publications, 1996).
Goodchild, Philip, "A Theological Passion for Deleuze," *Theology* 99 (1996): 357–65.

Goodchild, Philip, "Why is Philosophy so Compromised with God?" in Mary Bryden, ed., *Deleuze and Religion* (London: Routledge, 2001), 156–66.

Goodchild, Philip, ed., *Rethinking Philosophy of Religion: Approaches from Continental Philosophy* (New York: Fordham, 2002).

Goodchild, Philip, *Capitalism and Religion: The Price of Piety* (London: Routledge, 2002).

Goodchild, Philip, *Theology of Money* (Durham, NC: Duke University Press, 2009).

Goodchild, Philip, "Philosophy as a Way of Life: Deleuze on Thinking and Money," *SubStance* 39.1 (2010): 24–37.

Grant, Iain Hamilton, "'At the Mountains of Madness': The Demonology of the New Earth and the Politics of Becoming," in Keith Ansell Pearson, ed., *Deleuze and Philosophy* (London: Routledge, 1997), 93–114.

Guthrie, Stewart, *Faces in the Clouds: A New Theory of Religion* (New York: Oxford University Press, 1993).

Hallward, Peter, *Out of This World: Deleuze and the Philosophy of Creation* (London: Verso, 2006).

Hardt, Michael, *Gilles Deleuze: An Apprenticeship in Philosophy* (Minneapolis: University of Minnesota Press, 1993).

Hegel, G. W. F., *Lectures on the Philosophy of Religion*, three volumes, ed. P. C. Hodgson, trans. R. F. Brown et al. (Berkeley: University of California Press, 1985).

Holland, Eugene W., *Deleuze and Guattari's Anti-Oedipus: Introduction to Schizoanalysis* (London: Routledge, 1999).

Hughes, Joe, *Deleuze and the Genesis of Representation* (London: Continuum, 2008).

Hughes, Joe, *Deleuze's Difference and Repetition: A Reader's Guide* (London: Continuum, 2009).

Hughes, Joe, *Philosophy After Deleuze* (London: Bloomsbury, 2012).

Jensen, Casper Bruun and Kjetil Rodje, eds., *Deleuzian Intersections: Science, Technology, Anthropology* (New York: Berghahn Books, 2010).

Jun, Nathan and Daniel W. Smith, eds., *Deleuze and Ethics* (Edinburgh: Edinburgh University Press, 2011).

Justaert, Kristien, *Theology After Deleuze* (New York: Continuum, 2012).

Kant, Immanuel, *Critique of Pure Reason*, trans. N. K. Smith (New York: St. Martin's Press, [1787] 1965).

Kant, Immanuel, *Critique of Practical Reason*, trans. L. W. Beck (New York: Macmillan, [1788] 1993).

Kant, Immanuel, *Critique of Judgment*, trans. W. S. Pluhar (Indianapolis: Hackett, [1790] 1987).

Kant, Immanuel, *Religion Within the Limits of Reason Alone*, trans. T. M. Greene and H. H. Hudson (New York: Harper, [1793] 1960).

Kerslake, Christian, *Deleuze and the Unconscious* (London: Continuum, 2007).

Kerslake, Christian, *Immanence and the Vertigo of Philosophy* (Edinburgh: Edinburgh University Press, 2009).

Kirkpatrick, Lee A., *Attachment, Evolution, and the Psychology of Religion* (New York: The Guilford Press, 2005).

Klossowski, Pierre, *Roberte Ce Soir and The Revocation of the Edict of Nantes*, trans. A. Wainhouse (New York: Marion Boyars, [1953] 1997).

Klossowski, Pierre, *The Baphomet*, trans. S. Hawkes and S. Sartarelli (New York: Marsilio Publishers, [1965] 1988).

Klossowski, Pierre, *Nietzsche and the Vicious Circle*, trans. Daniel W. Smith (London: Continuum, [1969] 2005).

Kohn, Livia and Harold D. Roth, eds., *Daoist Identity: History, Lineage and Ritual* (Honolulu: University of Hawaii Press, 2002).

Lambert, Gregg, *In Search of a New Image of Thought: Gilles Deleuze and Philosophical Expressionism* (Minneapolis: University of Minnesota Press, 2012).

Laruelle, Francois, *Future Christ: A Lesson in Heresy*, trans. Anthony Paul Smith (New York: Continuum, 2010).

Latour, Bruno, *On the Cult of the Factish Gods* (Durham, NC: Duke University Press, 2010).

Leibniz, G. W. *Theodicy*, trans. E. M. Huggard (La Salle: Open Court, 1985).

Leibniz, G. W., *Philosophical Texts*, trans. and ed. R. S. Woolhouse and Richard Francks (Oxford: Oxford University Press, 1998).

Lewis-Williams, David, *Conceiving God: The Cognitive Origin and Evolution of Religion* (New York: Thames & Hudson, 2010).

McCauley, Robert N., *Why Religion is Natural and Science is Not* (New York: Oxford University Press, 2011).

McCauley, Robert N. and E. Thomas Lawson, *Bringing Ritual to Mind: Psychological Foundations of Cultural Forms* (Cambridge: Cambridge University Press, 2002).

Massumi, Brian, *A User's Guide to Capitalism and Schizophrenia: Deviations from Deleuze and Guattari* (Cambridge, MA: MIT Press, 1992).

May, Todd, *Gilles Deleuze: An Introduction* (Cambridge: Cambridge University Press, 2005).

Nail, Thomas, "Expression, Immanence and Constructivism: 'Spinozism' and Gilles Deleuze," *Deleuze Studies* 2.2 (2008): 201–19.

Nietzsche, Friedrich, *The Will to Power*, trans. Walter Kaufmann and R. J. Hollingdale (New York: Vintage, 1968).

Nietzsche, Friedrich, *Beyond Good and Evil*, trans. Judith Norman (Cambridge: Cambridge University Press, 2002).

Nietzsche, Friedrich, *The Anti-Christ, Ecce Homo, Twilight of the Idols*, trans. Judith Norman (Cambridge: Cambridge University Press, 2005).

Nietzsche, Friedrich, *Thus Spoke Zarathustra*, trans. Adrian del Caro (Cambridge: Cambridge University Press, 2006).
Patton, Paul, ed., *Deleuze: A Critical Reader* (Oxford: Blackwell, 1996).
Patton, Paul, *Deleuze and the Political* (London: Routledge, 2000).
Poxon, Judith, "Embodied Anti-theology: The Body without Organs and the Judgment of God," in Mary Bryden, ed., *Deleuze and Religion* (London: Routledge, 2001), 42–50.
Protevi, John, "The Organism as the Judgment of God: Aristotle, Kant and Deleuze on Nature (that is, on biology, theology and politics)," in Mary Bryden, ed., *Deleuze and Religion* (London: Routledge, 2001), 30–41.
Protevi, John, *Life, War, Earth: Deleuze and the Sciences* (Minneapolis: University of Minnesota, 2013).
Pyysiäinen, Ilkka, *How Religion Works: Towards a New Cognitive Science of Religion* (Leiden: Brill, 2003).
Pyysiäinen, Ilkka, *Supernatural Agents: Why we Believe in Souls, Gods and Buddhas* (Oxford: Oxford University Press, 2009).
Ramey, Joshua, *The Hermetic Deleuze: Philosophy and the Spiritual Ordeal* (Durham, NC: Duke University Press, 2012).
Rossano, Matt J., *Supernatural Selection: How Religion Evolved* (Oxford: Oxford University Press, 2010).
Schaff, Philip and Henry Wace, *Nicene and Post-Nicene Fathers*, second series, volume XIV, *The Seven Ecumenical Councils* (Grand Rapids: Eerdmans, 1988).
Schaller, Mark et al., eds., *Evolution, Culture, and the Human Mind* (New York: Psychology Press, 2010).
Sherman, Jacob Holsinger, "No Werewolves in Theology? Transcendence, Immanence, and Becoming-Divine in Deleuze," *Modern Theology* 25:1 (January 2009).
Shults, F. LeRon, "The Problem of Good (and Evil): Arguing about Axiological Conditions in Science and Religion," in Wesley Wildman and Patrick McNamara, eds., *Science and the World's Religions, Volume I: Origins and Destinies* (New York: Praeger, 2012), 39–68.
Shults, F. LeRon, "Science and Religious Supremacy: Toward a Naturalist Theology of Religions," in Wesley Wildman and Patrick McNamara, eds., *Science and the World's Religions, Volume III: Religions and Controversies* (New York: Praeger, 2012), 73–100.
Shults, F. LeRon, "Theology After Pandora: The Real Scandal of the Evangelical Mind (and Culture)," in Derek J. Tidball, Brian S. Harris, and Jason S. Sexton, eds., *Revisioning the Triune Center: Essays in Honor of Stanley J. Grenz* (Eugene: Cascade Books, forthcoming).
Shults, F. LeRon, *Theology After the Birth of God: Atheist Conceptions in Cognition and Culture* (New York: Palgrave-Macmillan, forthcoming).
Simpson, Christopher Ben, *Deleuze and Theology* (London: Bloomsbury, 2012).

Slone, D. Jason, *Theological Incorrectness* (Oxford: Oxford University Press, 2004).

Smith, Anthony Paul, "What Can be Done With Religion?: Non-philosophy and the Future of Philosophy of Religion," in Anthony Paul Smith and Daniel Whistler, eds., *After the Postsecular and the Postmodern: New Essays in Continental Philosophy of Religion* (Newcastle upon Tyne: Cambridge Scholars Publishing, 2010), 280–98.

Smith, Anthony Paul, "The Judgment of God and the Immeasurable: Political Theology and Organizations of Power," *Political Theology* 12.1 (2011): 69–86.

Smith, Daniel W., "From the Surface to the Depths: On the Transition from *Logic of Sense* to *Anti-Oedipus*," in Constantin Boundas, ed., *Gilles Deleuze: The Intensive Reduction* (New York: Continuum, 2009), 82–100.

Smith, Daniel W., *Essays on Deleuze* (Edinburgh: Edinburgh University Press, 2012).

Sosis, Richard, "Religious Behaviors, Badges, and Bans: Signaling Theory and the Evolution of Religion," in Patrick McNamara, ed., *Where God and Science Meet: Vol. 1, Evolution, Genes, and the Religious Brain* (Westport: Praeger, 2006), 61–86.

Stern, Jessica, *Terror in the Name of God: Why Religious Militants Kill* (New York: HarperCollins, 2003).

Stivale, Charles, J., ed., *Gilles Deleuze: Key Concepts* (Durham: Acumen, 2005).

Strozier, Charles B., David M. Terman, and James W. Jones, eds., *The Fundamentalist Mindset: Psychological Perspectives on Religion, Violence and History* (Oxford: Oxford University Press, 2010).

Teehan, John, *In the Name of God: The Evolutionary Origins of Religious Ethics and Violence* (Oxford: Wiley-Blackwell, 2010).

Tremlin, Todd, *Minds and Gods: The Cognitive Foundations of Religion* (Oxford: Oxford University Press, 2006).

Voss, Daniela, *Conditions of Thought: Deleuze and Transcendental Ideas* (Edinburgh: Edinburgh University Press, 2013).

Voss, Daniela, "Deleuze's Rethinking of the Notion of Sense," *Deleuze Studies* 7.1 (2013): 1–25.

Watson, Janell, "The Face of Christ: Deleuze and Guattari on the Politics of Word and Image," *The Bible and Critical Theory* 1:2 (2005): 04, 1–14.

Whitehouse, Harvey, *Modes of Religiosity: A Cognitive Theory of Religious Transmission* (New York: AltaMira Press, 2004).

Whitehouse, Harvey and James Laidlaw, *Ritual and Memory* (New York: AltaMira Press, 2004).

Widder, Nathan, *Genealogies of Difference* (Urbana: University of Illinois Press, 2002).

Widder, Nathan, "From Negation to Disjunction in a World of Simulacra: Deleuze and Melanie Klein," *Deleuze Studies*, 3.2 (2009): 207–30.
Widder, Nathan, *Political Theory After Deleuze* (New York: Continuum, 2012).
Wildman, Wesley, *Science and Religious Anthropology* (Farnham: Ashgate, 2009).
Williams, James, *Gilles Deleuze's Difference and Repetition: A Critical Introduction and Guide* (Edinburgh: Edinburgh University Press, 2003).
Williams, James, *Gilles Deleuze's Logic of Sense: A Critical Introduction and Guide* (Edinburgh: Edinburgh University Press, 2008).
Williams, James, *Gilles Deleuze's Philosophy of Time: A Critical Introduction and Guide* (Edinburgh: Edinburgh University Press, 2011).
Žižek, Slavoj, *Organs Without Bodies: Deleuze and Consequences* (London: Routledge, 2004).
Žižek, Slavoj, *The Parallax View* (Cambridge, MA: MIT Press, 2006).
Zourabichvili, François, *Deleuze: A Philosophy of the Event*, trans. Kieran Aarons, ed. Gregg Lambert and Daniel W. Smith (Edinburgh: Edinburgh University Press, 2012).

Index

Index